COMBINING PAID WORK AND FAMILY CARE

Policies and experiences in international perspective

Edited by Teppo Kröger and Sue Yeandle

First published in Great Britain in 2014 by

Policy Press
University of Bristol
1-9 Old Park Hill
Clifton
Bristol BS2 8BB
UK
t: +44 (0)117 954 5940
pp-info@bristol.ac.uk
www.policypress.co.uk

North America office:
Policy Press
c/o The University of Chicago Press
1427 East 60th Street
Chicago, IL 60637, USA
t: +1 773 702 7700
f: +1 773 702 9756
www.press.uchicago.edu
sales@press.uchicago.edu

British Library Cataloguing in Publication Data
A catalogue record for this book is available from the British Library

Library of Congress Cataloging-in-Publication Data
A catalog record for this book has been requested

ISBN 978 1 44730 682 5 paperback

Cover design by Andrew Corbett
Front cover: image kindly supplied by istock
Printed and bound in Great Britain by CMP, Poole
The Policy Press uses environmentally responsible print partners

Contents

Part Three: Working partner-carers

Conclusions

List of tables

List of abbreviations

CA	Carer's Allowance (UK and Australia)
CAOP	Carer Allowance for Older People (Taiwan)
CDC	Consumer Directed Care (Australia)
CDRD	Consumer Directed Respite Care (Australia)
CES	Carers, Employment and Services study (UK)
CP	Carer Payment (Australia)
DH	Department of Health (UK)
DLA	Disability Living Allowance (UK)
DoHA	Department of Health and Ageing (Australia)
DWP	Department for Work and Pensions (UK)
EPA	Economic Partnership Agreement (Japan)
EU	European Union
FaHCSIA	Department of Families, Housing, Community Services and Indigenous Affairs (Australia)
HACC	Home and Community Care (Australia)
HILDA	Household Income and Labour Dynamics survey (Australia)
JILPT	Japan Institute for Labour Policy and Training
LAs	Local Authorities
LASS	Assistance Benefit Act (Sweden)
LSS	Support and Services for Persons with Certain Disabilities Act (Sweden)
LTC	Long Term Care
LTCI	Long Term Care Insurance (Japan and Taiwan)
MBS	Medicare Benefits Schedule (Australia)
MHLW	Ministry of Health, Labour and Welfare (Japan)
MHSA	Ministry of Health and Social Affairs (Sweden)
MIAC	Ministry of Internal Affairs and Communication (Japan)
MOEA	Ministry of Economic Affairs (Taiwan)
MOI	Ministry of the Interior (Taiwan)
NDIS	National Disability Insurance Scheme (Australia)
NES	National Employment Standards (Australia)
NGOs	Non-Governmental Organisations
NHI	National Health Insurance (Taiwan)
NHS	National Health Service (UK)
NPOs	Non-Profit Organisations
NRCP	National Respite for Carers Programme (Australia)
PAs	Personal Assistants

SDAC   Survey of Disability, Ageing and Carers (Australia)
TAFC   Taiwan Association of Family Caregivers (Taiwan)
WoCaWo   Working Carers and Caring Workers Project

Notes on contributors

Bettina Cass is Emeritus Professor in the Social Policy Research Centre, University of New South Wales, Sydney, Australia. Her research interests include: employment and care-giving; workplace arrangements and transfer policies for work–care reconciliation; and family tax/benefit systems. Her recent work includes *Young carers in Australia* (FaHCSIA, 2009, with Smyth, Hill, Blaxland and Hamilton) and 'The marketisation of care: rationales and consequences in Nordic and liberal welfare regimes' (in the *Journal of European Social Policy*, 2012, with Brennan, Himmelweit and Szebehely).

Heng-Hao Chang is Associate Professor in the Department of Sociology, National Taipei University, Taiwan. His research interests include disability studies, social movements, sociology of health and illness, and quality of life studies. He has published widely in *Social Indicators Research, Taiwan: A Radical Quarterly in Social Studies, China Perspective, Asian Journal of Women's Studies, Taiwanese Journal of Sociology* and *Review of Disability Studies: An International Journal*.

Yueh-Ching Chou is Professor in the Institute of Health and Welfare Policy, National Yang-Ming University, Taipei, Taiwan. Her main research interests include: parents, families and carers of people with an intellectual disability; supporting individuals with intellectual disabilities living in the community; health issues among women with intellectual disabilities; and, most recently, the reconciliation between paid work and unpaid caring among mothers of adult children with intellectual disabilities. Chou has published widely in many international journals.

Kristina Engwall is Associate Professor of History and a Researcher in the Institute for Futures Studies, Stockholm, Sweden. Her research focuses on childhood, disability and families. Her publications include a chapter in *Gender and disability research in the Nordic countries* (Studentlitteratur, 2004), *Children's work in everyday life* (Institute for Futures Studies, 2007) and the first anthology on 'childfreeness' in a Nordic context, *Frivillig barnlöshet* (Dialogos, 2010).

Gary Fry is Research Fellow at the Centre for International Research on Care, Labour and Equalities (CIRCLE), School of Sociology and Social Policy, University of Leeds, UK. His research interests include the employment needs of unpaid carers, the use of information and communication technologies (ICTs) in social care and UK local authority services for unpaid carers. His publications include *Developing a clearer understanding of the Carer's Allowance claimant group* (Department for Work and Pensions, 2011, with Singleton, Yeandle and Buckner) and *Local authorities' use of carers grant* (Department of Health, 2009, with Price and Yeandle).

Trish Hill is Senior Research Fellow in the Social Policy Research Centre, University of New South Wales, Sydney, Australia. Her research interests encompass gender, poverty, social inclusion and the circumstances of carers across the life course. Her published work includes *The costs of caring and the living standards of carers* (FaHCSIA, 2011, with Cass and Thomson) and *Young carers: their characteristics and geographical distribution* (NYARS, 2009, with Cass, Smyth and Thomson).

Outi Jolanki is Postdoctoral Researcher at the Department of Social Sciences and Philosophy, University of Jyväskylä, Finland. Her research centres on the everyday life experiences of older people and their family members in relation to health, care, the living environment and paid work. Her publications include 'Talk about old age, health and morality', in *Valuing older people* (The Policy Press, 2009), and 'Agency in talk about old age and health' (in the *Journal of Aging Studies*, 2009).

Kaisa Kauppinen is Research Professor in the Finnish Institute of Occupational Health (FIOH), Helsinki, Finland. Her latest research focuses on women and ageing, showing that there is much need for workplace practices to support caregivers' work motivation and well-being. She leads a research group that evaluates the gender implications of the new Finnish care leave practices and is author of 'Who cares when grandmother gets sick?', in *Gender inequalities, households and the production of well-being in modern Europe* (Ashgate, 2010).

Teppo Kröger is Professor of Social and Public Policy in the Department of Social Sciences and Philosophy, University of Jyväskylä, Finland. His research focuses on local, national and global care policies and their outcomes for older people, disabled people, carers, families with children and care workers. His publications include: *Comparative research on social care: the state of the art* (European Communities, 2001); *Overstretched: European families up against the demands of work and care* (Blackwell, 2005, edited with Sipilä); and *Social work and child welfare politics: through Nordic lenses* (The Policy Press, 2010, edited with Forsberg).

Anu Leinonen is Postdoctoral Researcher in the Department of Social Sciences and Philosophy, University of Jyväskylä, Finland. Her research focuses on social networks of informal carers, retirement plans and future prospects of working carers and social care services for older people and informal carers. Her publications include 'Adult children and parental caregiving: making sense of participation patterns among siblings' (in *Ageing and Society*, 2011) and 'Masters of their own time? Working carers' visions of retirement' (in the *European Journal of Ageing*, 2011).

Li-Fang Liang is Assistant Professor at the Institute of Health and Welfare Policy, National Yang-Ming University, Taipei, Taiwan. Her academic interests include gender studies, care work, sociology of medicine and migration. Her PhD dissertation – *Constructing migrant care labour: a study of institutional processes and the discourses of migration and work* (Syracuse University, 2010) – examines how the coordination of migrant care labour is mediated by the gendered/racialised organisation of care work, which shapes the daily experiences of workers and care recipients.

Mei-Chun Liu is Professor at the Graduate Institute of Labour Research, National Chengchi University, Taipei, Taiwan. Her research focuses on employment issues in general and female employment in particular, with special attention to maternal protection issues. Her publications include *Working time: theoretical dialectics and experiential reflection* (Taiwanelites Press, 2001, in Chinese) and *Female labor policy White Paper* (Council of Labor, 2007, in Chinese).

Sonja Miettinen is Researcher at the Finnish Association on Intellectual and Developmental Disabilities, Helsinki, Finland. Her research focuses on the consequences of Finnish social and economic policies on people with intellectual disabilities and their families. She is author of 'Family care of adults with intellectual disabilities: analysis of Finnish policies and practices' (in the *Journal of Policy and Practice in Intellectual Disabilities*, 2012).

Toshiko Nakano is Professor in the Faculty of Sociology and Social Work, Meiji Gakuin University, Tokyo, Japan. Her research interests include social welfare policies, user-oriented approaches in social care and social work practices for people with intellectual disabilities and families with disabled children. She is author of *Perspectives of social* *welfare studies for people with intellectual disabilities* (Takasuga syuppan, 2009, in Japanese).

Machiko Osawa is Professor of Economics in the Faculty of Integrated Arts and Social Sciences, Japan Women's University, Tokyo, Japan. Her research focuses on the impact of globalisation in the labour market, changing women's labour force participation and family formation in economic development. Her publications include: *Non standard work in developed economies: causes and consequences* (Upjohn Institute, 2004); *Towards a work–life balance society* (Iwanami, 2006); and *Japan's working poor* (Iwanami, 2010).

Ann-Britt Sand is Researcher and Lecturer in the Department of Social Work, Stockholm University, Sweden. She also works at the Swedish National Family Care Competence Centre (NkA). Her research interests centre on welfare states and family care and maintenance. Her most recent research project ('The Cost of Care') focuses on working family carers. Her published work includes *The value of the work: on employment for family care in Sweden* (Nova Science Publishers, 2007) and *Family carers who combine work and care* (NkA, 2010, in Swedish).

Masaya Shimmei is Researcher in the Tokyo Metropolitan Institute of Gerontology, Tokyo, Japan. His research interests include the politics of community care, local care resource arrangement and differences in human service organisation. His published work includes *Municipalities and administration of the Long-term Care Insurance Scheme in Japan* (Minerva Books, 2010, with Creighton Campbell) and 'Finnish third sector activity for the elderly care and related institutions' (in *The Review of Comparative Social Security Research*, 1998).

Marta Szebehely is Professor of Social Work at Stockholm University, Sweden. Her research focuses on the shifting boundaries of care across time and place. Her recent publications include 'A caring state for all older people?', in *Welfare state, universalism and diversity* (Edward Elgar, 2012, with Vabø), and 'Equality in the social service state: Nordic childcare models in comparative perspective', in *Changing social equality* (The Policy Press, 2012, with Meagher).

Antti Teittinen is Adjunct Professor and Research Manager at the Finnish Association on Intellectual and Developmental Disabilities (FAIDD). He is Book Reviews Editor of the *Scandinavian Journal* *of Disability Research* and Vice-President of the Finnish Society for Disability Studies. He has been a board member of the Nordic Network on Disability Research and is a member of the Academic Network of European Disability Experts. He has edited two anthologies of disability studies in Finland and has published articles on ethical and social theories of disability, the structures of disability services, and inclusion in the school system.

Cathy Thomson is Research Fellow at the Social Policy Research Centre, University of New South Wales, Sydney, Australia. Her research interests include the costs of unpaid care, social inclusion and caring, ageing and community care, and gender and social policy. Her published work includes *The costs of caring and the living standards of carers* (FaHCSIA, 2011, with Hill and Cass) and 'Young carers: location, education and employment disadvantage' (in the *Australian Journal of Labour Economics*, 2011).

kylie valentine is Senior Research Fellow in the Social Policy Research Centre, University of New South Wales, Sydney, Australia. Her research interests include the politics of (and policies for) families, children and mothers, marginalised communities and individuals, and the translation of research into politics and practice.

Frank T.Y. Wang is Associate Professor in the Graduate Institute of Social Work, National Chengchi University, Taipei, Taiwan. His research interests span long-term care, the ageing experiences of lesbian, gay, bisexual and transgender (LGBT) people, and social work with indigenous communities. He was Chairperson of the Taiwan Association of Family Caregivers (TAFC) during 2008–12 and Editor in Chief of the journal *Taiwan: A Radical Quarterly in Social Science* during 2009–12.

Yoshiko Yamada is Deputy Director of International Relationships, Japan Workers' Cooperative Union, Tokyo, Japan. Her research interests include care workers, long-term care for older people and productive aging. Her published work includes 'Profile of home care aides, nursing home aides, and hospital aides' (in *The Gerontologist*, 2002) and 'Caregiving stress among elderly spouse caregivers' (in the *Japanese Journal of Social Welfare*, 2006).

Sue Yeandle is Professor of Sociology and Director of the Centre for International Research on Care, Labour and Equalities (CIRCLE), School of Sociology and Social Policy, University of Leeds, UK. Her research interests include the relationship between work and family life, employment and social policies relevant to work–care reconciliation, and the social organisation of paid and unpaid work. Her published work includes *Cash for care in developed welfare states* (Palgrave Macmillan, 2007, edited with Ungerson) and *Policy for a change: local labour market analysis and gender equality* (The Policy Press, 2009).

Acknowledgements

The editors are grateful for the support of their respective universities in preparing this book and in particular to the Academy of Finland, which funded the 'Working Carers and Caring Workers' (WoCaWo) project (2008–11, no 113340). Further details of the WoCaWo project are given in *Chapter One*, in which we also acknowledge the other institutions whose support and contributions made this book possible.

The book draws on the testimony of many people, in six countries, who gave research interviews and responded to surveys about the care they give to others. Although they cannot be named, we thank them very sincerely for their time and openness in helping the contributors to this book gain insights into their lives and social circumstances.

Our thanks go also to all the authors of the chapters in this book, for the ideas and energy they brought to the discussions and international meetings in which the book was planned and for the care that they have taken in writing and revising their chapters. We are also very grateful to Dr Keleigh Coldron, who assisted with the final preparation of the book, to the staff at The Policy Press for their cooperation and support in its planning and production, and to our friends, colleagues and family members for their support and patience throughout the preparation of this book.

Teppo Kröger, University of Jyväskylä, Finland
Sue Yeandle, University of Leeds, UK
October 2012

INTRODUCTION

ONE

Reconciling work and care: an international analysis

Teppo Kröger and Sue Yeandle

Introduction

In recent decades, the reconciliation of work and family life has become a key focus in social research and policymaking at both national and European levels. Thanks to the altered gender composition of the labour force and a new feminist-inspired understanding of the interconnections between work and family, many policymakers no longer see the public sphere of paid work and the private sphere of family life as two separate worlds. A long-standing resistance to any kind of intervention in family life in many welfare states, including most English-speaking and East Asian countries, has given way to new policy approaches addressing the needs of working families, and many areas of family policy, including childcare services and parental leave, have been reconceptualised as support measures for work–family reconciliation. The European Union (EU), aiming to increase overall employment rates and generate economic growth in Europe, has become an active advocate of women's labour force participation and has begun to require member states to develop and extend their reconciliation policies. Faced with struggling economies and falling birth rates, many European nations have adopted the reconciliation agenda and launched new measures to support families, especially working mothers of young children. These changes represent a remarkable policy shift and have led to the rapid development of family policies in Europe.

Despite its significance, the scope of this policy reorientation has nevertheless been limited. Research and policy on reconciliation have focused almost exclusively on parents of young children, even though, in most countries, it is not growing numbers of children that are putting pressure on families' capacity to provide care. Instead, as ongoing and anticipated changes in population structures confirm, it is people who are ill or disabled, especially in old age, whose numbers and needs are growing fast (Colombo et al, 2011). Previous research has shown that in virtually every nation, the bulk of care is overwhelmingly provided by the family. It is therefore hardly surprising that the growing needs of disabled and older people are expected to place greater demands on adult family members. Meanwhile, the 'adult worker model', with its expectation that everyone – including women, who in the past provided most family care unpaid – will participate in paid work (Lewis, 2001), has been adopted as a normative assumption almost everywhere. However, rising expectations about providing more family care do not fit well with the expectation that more people will be doing paid work. The mismatch is further aggravated by efforts in many welfare states to delay the effective retirement age. Care responsibilities, especially for those caring for elderly parents, are usually at their most demanding for 45–65 year olds, the very group now being discouraged from leaving the labour market (see *Chapters Three* to *Five*). Retirement options are reducing, and those who retire early face significant pension penalties (OECD, 2011a).

The mismatch experienced by individual families results from a major, macro-level mismatch in policy. Welfare states have focused their reconciliation policies on young adults early in their careers but have tended to disregard middle-aged and older workers in later working life, leaving them to cope alone with the problems of combining paid work with family responsibilities. Thus, in most cases, reconciliation policies remain fundamentally unbalanced.

The same can be said of most research. In literature searches, the keywords 'work–family reconciliation' or 'work–family balance' produce long lists of publications that are almost entirely about families with young children. Within this literature, problems in the work–family interface have rarely been viewed as issues that affect middle-aged or older workers. On the other hand, especially in English-speaking countries, where there has been a strong tradition of research on family care since the 1970s, caring and family carers are the subject of a huge research literature. Yet, even in these studies, it has been relatively rare to consider the employment of carers or the interplay between their roles and responsibilities as workers and carers.

Gradually, however, combining paid work with caring for a disabled or older family member has begun to attract the attention of researchers. In North America, in the context of high female labour force participation rates with limited welfare state support, family carers' difficulties in participating in paid work were the focus of research interest in the early 1990s (Neal et al, 1993; Martin-Matthews and Campbell, 1995). In Britain too, discussion of the implications of caring for employment and earnings featured at that time in an influential study of the costs of informal care (Glendinning, 1992), and some British researchers subsequently studied 'working carers' – as the new term had it – and their difficulties in combining work and care (Phillips, 1996, 1998; Yeandle, 1999; Arksey, 2002; Phillips and Bernard, 2002; Yeandle et al, 2002; Arksey and Kemp, 2006). Problems in the work–care interface were also recognised in the late 1990s in Australia and Germany (Beck et al, 1997; Watson and Mears, 1999). Perhaps surprisingly, research debate on working carers is only just beginning in the Nordic countries (Gautun, 2008; Leinonen, 2009; Sand, 2010; Kauppinen and Jolanki, 2012). Thus, while studies of reconciling paid work with caring for older or disabled family members do exist in some countries, the topic has remained rather marginal in the international literature on both reconciliation and caring.

Two international collections are nevertheless worthy of special mention: *Working carers* (Phillips, 1995) and *Work and caring for the elderly* (Lechner and Neal, 1999). The former comprised analyses of balancing working and care in Britain, Ireland, Germany, the US and Canada, while the latter offered a systematic review of support for employed caregivers in 11 countries, including not only the US, Canada and several European nations (Britain, Germany and Sweden), but also Brazil, China, Israel, Japan, Mexico and Uganda. Published in the 1990s, both books were opening up a previously untrodden path in social research, yet one that almost disappeared from view in the 2000s (see, however, Kröger and Sipilä, 2005; Martin-Matthews and Phillips, 2008; Saraceno, 2010). In an effort to once more carve a path towards new understanding based on an international analysis of combining work and care, the present volume both picks up the trail laid by these authors and aims for new ground, which is distinctive in its attention to the care of parents (older people), partners (with illness or disability) and disabled children.

The book's rationale

This book studies the experiences of working carers and the welfare and labour market policies that affect them in three different welfare systems: (1) the public sector-centred Nordic welfare model; (2) the private sector-dominated liberal democracies; and (3) the family-centred East Asian states. In each of these types of welfare system, two countries are analysed. The Nordic welfare model, or 'social democratic regime', is known for its generosity and extensive coverage, where both welfare benefits and publicly organised welfare services are concerned, and the Nordic countries, represented here by Finland and Sweden, are often ranked as having the world's most developed social policies. Australia represents the 'liberal' regime – seen in some anglophone democracies – in which social rights are rather limited, social welfare focuses primarily on people with low incomes and most families are expected to purchase the services they need from the market. Britain, also often categorised as a 'liberal' welfare system, is perhaps better understood as a 'mixed' model in which residual and market elements combine with universalism. Japan and Taiwan, both East Asian countries featuring familistic legislation, are influenced by Confucianist culture, in which families have traditionally provided the economic support and care needed by their members. East Asian welfare systems are often described as 'productivist', prioritising economic growth and providing only very limited public services and social security for their citizens. However, this image is now somewhat outdated, as these countries have recently launched universal long-term care insurance (Japan) and health care insurance (Taiwan) schemes.

These three types of welfare system were chosen for study to enhance understanding of dissimilarities and similarities in the situations of working carers under different welfare arrangements and in different parts of the world. Comparisons are made not only between, but also within, each type, enabling two versions of the same welfare model to be contrasted. This provides new material on the cases of England, Sweden and Japan, discussed in the two 1990s' volumes mentioned earlier, and brings working carers in Finland, Australia and Taiwan into comparative analysis for the first time. Reconciliation between work and family responsibilities is a global challenge and research needs to address it as such. The goal of this volume is to provide knowledge of the conditions of working carers that has relevance for the development of policies all over the globe.

The two international anthologies mentioned earlier – along with most existing research on combining work and family care – focused solely on one group of working carers: those providing support to older family members. This book distinguishes three different groups of carers: (1) those providing support to parents/parents-in-law[1] in their old age; (2) those caring for or helping a disabled son or daughter (or one with a serious illness or long-term condition); and (3) those caring for a partner affected by illness or disability. Caring for a disabled son or daughter is substantially different from caring for a partner, and both types of care differ in many respects from caring for an older parent. These three different sets of care relationships also reflect caring in different parts of the life course. Caring for disabled children usually starts early in parenthood when parents are in their late 20s, 30s or early 40s (although it may last for decades), while caring for older parents typically begins when offspring reach their late 40s or 50s. Caring for a partner often occurs in old age but is also a common experience in the decade or so before retirement for people of working age. This divergence in care relations and life phases means that the circumstances, difficulties and resources of these three groups of carers differ in important ways, with specific implications for the reconciliation of work and family life. The book gives each of these groups of working carers the attention they merit in their own right.

The book analyses the experiences of the three groups of working carers and the policies that affect them, offering a perspective on the relationship between the policy context and human agency. This is done through comparative analysis of public policies, employment practices and family behaviour. The book addresses issues of critical importance not only for how social care is delivered and framed in national policymaking, but also for how work is organised to enable women and men, across the life course, to combine paid work with the unpaid care of family members whenever long-term sickness, disability or frail old age is encountered. The ultimate goal of the volume is to offer empirical and conceptual insights as well as policy lessons that can contribute to the development of support to working carers in various national contexts and welfare state models.

The growing significance of work–care reconciliation

Why do working carers deserve particular attention from researchers and policymakers? Are carers not a group who, by definition, are outside the labour market? If some do manage a job and the care of an older or disabled person, surely they are few in number and do not need significant social policy attention and resources? Is that not correct?

That might indeed have been correct in the 1950s, but since that time, decade on decade, the world has been changing. Everywhere, the relationship between working and caring has been transformed, above all other influences, by two structural megatrends: (1) women's increasing participation in employment; and (2) the ageing of populations. These major transformations have brought working carers to the fore as a group of critical importance for societal well-being.

Changing labour markets

The transformation of the gender composition of the labour market has brought about many social changes in most societies. Within Organisation for Economic Co-operation and Development (OECD) nations,[2] the average employment rate for women rose from 45% in 1970 to 57% in 2010 (see Table 1.1). In the past four decades, this trend has been most emphatic in Australia: by 1970, most women in Finland, Japan and Sweden had already joined the labour force. Even after the economic crises of the 1990s and 2000s, when women's employment rates there fell, Finland and Sweden still had the highest female employment rates in our group. By 2010, Taiwan was alone among the six countries in having a female employment rate under 60%, although, even there, the trend was towards a gradual rise in women's labour market activity.

Table 1.1: Employment rates of working-age women (15–64), 1970–2010 (%)

	1970	1980	1990	2000	2010
Australia	41	48	57	61	66
Finland	62	66	72	65	67
Japan	53	51	56	57	60
Sweden	58	73	81	72	70
Taiwan	–	41	47	50	54
United Kingdom	53[a]	57	63	66	65
OECD	45	49	54	55	57

Note: [a] Figure for 1971.

Sources: OECD (2010a, 2011b); ONS (2011). Taiwan figures from secondary data analysis based on unpublished data set from the Directorate General of Budget, Accounting and Statistics, Executive Yuan, Taiwan.

Rising female employment rates imply, on the one hand, that women are no longer available to undertake unpaid family care responsibilities full-time, as many did in the past, making caring for an older or disabled family member with substantial needs problematic. Meanwhile, more feminised workforces necessarily contain more carers than ever before. With women, caring entered the world of paid work on a large scale; a development with implications for men as carers too.

Part-time employment offers one way of trying to combine work and care. The share of part-time work in total employment rose in OECD countries from 11% in 1990 to 17% in 2010 (see Table 1.2). The increase was most rapid in Finland, although part-time work remains less important there than in the other nations (except in Taiwan, where part-time work is also rare, although reliable data on it are not available). Part-time employment is most prevalent in Australia and the UK, where a quarter of all workers are 'part-timers'. Typically, part-time work is done by women: in 2010, the proportion of part-time workers who were female ranged from 62% (Finland) to 75% (UK) (OECD, 2011c).

Table 1.2: Part-time employment as a proportion of total employment, 1990–2010 (%)

	1990	2000	2010	2010 (women)
Australia	–	24[a]	25	39
Finland	8	10	13	16
Japan	–	18[b]	20	34
Sweden	15	14	14	19
United Kingdom	20	23	25	39
OECD	11	12	17	26

Note: From Taiwan there was no reliable, comparative data available. a Figure for 2001; b figure for 2002.

Sources: OECD (2010a, 2011c, 2011d).

In Australia and Britain, 39% of all employed women held part-time jobs in 2010, perhaps in part reflecting the problems women there face in combining care responsibilities with full-time work (see Table 1.2). As suggested earlier, caring for a disabled child – which is usually an unplanned and long-term responsibility – often begins for parents when they are in or around their 30s. It often requires care well into the child's adulthood, and may affect the whole working life of both parents. However, the more prevalent types of care – caring for a parent or partner – usually arise in later working life, making the employment of older workers particularly salient when working carers are discussed. Between 1990 and 2010, the employment rate among older workers (people aged 55–64) in OECD countries rose from 48% to 54% (see Table 1.3). Two decades ago, people in this age group were much more likely to be in employment in Japan and Sweden than in the four other countries, but convergence has been evident since then. Taiwan is an exception here since the employment of older workers has remained at around 40% across the decades. By 2010, the majority of older workers were employed in all five other nations, although there were still inter-country variations (eg between the two Nordic countries).

Table 1.3: Employment rates of older workers (55–64), 1990–2010 (%)

	1990	2000	2005	2010
Australia	42	46	54	61
Finland	43	42	53	56
Japan	63	63	64	65
Sweden	70	65	70	71
Taiwan	–	43	39	41
United Kingdom	49	50	57	57
OECD	48	48	52	54

Sources: OECD (2010a, 2011e). Taiwan figures from the Department of Statistics, Ministry of Interior, Taiwan.

The rising employment rates of older workers and women have similar implications: the number of people available to take on demanding care within the family decreases, while ever-growing numbers of people within the workforce are managing their jobs alongside some kind of caring role.

Table 1.4: Employment and part-time work among carers and non-carers, 2006/07 (%)

Country	Employed		Working part-time	
	Carer (%)	Non-carer (%)	Carer (%)	Non-carer (%)
Australia	53	66	15	10
Sweden	75	74	16	15
United Kingdom	78	81	28	21
OECD	69	74	25	21

Source: Colombo et al (2011: 92).

A recent OECD report (Colombo et al, 2011) compared the employment of people with and without family care responsibilities in 18 countries, including Australia, Sweden and the UK (see Table 1.4). In Australia and the UK, carers had lower employment rates than non-carers, while in Sweden – quite surprisingly, but probably due to the very high employment rate of older workers – carers were employed slightly more often than non-carers. Overall, within the OECD nations, participating in paid work seems to be more difficult for carers[3] than for people without care responsibilities. The report nevertheless observes that the impact of caring on labour force participation is only really evident when people provide high levels of care (Colombo et al, 2011: 93). Across the OECD nations, the data show that 69% of carers are employed: today, most carers are workers too. Part-time work is more usual among carers than among workers without family care responsibilities, especially in Australia and the UK, but, even there, most working carers are in full-time jobs (see Table 1.4).

Ageing populations

Alongside the rising employment rates of women and older workers, global ageing is the other megatrend turning the reconciliation of work and care into a burning social issue. The world's population is getting ever older: between 1950 and 2010, the share of people aged 65+ in the global population increased from 5% to 8%, and by 2050, it is projected to reach 16% (see Table 1.5). Within the OECD, the development is even more dramatic: estimates indicate that by 2050, a quarter of the population will be over 65. Of the nations included in this book, in 1990, it was in Sweden and the UK that more than 15% of the population had reached old age, the other countries were then much younger nations. Yet, in the short time since 1990, Japan has become the world's most aged society: in 2010, 23% of its people were aged 65+ and the startling projection is that by 2050, this figure will reach 40%. In 2015, Finland is projected to overtake Sweden on this measure, and Australia will do the same in 2037. Only Taiwan remains a young nation, with just 11% of its people aged 65+ in 2010.

Table 1.5: Population aged 65+ as a proportion of total population, 1950–2050 (%)

	1950	1970	1990	2010	2030[a]	2050[a]
Australia	8	8	11	14	22	26
Finland	7	9	13	18	26	28
Japan	5	7	12	23	32	40
Sweden	10	14	18	18	23	24
Taiwan	–	3	7	11	24	37
United Kingdom	11	13	16	17	22	24
EU27	9	12	14	17	24	29
OECD	8	10	12	15	22	26
World	5	6	6	8	12	16

Note: [a] Figures for 2030 and 2050 are estimations.

Sources: OECD (2010a, 2010b). Taiwan figures taken from the Council for Economic Planning and Development, Population in 2010 to 2060. Available at: www.cepd.gov.tw/ m1.aspx?sNo=0000455

However, even Taiwan's older population is expected to reach 37% by 2050, a huge transformation within a short time period.

These figures provide evidence of an unparalleled demographic transformation. Most noteworthy of all, ageing is revealed as an accumulating and accelerating process: while in the 1950s, the share of the world's population aged 65+ increased by just 0.1%, it grew by 0.8% between 2000 and 2010 and is projected to rise by 2.0% in the 2040s. The significance of this ongoing change is intensified by its other characteristic: within the 65+ population, it is the 'old old' whose number is increasing most rapidly. Between 1950 and 2050, the share of the world's population aged 65+ is projected to triple, yet the share of the population aged 80+ is set to increase by an astonishing 750% (Colombo et al, 2011: 62).

This huge demographic shift means that the number of older people needing support or care – which has already grown significantly in recent decades – will undergo ever more dramatic expansion in the coming years. Bringing a striking growth in care needs, it will have a profound impact on families, requiring family members to provide ever increasing amounts of care. In the 21st century, it cannot be expected that women will stay out of the labour market to provide unpaid and unsupported care. The growing reliance on both women and older workers in the workplace, while, at the same time, ever more care is needed, makes it crucial for public policy to focus on supporting working carers to balance their working and caring responsibilities.

Conceptualisation and numbers of working carers

As indicated earlier, this book focuses on people of working age and on three types of carers: (1) those caring for sick or disabled sons and daughters; (2) those caring for older parents; and (3) those supporting their partner through a period of sickness or disability, often in later working life. This trio of concepts covers most, but not all, carers of working age. While some people care for others in their kin group or for friends or neighbours, survey data suggest that their numbers are comparatively small, and their contributions likely to involve less intensive forms of care (Glendinning et al, 2009).

Qualitative research on carers – a feature of the work undertaken by all the contributors to this volume – shows the importance of understanding the nature of the caring relationship, and of appreciating differences between care provided by a co-resident carer or by one who lives elsewhere. All caring has demanding as well as rewarding aspects, but providing care within and outside the household are forms of caring that involve different forms of support, as does providing care to one's partner, one's father/mother or one's son/daughter. These forms of caring may last for different periods of time, impact on pre-existing roles and relationships in different ways, and encompass different configurations of love, concern, obligation, intimacy, responsibility and reciprocity. The chapters in this collection highlight many of these features, shedding light not only on the need for care and the challenges of providing and supporting care, but also on the value many working-age carers place on caregiving and their desire to find sustainable ways of including it in lives in which paid work and other family responsibilities also need to continue.

The difficulties of analysing statistical data on carers at the international level are widely acknowledged (Glendinning et al, 2009; Kotowska et al, 2010; Colombo et al, 2011). Definitions of who carers are differ and data collection methods vary: the term 'carer' or 'caregiver' is sometimes used to include *all* forms of unpaid care (including childcare), while in other statistics, it only includes care given to 'elderly relatives'. Sometimes, only care given within the carer's household is counted; in other cases, both co-resident and extra-household caring is covered. No single international comparative analysis exists that includes all the countries studied in this book, and it has not been possible to locate national data on caregiving in all six countries suitable for tabulated comparative presentation. In this book, 'carer' means someone providing care based in a relational, affective or neighbourly context to a person with care needs arising from disability, long-term or terminal illness, or frailty in old age. It includes the care of children with such needs, but not 'childcare' in its usual sense; that is, it excludes the care given by parents or by others to healthy children without disabilities.

Data on carers for the Nordic countries are limited compared with those available for Australia and England (see later) as the Nordic countries do not conduct population-wide censuses. In Finland and Sweden, specific surveys on caring based on large representative samples have also been rare, although some have recently been made. Kattainen et al (2008) found that 31% of 18 to 79-year-old Finns help family members or friends, usually with activities outside the home (21%) or household tasks (12%). Only 4% provide personal care and just 3% help with medical care. Of those providing help, according to this data, half (51%) support their parents and just a few their partners (4%) or children (5%), although 40% help 'other persons'. The intensity of support provided varies. Personal care is most often provided daily (39%) or a few times per week (24%) or month (23%); only a few (14%) give personal care less frequently. Men mostly help with activities outside the home and occasional household tasks, while women give most of the help with household tasks and with personal and medical care. Women aged 35–64 are especially active in giving help, but among people under 35 and over 65, men outnumber women as helpers, and co-resident support is rare (9%). Other surveys have shown that 22% of employees aged 45–63 look after someone needing help due to old age, illness or disability, and that 45% of employees aged 45–54 help an adult relative at least monthly (Kauppinen and Jolanki, 2012), with 21% doing so for a least 10 hours per month (Lehto and Sutela, 2008).

In Sweden, Clevenpalm and Karlsson (2010) found that among 16–84 year olds, 9% of men and 11% of women help an ill or old relative or friend with their daily activities. Caregiving was most common in the 45–64 age group, with 18% of women and 13% of men giving help. Other surveys using a wider definition find more caregiving. Olsson et al (2005: 45) note that 50% of 18–84 year olds helped with 'areas such as household work, driving, gardening, looking out for, tending or other forms of unpaid help', 28% helped someone without particular care needs (for nine hours per month on average) and 22% helped someone with care needs who lived in a separate household (for 14 hours monthly on average). Care recipients were often parents, but children, siblings and friends also received help: women were more likely to support someone with care needs.

Detailed data on carers have been collected in Australia and England since the 1980s, including in national population censuses since 2001 (England) and 2006 (Australia). Both countries also have survey data providing information on caring relationships (who carers care for), caring intensity (hours and length of time caring), caring tasks and whether caring is provided within or outside the carer's household.

In England, 5.3 million people (10% of the population) said that they were carers in 2001 (Buckner and Yeandle, 2006): eight in 10 were people of working age (Carers UK, 2009). Almost 6% of people aged 45–64 provided care for 20+ hours a week (Young et al, 2005: 30) and two thirds of carers of working age (74% of men; 60% of women) were in paid work (Yeandle and Buckner, 2007: 13). NHS Information Centre for Health and Social Care survey data (NHSIC, 2010: 110) showed that most carers in England were caring for their parents (40%), partners (26%) and children (13%); longitudinal data indicated that among carers in their 50s, 51% cared for parents, 15% for partners and 20% for children, with male carers being more likely than female carers to care for a partner (Vlachantoni, 2010: 11).

Among Australians, 12% (2.6 million people; 13% of women and 11% of men) were carers in 2009, and most carers (74% of all carers) were people of working age (18–64 years) (ABS, 2010). Among the population aged 45–64, 24% of women and 17% of men were carers. Over 1.1 million Australian carers said that their main source of income was wages or a salary; 864,500 carers had full-time jobs and 524,700 worked part-time. Nearly 30% of all carers were defined as 'primary carers'; that is, they were the person providing most of the informal help needed by a person with a disability or aged 60 years and over. In this group, 55% lived with the person they cared for. Among 'primary carers' of working age, over 190,000 were carers of their partner (mostly people aged 45–64), some 160,000 were carers of a parent (over 100,000 of them people aged 45 or older) and over 150,000 cared for a disabled child (over 95,000 were younger than 45) (ABS, 2010).

In the East Asian states, few national data sets on carers exist, although estimates suggest that 85% of older people receiving care at home in Japan are cared for by female relatives (Harris and Long, 2000; Long and Harris, 2000). Other estimates, also indicating the breadth of family care in Japan, note that the Japanese working population included 2.34 million carers (MoPM, 2006). A more recent survey found that within the home, care was mostly provided solely by women, with just 30% of husbands and wives sharing this work, and only 8% using eldercare services provided by the government or private businesses (Rengo Tochigi Research Institute of Lives, 2009). However, care at home for parents appears to be in decline, being linked to significant change in residential patterns in Japan: between 1980 and 2010, the proportion of older people living with a child fell from 70% to 41%, while those living alone rose from 9% to 16% (Tamiya et al, 2011).

Data for Taiwan indicate that in 2007, about 3% of Taiwanese people had caring responsibilities (TAFC, 2011). Older people needing assistance were mostly (80% of cases) helped by unpaid carers, the majority of whom (68%) were under 65, typically children, daughters-in-law and spouses. Almost all disabled children (97%) and most non-elderly disabled adults (89%) lived with family members, with 79% of them primarily cared for by their parents, the vast majority by mothers (MoI, 2007). Among primary carers of working age, 69% were female and over a third of those caring for a disabled child (37%) had full-time paid work. In all, 6% of the working population had a family member with disabilities and 2% were the primary carers of such a relative (Council of Labour, 2007).

The ubiquity of caring is not fully captured by cross-sectional data, as many people experience several episodes of caring during their lives. Clearly, however, caring is both prevalent and mainly undertaken by people of working age in all the countries studied here.

The background and structure of the book

This book arises from a four-year international research collaboration originally based on the Finnish research project 'Working Carers and Caring Workers' (WoCaWo), coordinated by the University of Jyväskylä and funded by the Academy of Finland from 2008 to 2011. From its inception, the project brought together an international group of researchers who were conducting studies on combining paid work with unpaid caring in their respective countries. This global network of researchers collaborated closely over four years to study and analyse the situation of working carers.

In its first phase, the network brought together research teams from Finland (University of Jyväskylä), Britain (University of Leeds), Sweden (Stockholm University) and Taiwan (National Yang-Ming University). In Britain, the Centre for International Research on Care, Labour and Equalities (CIRCLE) research team had developed a programme of research on working carers, including the 'Carers, Employment and Services' (CES) study commissioned by Carers UK (Yeandle and Buckner, 2007). In Finland, Sweden and Taiwan, work–family issues faced by people who simultaneously participate in paid work and care for family members were just coming on to the research and policy agenda. Japanese (primarily the Tokyo Metropolitan Institute of Gerontology) and Australian (the Social Policy Research Centre of the University of New South Wales) researchers later joined the network. In Australia, the collaboration built on earlier work in the 'Negotiating Caring and Employment' project funded by the Australian Research Council. The work of the national research teams also had financial support from the National Science Council in Taiwan, the Swedish Council for Working Life and Social Research (FAS) and from each university. REASSESS – the Nordic Centre of Excellence 'Reassessing the Nordic Welfare Model' – also gave financial support to assist in the production of the book.

Between 2008 and 2011, the research network held meetings in Finland, Sweden, Britain and Taiwan. It organised a major international conference on work–care reconciliation in Taipei in 2010, gathering over 200 participants, and a final international conference in Jyväskylä in 2011. This book represents the core objectives and activities of the WoCaWo international collaboration. From the start, producing a collaborative international anthology was one of the network's three ambitions. The structure of the collection results from the joint discussions and collective decision-making that took place during network meetings. This included the decision to prepare a book in three main parts, each focusing on a specific group of working carers, and each with three chapters covering the different welfare systems. The group wanted to give specific attention to the three groups of working carers identified, but also to make each chapter comparative, covering two countries. Every chapter was prepared by a small, two-country author group, some additional authors being invited to join the group to ensure expert coverage of the three types of carers in all six countries. The book is thus the outcome of intensive research collaboration between six national research teams from Europe, Asia and Australia over four years.

It is necessary to emphasise here that the funding available to the network did not cover conducting new empirical studies outside Finland. As a result, most authors had to draw on related studies of shared topics and issues, which – necessarily, given the lack of attention to many aspects of our topic in previous research and published work – meant that comparable data was not always available. In particular, the balance between statistical evidence and qualitative research data varied, and the qualitative data drew on a variety of research methods in which definitions and approaches sometimes differed. The book does not attempt to provide a comprehensive or unified theoretical analysis as the contributors were not asked or expected to develop their chapters within a single theoretical framework. The book is based on a common thematic approach, addressing the reconciliation between working and caring among the three different carer groups. The primary aim of the book is, using the best available relevant data and information from the six countries, to focus on the reconciliation issues arising for carers in different relational contexts as parents, children or partners.

The book is in three main parts. Following two introductory chapters outlining the welfare and employment policy contexts that structure working carers' experiences in the six countries, *Part One* analyses the situations and experiences of working carers of older family members, that is, children caring for frail or disabled parents. In *Chapter Three*, Outi Jolanki, Marta Szebehely and Kaisa Kauppinen ask if the Finnish and Swedish welfare states have really become aware of the importance of reconciling work and care for older people and adjusted their health and social care and benefit systems accordingly. *Chapter Four*, by Sue Yeandle and Bettina Cass, poses a similar question and analyses the adequacy of the support that has been developed to assist working carers of older family members in Australia and England. *Part One* closes in *Chapter Five* with an examination of the struggle, led by carers' groups in Taiwan and Japan, to place the needs of working carers of older people on the policy agenda in East Asia and is written by Frank T.Y. Wang, Masaya Shimmei, Yoshiko Yamada and Machiko Osawa.

Part Two turns the discussion to issues of disability, often absent in research on working carers, and thus to 'parent-carers'. Disabled children, albeit a smaller group than older people, in some ways represent an extreme example of caring. It is often mothers who become the carers of their disabled children, giving care that differs in many ways from ordinary childcare and often lasts for decades. Caring for both adult and non-adult groups of disabled children is included in this book. Participating in paid employment can be extremely difficult for the mother, especially if the child has a serious illness or substantial impairment. *Chapter Six*, by Sonja Miettinen, Kristina Engwall and Antti Teittinen, analyses the needs and difficulties of parent-carers in Finland and Sweden. In *Chapter Seven*, Sue Yeandle and kylie valentine consider work–care reconciliation issues as they affect parent-carers in Australia and England. In *Chapter Eight*, Yueh-Ching Chou, Toshiko Nakano, Heng-Hao Chang and Li-Fang Liang ask how the familistic welfare systems of Taiwan and Japan affect the opportunities parent-carers of disabled children have to participate in paid employment.

Part Three brings into focus the third group of carers – partners of a sick or disabled partner – a group usually neglected in discussions of work–care reconciliation. Partner-care is a remarkably normal phenomenon that often arises in old age, when both partners have retired. A substantial minority of partner-carers are people of working age and in the workforce, however, and as welfare states increasingly focus on delaying retirement, these carers' needs have become a more important policy concern. In *Chapter Nine*, Anu Leinonen and Ann-Britt Sand analyse the uniqueness and diversity of the experiences of Finnish and Swedish partner-carers. *Chapter Ten*, by Gary Fry, Cathy Thomson and Trish Hill, examines the effects of partner-caring on employment, income and stress and the strategies developed by Australian and English couples faced with a partner's illness or disability. *Chapter Eleven*, by Mei-Chun Liu and Machiko Osawa, highlights the importance of workplace flexibility and informal support networks for Taiwanese and Japanese partner-carers.

In *Chapter Twelve*, the editors reflect on the lessons learned from the comparative analyses considered in the book. Experiences of the three different groups of working carers are juxtaposed and the significance of available policies to support the reconciliation of work and care is discussed within each welfare system. The book concludes with suggestions about ways of developing both policy options and international research on working carers.

Notes

[1] Throughout this book, the care of both parents and parents-in-law is captured by reference to 'parents', except where otherwise indicated.

[2] Of the six countries included in this study, Taiwan is alone in not being an OECD member. OECD sources are used here, with Taiwanese data added using the best reasonably comparable data available.

[3] Defined here as people 'providing long-term care services on a regular basis, often unpaid and without contract, for example spouses/partners, family members, as well as neighbours or friends' (Colombo et al, 2011: 11).

References

ABS (Australian Bureau of Statistics) (2010) *Disability, ageing and carers, Australia: summary of findings 2009*, Canberra: Australian Bureau of Statistics.

Arksey, H. (2002) 'Combining informal care and work: supporting carers in the workplace', *Health and Social Care in the Community*, vol 10, no 3, pp 151–61.

Arksey, H. and Kemp, P.A. (2006) 'Carers and employment in a work-focused welfare state', in C. Glendinning and P.A. Kemp (eds) *Cash and care: policy challenges in the welfare state*, Bristol: The Policy Press, pp 111–24.

Beck, B., Naegele, G. and Reichert, M. (1997) *Vereinbarkeit von Erwerbstätigkeit und Pflege* [*Reconciliation of paid work and care*], Köln: Verlag W. Kohlhammer.

Buckner, L. and Yeandle, S. (2006) *Who cares wins: the social and business benefits of supporting working carers: statistical analysis – working carers, evidence from the 2001 Census*, London: Carers UK.

Carers UK (2009) 'Facts about carers', in Carers UK (ed) *Policy Briefing*, London: Carers UK.

Clevenpalm, J. and Karlsson, A.S. (2010) *På lika villkor. Resultat från Nationella folkhälsoenkäten – 2009* [*On equal terms: results from the National Survey of Public Health – 2009*], Stockholm: Swedish National Institute of Public Health.

Colombo, F., Llena-Nozal, A., Mercier, J. and Tjadens, F. (2011) *Help wanted? Providing and paying for long-term care*, Paris: OECD Publishing.

Council of Labour (2007) *National survey for working people 2007*, Taipei: Council of Labour, Executive Yuan.

Gautun, H. (2008) 'Hvordan kombinerer eldre arbeidstakere jobb med omsorgsforpliktelser for gamle foreldre?' ['How do older workers combine work with care responsibilities for older parents?'], *Søkelys på arbeidslivet*, vol 25, no 2, pp 171–85.

Glendinning, C. (1992) *The costs of informal care: looking inside the household*, London: HMSO.

Glendinning, C., Arksey, H., Tjadens, F., Morée, M., Moran, N. and Nies, H. (2009) *Care provision within families and its socio-economic impact on care providers across the European Union*, York: Social Policy Research Unit.

Harris, P.B. and Long, S.O. (2000) 'Recognizing the need for gender-responsive family caregiving policy: lessons from male caregivers', in S.O. Long (ed) *Caring for the elderly in Japan and the US: practices and policies*, London: Routledge, pp 248–71.

Kattainen, E., Muuri, A., Luoma, M.L. and Voutilainen, P. (2008) 'Läheisapu ja sen merkitys kansalaisille' ['Informal care and its meaning to citizens'], in P. Moisio, S. Karvonen, J. Simpura and M. Heikkilä (eds) *Suomalaisten hyvinvointi 2008*, Helsinki: Stakes, pp 218–31.

Kauppinen, K. and Jolanki, O. (2012) 'Työn sekä omais- ja läheishoivan yhdistäminen – työssäjatkamisajatukset' ['Reconciling work and care giving – to continue working or retire?'], in M. Perkiö-Mäkelä and T. Kauppinen (eds) *Työ, terveys ja työssäjatkamisajatukset*, Helsinki: Finnish Institute of Occupational Health, pp 133–56.

Kotowska, I.E., Matysiak, A., Styrc, M., Pailhé, A., Solaz, A. and Vignoli, D. (2010) *Family life and work: second European quality of life survey*, Luxembourg: Office for Official Publications of the European Communities.

Kröger, T. and Sipilä, J. (eds) (2005) *Overstretched: European families up against the demands of work and care*, Oxford: Blackwell.

Lechner, V.M. and Neal M.B. (eds) (1999) *Work and caring for the elderly: international perspectives*, Ann Arbor, MA: Brunner/Mazel.

Lehto, A.-M. and Sutela, H. (2008) *Työolojen kolme vuosikymmentä* [*Three decades of working conditions*], Helsinki: Statistics Finland.

Leinonen, A. (2009) 'Tutkittavana työssäkäynnin ja omaishoivan yhdistäminen: keskiarvoja, kokemuksia ja käsitteellistämisen tarpeita' ['Research on combining caring and working: numbers, experiences and need of conceptualisations'], *Gerontologia*, vol 23, no 1, pp 14–22.

Lewis, J. (2001) 'The decline of the male breadwinner model: implications for work and care', *Social Politics*, vol 8, no 2, pp 152–69.

Long, S.O. and Harris, P.B (2000) 'Gender and elder care: social change and the role of the caregiver in Japan', *Social Science Japan Journal*, vol 3, no 1, pp 21–36.

Martin-Matthews, A. and Campbell, J. (1995) 'Gender roles, employment and informal care', in S. Arber and J. Ginn (eds) *Connecting gender and ageing: a sociological approach*, Buckingham: Open University Press, pp 129–43.

Martin-Matthews, A. and Phillips, J. (eds) (2008) *Aging and caring at the intersection of work and home life: blurring the boundaries*, New York, NY: Lawrence Erlbaum Associates/Psychology Press.

MoI (Ministry of Interior) (2007) *National survey of women 2006*, Taipei: MoI, Department of Statistics.

MoPM (Ministry of Public Management) (2006) *Survey on time use and leisure activities*, Tokyo: MoPM, Home Affairs, Posts and Telecommunications.

Neal, M., Chapman, N., Ingersoll-Dayton, B. and Emlen A. (1993) *Balancing work and caregiving for children, adults and elders*, New York, NY: Sage.

NHSIC (NHS Information Centre for Health and Social Care) (2010) 'Survey of carers in households 2009/10', The NHS Information Centre for Health and Social Care. Available at: http://www.ic.nhs.uk/pubs/carersurvey0910

OECD (Organisation for Economic Co-operation and Development) (2010a) *OECD factbook 2010: economic, environmental and social statistics*, Paris: OECD Publishing.

OECD (2010b) *Labour force and demographic database, 2010*, OECD, doi: 10.1787/888932400893.

OECD (2011a) *Pensions at a glance 2011*, Paris: OECD Publishing.

OECD (2011b) 'Employment rate of women', in OECD (ed) *Employment and labour markets: key tables from OECD, No. 5*, Paris: OECD Publishing.

OECD (2011c) *OECD employment outlook 2011*, Paris: OECD Publishing.

OECD (2011d) 'Part-time employment', in OECD (ed) *Employment and labour markets: key tables from OECD, No 7*, Paris: OECD Publishing.

OECD (2011e) 'Employment rate of older workers', in OECD (ed) *Employment and labour markets. key tables from OECD, No 6*, Paris: OECD Publishing.

Olsson, L.-E., Svedberg, L. and Jeppsson Grassman, E. (2005) *Medborgarnas insatser och engagemang i civilsamhället – några grundläggande uppgifter från en ny befolkningsstudie* [*Citizens' contributions and engagement in civil society – some main results from a new population study*], Stockholm: Justitiedepartementet.

ONS (Office for National Statistics) (2011) *Social Trends 41*, London: Office for National Statistics.

Phillips, J. (ed) (1995) *Working carers: international perspectives on working and caring for older people*, Aldershot: Avebury.

Phillips, J. (1996) *Working and caring: developments at the workplace for family carers of disabled and older people*, Dublin: European Foundation for the Improvement of Living and Working Conditions.

Phillips, J. (1998) 'Paid work and care of older people: a UK perspective', in E. Drew, R. Emerek and E. Mahon (eds) *Women, work, and the family in Europe*, London and New York, NY: Routledge, pp 66–75.

Phillips, J. and Bernard, M. (2002) *Juggling work and care: the experiences of working carers of older adults*, Bristol: The Policy Press.

Rengo Tochigi Research Institute of Lives (2009) *Danjo kyôdô sankaku shakai to Wâku raifu balansu shakai no jitsugen no tameno kadai to taiô ni kansuru chôsa kenkyû hôkoku* [*Research on task and response to actualise gender-equal society and work–life balance*], Tokyo: Rengo Tochigi.

Sand, A.-B. (2010) *Anhöriga som kombinerar förvärvsarbete och anhörigomsorg* [*Family members who combine paid work and family care*], Stockholm: Nationellt kompetenscentrum Anhöriga.

Saraceno, C. (2010) 'Social inequalities in facing old-age dependency: a bi-generational perspective', *Journal of European Social Policy*, vol 20, no 1, pp 1–13.

TAFC (Taiwan Association of Family Caregivers) (2011) *Survey on family caregivers in 2011*, Taipei: TAFC.

Tamiya, N., Noguchi, H., Nishi, A., Reich, M.R., Ikegami, N., Hashimoto, H., Shibuya, K., Kawachi, I. and Creighton Campbell, J. (2011) 'Population ageing and wellbeing: lessons from Japan's Long-Term Care Insurance policy', *The Lancet*, vol 378, no 9797, pp 1183–92.

Vlachantoni, A. (2010) 'The demographic characteristics and economic activity patterns of carers over 50: evidence from the English Longitudinal Study of Ageing', *Population Trends*, no 141, pp 1–23.

Watson, E.A. and Mears, J. (1999) *Women, work and care of the elderly*, Aldershot: Ashgate.

Yeandle, S. (1999) *Supporting employed carers: new jobs, new services?*, Sheffield: Sheffield Hallam University.

Yeandle, S. and Buckner, L. (2007) *Carers, employment and services: time for a new social contract?*, London: Carers UK.

Yeandle, S., Wigfield, A., Crompton, R. and Dennett, J. (2002) *Employed carers and family-friendly employment policies*, Bristol: The Policy Press.

Young, H., Grundy, E. and Kalogirou, S. (2005) 'Who cares? Geographic variation in unpaid caregiving in England and Wales: evidence from the 2001 Census', *Population Trends*, no 120, pp 23–34.

TWO

The emergence of policy supporting working carers: developments in six countries

Sue Yeandle and Teppo Kröger, with Bettina Cass, Yueh-Ching Chou, Masaya Shimmei and Marta Szebehely

Introduction

This chapter presents the key features of the welfare state and policy context, as they affect carers, for each of the six nations included in the book – Australia and England, Finland and Sweden, and Japan and Taiwan – providing a point of reference for readers of later chapters. Outlining similarities and differences between the six countries, the chapter presents an overview of how carers and the support they may need have been conceptualised in the public policy sphere in three welfare systems (referred to in this book, as already explained, as 'liberal-democratic', Nordic and East Asian welfare systems).

Chapter One has already outlined basic information about people requiring care and carers in the six countries and has shown that care needs are expected to increase. This chapter considers the policy background and context affecting people of working age who help or care for relatives or friends who are sick, disabled or old, focusing on how far they are recognised and responded to in policy provisions. It outlines the support and services available to them in each country, noting any financial support carers receive and any employment options and rights accorded to them. At the end of the chapter, the focus turns to advocacy and the role played by carers' organisations in framing public policy in this field.

In each country, giving at least some kinds of care to sick, frail or disabled family members, friends or neighbours is normal and ubiquitous for people of working age, especially, but by no means exclusively, by women (see *Chapter One*). As the roles and activities of carers have come to the attention of policymakers in recent decades, each nation has chosen to adopt measures covering at least some of the types of support for carers identified in other international analyses

(Colombo et al, 2011). The chapter considers three types of support relevant to the reconciliation of work and the care of frail, elderly, sick or disabled people: (1) the *services* carers can access; (2) the *financial assistance* available to carers if they give up, take leave from or reduce their hours of paid work (or to remunerate their caring labour); and (3) their *rights and entitlements in employment*, which may protect carers from dismissal or unfair treatment and/or enable them to vary their working arrangements to facilitate caring activities.

After a brief review of how public policy affecting carers has developed in each pair of countries, these three types of carer support are discussed in this chapter. The boundary between 'carer-specific' support and support to the people carers assist is necessarily somewhat blurred. At one extreme, all services for a person with care needs can be conceptualised as a form of support for carers; at the other, 'carer support' is a concept covering *only* payments, services or rights accorded directly to carers. In this chapter, we focus mainly on the latter, since to fully explore all social care support in six countries and assess its significance for carers would not be possible in a single chapter. Some services, such as carers' 'breaks' or 'respite' services, self-evidently fall between these two categories, however.

Development of public policy on carers

The main public policy measures enacted or implemented in the six countries studied here are presented in summary form in Table 2.1. This shows changes and policy developments at the national level in each country. It concentrates on *legislation* relating to social services, social security or employment that addresses the circumstances of people with unpaid caring roles or responsibilities; any state *financial* support available to carers (sometimes organised by permitting local authorities [LAs] to make such help available); and *policies* promoted nationally that encourage the delivery of services and support to carers. As elsewhere in the book, each pair of countries is considered together: the liberal democracies; the Nordic states; and the East Asian countries. In each case, there are similarities, but also differences of approach, emphasis and policy objectives. This chapter highlights the timescales and main influences on the development of carer awareness and of policies and support (or lack of it) for carers, and explores the main features of each type of carer support in each country. It focuses on aspects that are especially relevant to the work–care reconciliation challenges that face carers of working age. The significance of the developments described is briefly considered at the end of the chapter and discussed in more detail in *Chapter Twelve*.

Table 2.1 Legislation and national policy on carers: a chronology covering six countries

	Australia	England	Finland	Sweden	Japan	Taiwan
1960s		1967: Dependent Relative's Tax Allowance.		From 1950s: LAs are allowed to pay care allowances and to employ family members as paid kin caregivers. 1964: National care allowance for parents to disabled children.		
1970s	1972: Wife's Pension (WP) for wives of Age and Invalid pensioners. 1973: Domiciliary Nursing Care Benefit for carers of frail aged/disabled people. 1974: Handicapped Child Allowance (HCA).	1975: Invalid Care Allowance (ICA).				
1980s	1983: Spouse Carer Pension (SCP, men only). 1985: Carer Pension (CP) (amalgamated WP/SCP) for carers of a spouse, parent, other close relative, offspring or friend. 1987: Child Disability Allowance replaced HCA.	1986: ICA available to married women.	1982: Social Welfare Act enabled municipalities to fund carer support and pay carer's allowance.	1989: Allowance for Care of Close Relatives: legal right to paid leave when a relative is severely ill (maximum 6 weeks).		
1990s	1996: Carer Payment replaced Carer pension. 1999: Carer Allowance (combined Child Disability Allowance and Domiciliary Nursing Care Benefit).	1995: Carers (Recognition and Services) Act. 1999: National Carers' Strategy. 1999: Employment Relations Act gave employees the right to 'reasonable time off' to deal with family emergencies.	1993: Decree on Support for Informal Carers 1995: Job Alternation Leave Experiment Act: allowed career breaks of 90-359 days. 1997: Social Welfare Act (revision): 1 free day per month for recipients of carer's allowance.	1994: Allowance for Care of Close Relatives (extended to 12 weeks). 1994: Disability Act: right to employ family member as personal assistant. 1998: Social Services Act (Revised): LAs encouraged to provide support for family carers. 1998: National Action Plan on carers (included state subsidy to municipalities).	1995: Childcare and Family Leave Act (Revised) extended to care of 'other family members' in addition to childcare, employers recommended to offer family care leave. 1999: Childcare and Family Leave Act (Revised) obliged employers to offer family care leave.	1993: Respite care initially introduced (in Taipei City). 1997: Disabled Persons (Respite Care) Act.

	Australia	England	Finland	Sweden	Japan	Taiwan
2000s	2004-11: One-off carer bonuses to CA and CP recipients. 2006: National Respite for Carers programme. 2007: Carer Adjustment Payment (interim measure, pending review of CP Child).	2000: Carers and Disabled Children Act (strengthened right to Carer's Assessment; carers eligible to receive services/direct payments. 2002: Employment Act: parents of disabled children gain 'right to request' flexible working. 2003: ICA re-named Carers' Allowance, carers aged 65+ able to claim. 2004: Carers (Equal Opportunities) Act: LAs must inform carers of rights/consider their wish to work in carers' assessments. 2006: Work and Families Act extended right to request flexible working to carers of adults. 2007: Pensions Act: pension credit for carers. 2008: National Carers' Strategy.	2001: Social Welfare Act (Revised): 2 free days per month for recipients of carer's allowance. 2002: Job Alternation Leave Act: 90-359 days' financially supported leave made permanent. 2005: Support for Informal Carers Act: 3 free days per month for recipients of carer's allowance.	2006: Increased state subsidies to LAs to develop support for family carers. 2009: Social Services Act (Revised) obliged LAs to provide support for family carers. 2010: Allowance for Care of Close Relatives extended to maximum of 20 weeks.	2000: Long Term Care Insurance Act: (included a family carer support programme). 2001: Family Care Leave extended / amended. 2002: Family Care Leave extended / amended. 2004: Family Care Leave extended / amended. 2005: Family Care Leave extended / amended.	2002: Gender Equality in Employment Act: unpaid leave to care for relatives. 2004: 5 days per year paid care leave (government officials only). 2007: Welfare of Disabled People Act: included Special Care Allowance to mid- or low-income senior citizens. 2007: Welfare of People with Disabilities Act: LAs to co-operate with NGOs on respite/ carers' services. 2009: Employment Insurance Act: unpaid care leave for carers of family members. 2009: Welfare of Older People Act: LAs to co-operate with NGOs on respite/carers' services.
2010s	2010: Fair Work Act: NES (National Employment Standards), right to request flexible work arrangements for carers of disabled children under 18; carer's leave. 2010: Carer Recognition Act. 2011: National Carer Strategy.	2010: National Carers' Strategy. 2010: Equality Act: prevents carers from discrimination (including at work) because they care for a disabled person.	2011: Support for Informal Carers Act (Revised): LAs may contract with a 'respite care' worker to replace family carer on 'days off'. 2011: Employment Contracts Act (Revised): right to request unpaid leave to care for family member.			

Note: Includes national legislation and policy. Date given is when measure introduced, except where otherwise stated.

The liberal democracies

England was the first of the countries studied in this book to pay serious policy attention to the needs of carers of adults with care needs by explicitly addressing their situation in state financial benefits and legislation (see Table 2.1). Carers were recognised in national policy on taxation and income support in the 1960s and 1970s; they became the subject of official data collection in the 1980s; and began to acquire limited rights in national social care and employment systems in the 1990s and 2000s. A clearer focus on carers, under pressure from the carers' movement, found expression in the first National Carers' Strategy (DH, 1999), introduced by a Labour government as a cross-departmental policy initiative. This acknowledged carers' need for services and support and their difficulties in reconciling work and care. In 2008, a revised National Carers' Strategy focused on carers' health, incomes and rights and drew specific attention to the needs of carers who wish to combine work and care (DH, 2008). In 2010, the incoming Conservative–Liberal Democrat government's 'vision' for carers also identified priorities that included 'enabling carers to fulfil their educational and employment potential' (DH, 2010: 5).

In Australia, carers in advocacy associations have made claims over the last 25 years for recognition and respect for carers, through income support, entitlements to support services and statutory recognition of caring responsibilities. Carers gained legislative recognition in the Australian social security system in 1985 (see Table 2.1) and from the 2000s, the lobbying and advocacy of carers' associations has led to an increased emphasis on carer support, primarily through community services (Carers Australia, 2007). More recently, a parliamentary inquiry ('Better Support for Carers') recommended further improvements, including a nationally consistent carer recognition framework and strategy, enhanced respite care services, the right to request flexible employment arrangements for all employees with care responsibilities, and support for carers seeking to enter or re-enter the workforce (HRSCFCH&Y, 2009: xxi–xxx). Although the Carer Recognition Act 2012 that followed established new principles for the recognition of carers and how they should be treated by public service agencies, it did not establish carers' rights or create legally enforceable obligations relating to carers (Phillips and Magarey, 2010). However, the National Carer Strategy identified carers' 'economic security' as a priority area for policy action, and emphasised the need to provide more options and support for carers to participate in paid work (Australian Government, 2011: 23).

The Nordic states

Until the 1990s, the main focus of care policy in Finland was on developing public care services, although an experiment in some LAs in the early 1980s introduced specific support – notably, a Carer's Allowance – for carers of older and disabled family members. This support was included in the Social Welfare Act 1982, the centrepiece of Finnish social welfare legislation, in force from 1984. It provided a legal framework for actions some LAs had already initiated, but did not *require* LAs to provide support for carers. Family care began to receive more attention in the late 1980s and early 1990s, as the first Finnish studies on carers were being undertaken. The 1993 Decree on Support for Informal Carers called on LAs to develop carer support, including respite care, access to a Carer's Allowance and individual service planning. Policy on care continued to be framed by the Social Welfare Act, revised in 1997 and 2001 to provide monthly 'days off' from caring for carers receiving Carer's Allowance from their LAs. Municipalities remained free to choose which carers to support, however, and despite the Support for Informal Carers Act 2005 (discussed later), arrangements have changed little in recent years.

In Sweden, municipal programmes of payments for family care of older people were first introduced in the 1950s: a modest attendance allowance and the employment of family members as home-helpers (Ulmanen, 2013). However, carers barely featured in policy documents until the early 1990s, when policymakers 'rediscovered' the family (Kröger, 2005; Johansson et al, 2011). Since then, political interest in family carers has increased dramatically, in a period when publicly funded care services have declined in coverage and expenditure, while the care of older people by family members, especially those with lower levels of formal education, has increased (Johansson et al, 2003; Szebehely and Trydegård, 2012). Family carers were first mentioned in Swedish legislation in the Social Services Act 1998, which stated: 'social services should support and provide relief for families who care for next of kin with chronic illnesses, elderly people or people with disabilities' (Johansson et al, 2011). At this time, the state recommended – but, like Finland, did not require – municipalities to develop services to support carers. To encourage this, the national government allocated SEK300 million (approximately €35 million) in 1999–2001, Sweden's first, very modest, financial investment in supporting carers. All subsequent governments have provided similar subsidies, aiming to show 'society's appreciation' of families who choose to care for sick, frail or disabled family members, enhance carers' quality of life, and reduce the risk that carers will 'burn out' or feel that they cannot continue caring (Johansson et al, 2011).

The East Asian states

Japan's Civil Code places a duty on relatives to support each other, and this fundamental legal position remains in place today. The Code normalises familial care and limits citizens' expectations of the state when care needs arise. In recent decades, however, increased longevity and a falling birth rate have brought care issues, especially the care of older people, into sharp focus in Japan. In the 1990s, this led to a debate and new policy on Long Term Care Insurance (LTCI), a radical shift in Japanese public policy. Since the 2000 LTCI Act, all workers aged over 40 must contribute to the LTCI scheme, designed to cover the rising costs of care, including home care. Carers in Japan have gradually become recognised in public policy since 1995, initially through legislation on the welfare of workers, when rights given originally to working parents were extended to include workers caring for other family members.

In Taiwan too, care for children, frail older people and disabled people is seen primarily as a family responsibility and defined as such in the Civil Code, which places legal responsibility for care on lineal family members (parents, spouses, siblings and children). Those needing care mostly live with their families: 60% of older people and 90% of disabled people (MoI, 2012). Several types of social services support – home care, day care, respite or residential care – are available, although relatively few families use them, not least because family members are expected to cover, or contribute to, their cost. Instead, many families employ a live-in migrant care worker to support older relatives. Legislation and official policy documents do not include any general recognition of the needs of carers, nor is the term 'carer' in general use. Welfare policies and legislation relating to older and disabled people (the Welfare of Disabled Persons Act 2007 and the Welfare of Older People Act 2009), a proposed Long Term Care Services Act and a planned Long Term Care Insurance Scheme all focus on the needs of older, sick and disabled people, but take no account of the needs of those caring for them.

Services available to carers

Given their different cultures and backgrounds, it is unsurprising that the services and support available to carers differ in each country.

Patterns are discernible across the three welfare systems, although some services, such as limited respite care, exist in all six states.

The liberal democracies

In Australia, family carers provide the majority of care to disabled and frail older people, often playing a key role in coordinating formal care services (AIHW, 2011). Nevertheless, most receive no formal services: 56% of primary carers supporting a disabled person under 65 and 65% of primary carers of older people had no such assistance in 2009 (AIHW, 2011: 218–21). Access to appropriate services is constrained by inadequate provision and lack of information. An official 2011 report concluded that carer support is 'administered in an ad hoc way across a number of programs and jurisdictions' (Productivity Commission, 2011a: 333), and a report on the welfare of Australians found that 38% of primary carers felt that they needed more support, including respite care and support in maintaining their own health, as well as physical, emotional and financial support (AIHW, 2011: 218–19).

Although services targeted at care recipients – including the Home and Community Care (HACC) services first introduced in 1985 – have a 'respite effect' for some carers (AIHW, 2011: 224), in 2008, 90% of HACC recipients had only two hours' help weekly, with just a few getting 'intensive' support (five to six hours per week) (AIHW, 2009). Australia's National Respite for Carers Program (NRCP) assists some carers, providing short-term or emergency respite, but while this supported one in five 'primary carers' in 2009/10, most carers never use respite services (ABS, 2011). Australia also has a long-standing practice of delivering services through government-funded non-governmental organisations (NGOs), including funding Carers Australia's network of associations to provide advice, education and training about caregiving (Productivity Commission, 2011a: 330).

Carers do not have a right in Australia to be assessed for or to receive support services, and significant problems in obtaining assessments for respite care and gaining access to planned and emergency respite have been reported (Productivity Commission, 2011a: 336). Responding to this, the Commonwealth (that is, national) government has announced the expansion of respite services and counselling for carers and the establishment of a regional network of carer support centres from 2014, although it remains silent on the issue of carers' assessment (Commonwealth of Australia, 2012: 7–8).

While publicly funded services for carers still reach only a minority of carers in England, in the 2000s, a national policy emphasis on building carers' services – following the 1999 National Carers' Strategy – increased the range and volume of support. Developments include 'carers grant' funding to LAs to develop respite and local support services for carers (Fry et al, 2009; Clements, 2010) and national programmes offering carers improved access to information, advice and training (Yeandle and Wigfield, 2011, 2012).

Legislation enabling carers' services to develop in England includes the Carers and Disabled Children Act 2000 and the Carers (Equal Opportunities) Act 2004. Both strengthened policy on carers' assessments, which are delivered through local authority social services departments and were first introduced via the Carers (Recognition and Services) Act 1995. The 2004 Act requires carers' assessments to take a carer's wish to continue in, or re-enter, paid work into account. In 2007, a New Deal for Carers programme signalled a greater national policy emphasis on social care support for carers, with implementation monitored at the national level (CSCI, 2009), and a new Standing Commission on Carers was established to advise government.

Most publicly funded services for carers are accessed via a carers' assessment, which LAs have a statutory duty to undertake where required (CSCI, 2009). Carers' services funded by LAs include direct payments to carers, respite care and breaks for carers, support groups, health checks, and training (Yeandle and Wigfield, 2011, 2012). Some LAs have developed local carers' strategies and appointed 'carers' lead officers' to champion change (Fry et al, 2009), often working with voluntary agencies.

Operating independently as voluntary organisations, 'carers' centres' also provide carers' services in some localities (Fry et al, 2009). In 2006/07, data on about half of English LAs found that they had allocated £44 million (€55.5 million) to local carers' organisations, through which 35,000 carers had been supported in a sample week (CSCI, 2009: 29, 40). Following the 2008 National Carers' Strategy, over 10,000 carers participated in a national programme of training that operated in 2008–10 and a programme of health and well-being support for carers assisted 19,000 carers, including 4,000 working carers, in 2009–11 (Yeandle and Wigfield, 2011, 2012).

Despite these developments and investments, most carers in England still care without receiving financial support, carers' services or accessing their modest employment rights. Reasons for this include: the complexity of carers' circumstances; low awareness of available support; worsening financial pressures on LAs, which limit service availability; restrictions on eligibility criteria for Carer's Allowance

(CA); and the large number of carers, whose care is costly to replace or support (Buckner and Yeandle, 2011).

The Nordic states

Carers have come into much greater focus in Finnish policy since the early 1990s, with carer support being one of the few welfare programmes to expand, while the numbers of people receiving residential or home-based care have declined. Policymakers seem to see carer support as a way of reducing demand for formal care services, especially for people aged 65 to 85. Such support is now institutionalised in Finnish law through the Support for Informal Carers Act 2005, but the considerable discretion that LAs retain has resulted in significant local variations in carer support and services.

In force from 2006, the 2005 Act has become the foundation of subsequent carer policy. It defined the criteria against which LAs could contract with carers and made such carers eligible for pension and accident insurance. The Act established minimum rates at which CA was payable, from €300 per month (from €600 per month for carers temporarily unable to participate in employment). The allowance is accompanied by respite care, allowing carers to have three days per month free from their caring responsibilities.

Although Finnish carers now receive greater policy attention, evidence about the support and services they receive is limited. Official statistics show that between 1990 and 2010, the coverage of home-based care services for people aged 65 or over decreased by 40%, but that during the same period, support for carers increased by 30% (Kröger and Leinonen, 2012). The reductions in services seem mainly to have affected people aged 65–84, increasing their reliance on family support. This shift towards carer support in Finland seems to be part of a larger move whereby responsibility for people under 85 is increasingly left to family carers, while only those with the greatest care needs receive formal support (Kröger and Leinonen, 2012).

In Sweden, an amendment to the Social Services Act 1998 in 2009 required municipalities to offer services to support family carers, and gave all caregivers the right to an assessment of their needs. However, it did not entitle them to support, which municipalities are not obliged to provide (Johansson et al, 2011). Swedish legislation explicitly mentions different groups of people in need of care, but, in practice, municipal support to carers has focused overwhelmingly on those caring for an older family member, with family and informal care to younger disabled people virtually invisible in Swedish social policy (Jeppsson

Grassman et al, 2009). Notable is the very limited attention to carers of working age, with most support focused on older carers, especially those caring for an older spouse (Sand, 2010). Municipal expenditure has mainly sought to address carer 'burnout', by offering carers training, mentoring, advice and support and by attending to carers' health needs, with helping carers to keep well seen as a means of sustaining family caregiving and controlling costs (Johansson et al, 2011).

Sweden collects detailed statistics on care services but these do not routinely include data on support to family carers. Care by family members has increased steadily since the late 1980s, however, indicating that formal care services are not meeting the increasing needs of an ageing population (Kommunal, 2011; Szebehely and Trydegård, 2012). Most Swedish municipalities have a contact person for family carers, who provides information about services available; these usually include respite care, counselling and personal assistance.[1] There are no national statistics on how many family carers receive this type of support, however. Under Swedish family and welfare legislation, responsibility for providing the care needed by disabled or older adults rests not with the family, but with the municipality, with services offered irrespective of whether there is a family member available (MHSA, 2008). Some municipalities – but far from all – also offer financial support for family carers. Most services for carers are free, but modest user fees (4–5% of the actual cost) are charged for care services provided to older people (Johansson et al, 2011; Szebehely and Trydegård, 2012: 301).

The East Asian countries

In Japan, family carer support was introduced as part of a community support programme linked to the Long Term Care Insurance Act 2000 (LTCI). Delivered by municipalities, this gave some carers access to respite care (Colombo et al, 2011: 129) and allowed LAs to deliver support to family carers if they wished, but did not oblige them to do so. The programme includes: education and training for carers; an 'exchange programme' among carers; and a support service for carers of older people with memory problems. Further measures to strengthen the LTCI service infrastructure, including establishing community general support centres, were adopted in 2011, when the Act was revised (MHLW, 2012). The changes made also aimed to improve 'caregiver compensation' within the LTCI system.

In Taiwan, service developments for carers are very recent. Both the Welfare of Disabled People Act 2007 and the Welfare of Older People Act 2009 require LAs to provide, in cooperation with NGOs, services such as respite, carer training, counselling, support groups and information about access to services, with the aim of sustaining family care and improving the quality of life for carers and older and disabled people. Not all LAs provide the full range of services, however, and few older and disabled people or their family carers actually use such services. Respite care users account for less than 1% of the population of older and disabled people with care needs, and the available budget is equivalent to less than 1% of overall spending on disability services (Chou et al, 2008: 19).

Financial support available to carers

State financial support for carers takes a variety of forms: specific carers' benefits (as in Australia and England); other income support in circumstances where caring leads to poverty or disconnection from the labour market (as in England); payments to care (as in Finland and Sweden); direct cash-for-care payments to carers (as in England); or payments to offset the costs of caring (as in Australia). As noted later, most carers of working age do not receive such financial support, even where it has existed for many years. Overwhelmingly, carers of working age support themselves and their families by undertaking paid work.

The liberal democracies

Australia introduced Carer Pension, later Carer Payment (CP), in 1985 (Ganley, 2009). This provides income support for carers unable to support themselves through substantial paid employment. It is means-tested on the income of both the care provider and the care receiver, who must also meet an assessment of disability (AGDHS, 2012). CP provides substantially higher rates and more liberal conditions than most other forms of income support for Australians of workforce age, but, in 2008, was paid to only a very small proportion of all carers (Ganley, 2009). However, it is not subject to activity testing and not included in the 'activation' policies applied to most other forms of income support for working-age people. While CP recipients may participate in paid work, unpaid work, education or training for up to 25 hours per week, in 2006, only 23% had earnings while receiving it (Ganley, 2009: 39). Reasons included the strain of caring responsibilities, inadequate skills and training (for some), and the carer's own health problem or disability: about 40% of recipients had not been in employment when they started caring and/or receiving CP (Ganley, 2009: 46). Some Australians also get a small non-means-tested CA, introduced in 1999, replacing other small payments introduced in 1973 and 1974. CA is paid to people who provide daily care and attention to a dependent child or adult with a disability or medical condition in partial recognition of the additional costs of care. Many carers rely on government income support as their main source of income, however, reflecting their lower rates of labour force participation and concentration in part-time work. In 2003, income support was the main source of personal cash income for 40% of Australian carers, compared with 24% of other people (ABS, 2008: 53).

Introduced in 1976, Invalid Care Allowance – available at first only to single women caring for their parents – was the first financial support for carers in England. Subsequently renamed CA, this still provides financial assistance (£241 [€300] per month in 2012) to those whose ability to support themselves through paid work is negatively affected by substantial caring responsibilities. In 2011, it was paid to almost half a million carers of working age in the UK (130,000 men and 349,000 women) (DWP, 2012). Recipients must provide care for 35 or more hours per week for someone receiving a state disability benefit. Their personal earnings from paid work must be under £100 (€125) per week, and if studying, they must be doing so for less than 21 hours per week (Fry et al, 2011). Since 2004, a very small number of carers have received a direct payment (cash to purchase services) from their LA following a carer's assessment: this is not intended to replace or supplement forgone income. Many carers, as in Australia, live in low-income households and depend on the other forms of income security available to all citizens. A parliamentary inquiry recently noted that CA 'makes a modest contribution to reducing poverty among carers' (HCWPC, 2008: 33).

The Nordic states

Finland has also offered a CA from the early 1980s. Since the Social Welfare Act 1982, it has been directed to carers of older and disabled family members. Currently, this carer support is framed by the Support for Informal Carers Act 2005. In 2011, the minimum allowance was €353 per month. The allowance is taxable income but it is not affected by the income or assets of either the carer or the care receiver. The legal framework leaves wide discretion to municipalities concerning both eligibility and the level of support, however. The allowance is not really meant as a compensation for forgone earnings, unlike the job alternation compensation, which provides a benefit of 70–80% of the level of earnings-related unemployment benefits. Parents of disabled or sick children can also receive a special care allowance for a maximum of 90 working days per year, compensating 70% of lost income.

Besides modest levels of municipal cash allowances for carers, Sweden has also had a unique model of carer support since the 1950s. LAs have been able to employ family carers on the same terms and employment conditions as home care workers. Thus, these family carers have become municipal employees with the task of providing care for their family members. The use of this support model has nevertheless decreased considerably in recent decades, although increasing numbers of family members of severely disabled people are now employed as personal assistants following the implementation of changes in disability policy (see *Chapters Three, Six* and *Nine*). Sweden's payment for 'end of life care leave' offers a good level of compensation – 80% of normal income – and the care allowance for parents with a disabled child provides an average benefit of €500 per month.

The East Asian countries

In Japan, about 40% of municipalities offer some carers of older people a cash allowance designed to help pay for their care. Although these cash benefits are not part of the universal national system, some municipalities and prefectural governments choose to pay them (Kikuchi, 2010). Prior to the introduction of the LTCI system, these formed a major source of support for carers: before 2000, 23 of Japan's 47 prefectural governments provided such allowances, although only five still offered these at the end of the decade (Kikuchi, 2010: 168).

Taiwan provides a special care allowance for some family carers, worth between NT$3,000 and $5,000 (€75–€125) per month. The eligibility criteria are tight: although they need to be of working age, recipients are not allowed to be in full-time paid work. The allowance is means-tested and older people cared for by family carers who receive it are not permitted to use publicly funded care services.

Carers' rights and entitlements in employment

The liberal democracies

In Australia, two of the 10 National Employment Standards (NES) set out in the Fair Work Act 2009 are directly applicable to the employment circumstances of some carers: the NES on requests for flexible working arrangements and the NES on personal/carer's leave and compassionate leave (AGFWO, 2010). The flexible working NES gives certain employees, including those responsible for the care of a disabled child aged under 18, the right to request a change in working arrangements, such as different hours or a different pattern or location of work (AGFWO, 2010: 85). Employers are not obliged to approve the request, but must give a written business case for not doing so within 21 days. To be eligible, employees must already have 12 months' continuous service or have had long-term casual employment with the employer and 'reasonably expect' this to continue, criteria that carers with intermittent employment or seeking to enter or return to work after a break cannot meet. This NES is not applicable to carers of disabled adults, despite strong calls for this in several official reports and by carers' associations (HRSCFCH&Y, 2009; Productivity Commission, 2011a): the 2011 National Carer Strategy commits the Australian government to consulting with 'stakeholders' on making such a change (Australian Government, 2011: 24), but no further announcements have been made.

The second NES gives employees – excluding casual employees – 10 days' *paid* personal/carer's leave that accrues progressively during a year of service and can accumulate from year to year (AGFWO, 2011: 1). An employee may take paid carer's leave to care for a member of their close family or household who needs care or support because of an illness, injury or an unexpected emergency (AGFWO, 2010: 111). In these circumstances, employees are also entitled to two days' *unpaid* carer's leave for each occasion when a member of their family/household needs care and to two days' *paid* compassionate leave for each occasion when a member of their immediate family or household contracts an illness or sustains an injury posing a serious threat to his or her life (AGFWO, 2010: 113). While these entitlements are of considerable benefit to employees with caring responsibilities, those with continuous responsibilities that periodically become more intensive find them insufficient to meet their employment and caregiving responsibilities. Some carers use all their annual paid leave entitlement for caring activities, leaving them with no remaining holiday entitlement or opportunity for rest, a significant problem that may help to explain carers' relatively high rate of sickness and disability (Ganley, 2009; HRSCFCH&Y, 2009; ABS, 2011).

Carers seeking to enter or re-enter the workforce can access Job Services Australia – the national network covering non-government employment services – for support in finding training, skills development, work experience and tailored assistance (Australian Government, 2011: 23), but their lack of any rights to flexible working options are often a sticking point that they struggle to overcome.

In England, employed carers acquired modest legal rights in the 2000s. They may take a few days' *unpaid* leave for a 'family emergency' – such as a sick parent or spouse or a crisis with a disabled child – without fear of dismissal from their job (the Employment Act 2002). Some employers, especially in the public sector, offer this (at their discretion) without loss of pay. If carers have been in their job for at least six months, they can invoke a formal procedure, the 'right to request flexible working'. Employers must comply with this within a fixed time period: they can reject requests but must give a reason for this. This right was initially granted to parents of young children and of disabled children under 18 in the Carers and Disabled Children Act 2000, but was later extended to most other carers through the Work and Families Act 2006. Under the Equality Act 2010, carers are also protected from discrimination in association with a disabled person, following a ruling in the European Court of Justice in which the complainant was the mother of a disabled child who had been unfairly treated in her place of work (*Coleman v Attridge Law* [2008] C-303/06).

Carers outside the labour market who wish to return to work can obtain assistance from the official employment agency in England. Since 2010, this has funding to cover their alternative care expenses while they train to return to work. Carers, unlike other job-seekers, do not face benefit penalties if they fail to look for work. Those eligible for CA may claim this while working, provided their earnings from their employment remain below £100 (€125) per week, effectively restricting them to low-paid, part-time work (Fry et al, 2011).

Some employers and trade unions in England have shown an interest in supporting the reconciliation of work and care since at least the mid-1980s (OFW, 1990), but real attention to carers' need for help in reconciling the demands of care and work came first in the voluntary sector. With EU funding, Carers UK's 'Action for Carers and Employment' project engaged employers, trade unions and policymakers as well as social care agencies between 2002 and 2007. This established the relevance of carers to the broader labour market activation agenda, created the Employers for Carers group and pressed the government to respond to working carers (Yeandle and Starr, 2007).

The Nordic states

In 1996, a Finnish experiment in employment policy – the Job Alternation Scheme – enabled some carers (and others) to obtain a temporary break, from three months to a year, from their paid jobs, with the support of an earnings-related benefit that partially compensated for their forgone earnings. The scheme, which is still available, was not designed as a carer support measure, however; its main purpose was to boost employment by requiring employers to recruit an unemployed person while an existing employee took a break. In 2011, Finnish working carers were also accorded a right to request 'care leave' from their employers, but without earnings compensation.

There is almost no research and very little discussion of the issues faced by working carers in Sweden (Sand, 2010; Ulmanen, 2013). The only form of leave available for carers is the 'end of life leave' that gives workers a right to paid leave of up to 20 weeks if a family member is terminally ill. In a recent report, the Municipal Workers' Union noted the increase in family caregiving and the particular impact caring for a parent has on women with lower levels of formal education (Kommunal, 2011). This called on the state to increase investment in eldercare services to enable family members of frail older people to remain in paid work without worrying if their relatives are receiving adequate care. It did not advocate direct support for carers, however, citing the 'official' Swedish position that good publicly funded care services offer carers the best form of support.

The East Asian countries

Since 1995, the law in Japan has required employers to make an effort to introduce a family care leave system, a measure strengthened in 1999 when employers became obliged to do this. Part of a wider set of measures on gender equality and parental rights in Japan, these arrangements included legislation for the equal opportunity and treatment of male and female workers. This gave employees meeting specified criteria the right to 93 days' leave for 'each occurrence of circumstances in which a family member's condition requires constant care' (Colombo et al, 2011: 122; see also MHLW, 2009). Subsequent measures aim to protect workers with family care responsibilities from disadvantageous treatment, entitle them to apply for reduced working hours and put arrangements in place to assist parents of sick or disabled children.

These measures arose from concerns in Japan about population ageing, fertility and the size of the active workforce as well as evidence that some 455,000 Japanese workers, many aged under 59, had left or changed their jobs 'for family care' between 1997 and 2002 (MHLW, 2009). By 2008, most Japanese companies had employment policies providing for family care and almost half had in place a care leave system for sick or disabled children (MHLW, 2008), although these measures were better integrated in larger than in smaller firms. In 2009, an official report on work–life balance led to a new short-term leave system for family care that enabled workers to accompany a family member to hospital or care for him/her for five days per year and established dispute resolution procedures for care leave (MHLW, 2009).

In Taiwan, official policy supporting the reconciliation of paid work and family care remains limited, although the Gender Equality in Employment Act 2002 has allowed employees to take unpaid parental leave or unpaid leave to care for relatives. However, when the Employment Insurance Act 2002 was amended in 2009 to introduce a government subsidy (60% of salary for up to six months) for workers taking parental leave to care for children under three, this was not extended to carers of other family members, whose leave remains unpaid.

Voluntary organisations supporting carers

The role of voluntary organisations in developing carers' services and highlighting the importance of carers' role is significant in all six countries and especially prominent, over a long period, in the two liberal democracies. As already noted, in England and Australia, campaigning on behalf of carers and providing services to support them has led to strategic policy commitments to help carers who wish to combine work and care, although in Australia, the measures are considerably less extensive with respect to flexible work arrangements than in England (DH, 1999, 2008, 2010; Australian Government, 2011). Finland's and Sweden's main carers' organisations emerged later than in England and Australia – in 1991 and 1996, respectively – but both have influenced the development of local services for carers and campaigned nationally for policies beneficial to carers. In the East Asian states, especially Taiwan, voluntary organisations have recently become important in building support for carers, pressing for innovative carer support and public funding of suitable policies. As discussed later, however, it is in England that the strongest link has been made between a voluntary sector carers' organisation, employers and the reconciliation of work and care. This reflects a particular emphasis in that country, although there are emerging parallels elsewhere and a focus on carers and employment has begun in recent years to feature in the work of carers' organisations in most countries.

The liberal democracies

Over the past 25 years, Australian carers' associations – operating throughout Australia and connected as a national network through Carers Australia – have placed the needs of carers on the political agenda and ensured that their voices are heard in official inquiries concerned with health care, aged care and disability services reform, as well as on issues and services directly concerning carers (HRSCFCH&Y, 2009; NHHRC, 2009; Productivity Commission, 2011a, 2011b). They have advocated for carers' interests and needs for income support, community services, information and counselling, and highlighted carers' circumstances and the costs and value of their care (Access Economics, 2005; Cummins et al, 2007). These associations helped establish the 2009 parliamentary inquiry on carer support (HRSCFCH&Y, 2009), which paved the way for the 2011 National Carer Strategy and the Carers Recognition Act 2012. They have argued for carers' assessments, 'consumer-directed' eldercare and disability care, with particular emphasis on carers' requirements within such arrangements, and for carers' rights and recognition (Carers Australia, 2010).

Carers Australia also advocated vigorously on carers' behalf during the deliberations of the 2008 National Health and Hospitals Reform Commission, which considered the future design of Australia's health system. Describing unpaid carers as the invisible health workforce, the Commission recommended that carers be supported through educational programmes, information, mentoring, timely advice and, subject to the consent of those they care for, engagement in health decisions as well as respite care, and emphasised that carers' health should be a priority for primary health care services (NHHRC, 2009).

England is home to Carers UK, probably the world's first carers' organisation (initially established in 1965). It has campaigned on carers' issues for almost 50 years, latterly alongside other carers' organisations (Cook, 2007). The initial focus of the carers' movement was on the financial well-being of women who had given up a career to care, with the needs of full-time carers dominating public debate and policymaking about carers. In the 1990s, as evidence on carers' circumstances revealed that most carers provide unpaid care alongside paid work, 'working carers' became an important focus for the carers' movement.

Carers UK's impact on the work–care reconciliation agenda has been important. It established an influential group, Employers for Carers, in 2002 and led the Action for Carers and Employment (ACE) project (during 2002–07). This EU-funded, multi-agency policy and delivery partnership project addressed the barriers carers face in entering, re-entering or remaining in the labour market and explored the development, design and delivery of alternative care services that enable carers to work (Yeandle and Starr, 2007). Labour market conditions were receptive to thinking on employee recruitment and retention in the 2000s, with the ground prepared for new policy on reconciling work and care by significant investment in support for working parents (Williams, 2001; Yeandle and Buckner, 2007). Evidence from ACE helped shape the Carers (Equal Opportunities) Act 2004, the focus on working carers in the 2008 National Carers' Strategy and national policy on carers and employment after 2010.

Voluntary organisations in England also offer advice lines, online forums, training and other services for carers, run annual events and campaign vigorously on carers' issues. As noted earlier, a network of 280 local carers' organisations[2] also provides services – including carers' breaks and respite – in many localities.

The law on carers in England has been strongly influenced by Carers UK and other organisations representing older and disabled people and their carers. This has been achieved by providing evidence and support to parliamentarians, through the All-Party Parliamentary Group on Carers at Westminster, and by assisting MPs to develop and introduce three parliamentary Private Member's Bills. The latter passed into law as the Carers (Recognition and Services) Act 1995, the Carers and Disabled Children Act 2000 and the Carers (Equal Opportunities) Act 2004 (Clements, 2010).

The Nordic states

Although Finland is a Nordic welfare state in which public services have been central for several decades, it also has a strong tradition of voluntary action and voluntary associations, dating back to the 19th century. Many nationally provided welfare services of today were originally created and developed by voluntary associations, which have been important in lobbying for new welfare support and services, including support for carers. The Association of Care Giving Relatives and Friends, the main national organisation of carers – with 10,000 members, founded in 1991 – has maintained close relationships with politicians and other policymakers. Its campaigning influenced the Support for Informal Carers Act 2005, although it has expressed disappointment in its implementation, particularly the unwillingness of LAs to make larger investments in carer support.

The Association has many local branches that organise home-based respite care, peer support groups and other forms of carer support. However, these suffered a major blow in 2006 when the Finnish Slot-Machine Association changed its funding policy, leaving many groups without monies.[3] Several branches had to close their services, including home-based respite care. The Association and its local branches nevertheless continue their major role as sources of peer support and advocacy for their members (Salanko-Vuorela et al, 2006; OLL, 2011).

In Sweden too, voluntary organisations have played a significant role as initiators of various welfare programmes that municipalities have later taken over. The Red Cross, for example, organised the first home care services in 1950. Latterly, the role of voluntary organisations has been more limited than in Finland, although when public funds for carer support were allocated to municipalities in 1999–2001, they were required to collaborate with voluntary organisations to develop new support, an arrangement somewhat unusual in Sweden (Jegermalm, 2003: 758).

Today, Swedish voluntary organisations support carers mainly by organising support groups and providing carer training. The two most significant organisations in this respect are Carers Sweden (Anhörigas Riksförbund), established in 1996, and the Dementia Association (Demensförbundet), founded in 1984. Carers Sweden campaigns for additional tax-funded support for family carers (including advisory services and respite care), paid short-term leave for carers ('contact days') and pension credits for caring. In 2011, it operated through a network of 63 local branches across Sweden. The Dementia Association, which claims to be the largest national organisation for carers, has 11,000 members and 130 local branches. Its principal aim is to protect the interests of people with dementia and it campaigns primarily for better services for them, pressing also for improvements in support for their families.

The East Asian countries

Japan's Promotion of Specified Non-profit Activities Act 1998 enabled eligible non-profit organisations to become legal entities. After the LTCI system was established in 2000, many grassroots voluntary organisations became non-profit organisations (NPOs) and began to provide services. Most supply home-help or day care services and some began to hire care managers to help families with care planning. Because the LTCI system takes no account of carers involved in the caring situation when assessing eligibility, any carer involvement is first considered only when an eligible older person needs a care plan. Many NPOs become involved in supporting carers in this way: some also provide services not covered by the LTCI scheme. NPOs are growing rapidly in all areas of social service provision but their overall share is still small – less than 5% among LTCI service providers – relative to the role of private and quasi-public welfare organisations (Kôsei Tôkei Kyôkai, 2009: 80). Some have commented that NPOs, becoming too close to private services, are losing their voluntary and independent missions (Suda, 2006).

The Taiwan Association of Family Caregivers (TAFC), established in 1996 by a group of health professionals, scholars and carers, was the country's first voluntary group working for the rights of carers (TAFC, 2011). Campaigning on carers' issues began in earnest in 2010 and by 2011, TAFC branches had developed in 10 Taiwanese LAs. The TAFC campaigns on four main issues: one day a week respite for family carers; paid family care leave; inclusion of family carers in the forthcoming Long-term Care Services Act (LTC; drafted in 2011); and economic security for carers. The TAFC and 26 other NGOs have established a 'LTC Coalition' to monitor the government's design of its planned LTC scheme. Carers' issues were not initially included in planning for the scheme and the TAFC and LTC Coalition have pressed for additional measures, including: universal LTC services to meet the needs of care recipients and family carers; LTC inspection and ombudsman systems; and family support services. They also argued for domestic and 'live-in' migrant care workers, with appropriate training, to be integrated into Taiwan's LTC system.

Policy variations

The liberal democracies studied here, Australia and England, are distinctive in having first adopted measures specifically designed to support carers in the 1960s and 1970s, and in initially offering carers in particular circumstances payments and allowances to compensate them for forgone income from paid work. This chapter has described how, over several decades and spurred on by an active carers' movement, both countries developed a range of carer support and services, which are still received by only a minority of carers. Each also enacted legislation with specific reference to carers, built a database of official statistics about carers and adopted a strategic approach to supporting carers through explicit policy statements with a focus – especially in England, and increasingly so in Australia – on working carers.

Support for carers in Finland and Sweden came initially through the strong emphasis in their 20th-century Nordic welfare states on universal, publicly funded services for all with care needs. In theory, these were designed to ensure that family members did not feel under pressure to take on unpaid caring responsibilities for their sick, frail or disabled relatives, and could – initially in Sweden, and later in Finland – be remunerated if they did so. However, when Nordic public services came under pressure in the final decades of the 20th century, the previously rather hidden role of family carers became visible. In both countries, this led to the development of explicit policies and support for carers whose needs received new attention, especially in the 1990s and 2000s, in altered public policy arrangements.

In East Asian societies, with their historical lack of welfare state support, the traditional reliance on family systems came under significant strain towards the end of the 20th century, as exemplified in Japan and Taiwan. In the 1990s and 2000s, policy in these countries responded to rapid population ageing, changes in gender relations and difficult labour market pressures, beginning in both cases with new public policy developments affecting employment. Here, the initial focus in work–care reconciliation policy was on fairness at work for women, and, in Japan, on funding long-term care. In the 1990s and 2000s, both countries adopted measures allowing leave for family care and permitted LAs to fund some support and services for carers.

These policy developments relating to carers can be conceptualised in a variety of ways. In the liberal democracies studied, they are probably best seen as 'enhancements' of the mainly means-tested safety-net care provision available to those in greatest need. A focus on carers' needs in the workplace was also encouraged by labour market pressures in the 1990s and 2000s in England and, more recently, in Australia. In the two Nordic states, support for carers increasingly offers 'alternative options' in hard-pressed universal welfare systems. Recent pressures have led in Finland and in Sweden to a variety of new arrangements for carer support, including in employment policy. In East Asia, state support for carers is a novel feature of public policy, mainly evident in new employment arrangements. Here, scholars and activists concerned about women overburdened with family care and paid work have pressed for these changes, which the state has started to accept in the face of rapid population ageing, decreasing birth rates and economic change.

Notes

[1] From 1994 in Sweden, a group of disabled people – those who need personal help to take care of hygiene, to get dressed and undressed, to have

meals, or to communicate with others – have had a legal right to personal assistance and to have the costs of the assistant covered from public funds. The disabled person can choose whether he/she wants to buy hours from personal assistance entrepreneurs, arrange them through a cooperative, become a private employer or simply demand this type of service from the municipal welfare administration (Berg, 2003). Since 2009, Finland has also offered a group of disabled people the right to personal assistance.

[2] Comprising 144 Princess Royal Trust for Carers (PRTC) and 76 Crossroads centres (see: www.carers.org) and 60 'Carers UK' local branches (see: www.carersuk.org).

[3] In Finland, the Slot-Machine Association has the monopoly for slot-machines and casinos and is the main funder of voluntary associations. In 2006, it ceased funding activities that could also be provided by for-profit providers, responding to concerns that its semi-public funding could distort market competition.

References

ABS (Australian Bureau of Statistics) (2008) *A profile of carers in Australia*, Canberra: ABS.

ABS (2011) *Caring in the community*, Canberra: ABS.

Access Economics (2005) *The economic value of informal care*, Canberra: Access Economics/Carers Australia.

AGDHS (Australian Government Department of Human Services) (2012) 'Carer payment'. Available at: www.humanservices.gov.au/customer/services/Centrelink/carer-payment

AGFWO (Australian Government Fair Work Ombudsman) (2010) *National Employment Standards: the Fair Work Act 2009*, Canberra: AGFWO.

AGFWO (2011) 'Personal/carer's leave and compassionate leave and the National Employment Standards', FWOFS27. Available at: www.fairwork.gov.au

AIHW (Australian Institute of Health and Welfare) (2009) *Australia's welfare*, Canberra: AIHW.

AIHW (2011) *Australia's welfare 2011*, Canberra: AIHW.

Australian Government (2011) *National carer strategy*, Canberra: Commonwealth of Australia.

Berg, S. (2003) 'Personal assistance in Sweden', plenary speech at the Personal Assistance in Practice Conference organised by the Swiss Association for Social Policy, 20 May, Bern. Available at: http://www. independentliving.org/docs6/berg20030520.html

Buckner, L. and Yeandle, S. (2011) *Valuing carers 2011: calculating the value of carers' support*, London: Carers UK.

Carers Australia (2007) *Federal budget submission 2008–2009*, Canberra: Carers Australia.

Carers Australia (2010) *Federal budget submission 2011–2012: from recognition to action*, Canberra: Carers Australia.

Chou, Y.C., Tzou, P.Y., Pu, C.Y., Kröger, T. and Lee, W.P. (2008) 'Respite care as community care service: factors associated with the effects on family carers of adults with intellectual disabilities in Taiwan', *Journal of Intellectual and Developmental Disability*, vol 33, no 1, pp 12–21.

Clements, L. (2010) *Carers and their rights* (4th edn), London: Carers UK.

Colombo, F., Llena-Nozal, A., Mercier, J. and Tjadens, F. (2011) *Help wanted? Providing and paying for long-term care*, Paris: OECD Publishing.

Commonwealth of Australia (2012) *Living longer: living better*, Canberra: Commonwealth of Australia.

Cook, T. (2007) *The history of the carers' movement*, London: Carers UK.

CSCI (Commission for Social Care Inspection) (2009) *The state of social care in England*, London: CSCI.

Cummins, R.A., Hughes, J., Tomyn, A., Gibson, A., Woerner, J. and Lai, L. (2007) *The wellbeing of Australians: carer health and wellbeing*, Victoria: Deakin University.

DH (Department of Health) (1999) *Caring about carers: a national strategy for carers*, London: DH.

DH (2008) *Carers at the heart of 21st-century families and communities: a caring system on your side, a life of your own*, London: DH.

DH (2010) *Recognised, valued and supported: next steps for the Carers' Strategy*, London: DH.

DWP (Department for Work and Pensions) (2012) 'Carers Allowance quarterly statistics (Carers Allowance cases in payment)', DWP tabulation tool. Available at: http.//research.dwp.gov.uk/asd/index. php?page=ca

Fry, G., Price, C. and Yeandle, S. (2009) *Local authorities' use of carers grant*, London: DH.

Fry, G., Singleton, B., Yeandle, S. and Buckner, L. (2011) *Developing a clearer understanding of the Carers' Allowance claimant group*, London: DWP.

Ganley, R. (2009) 'Carer Payment recipients and workforce participation', *Australian Social Policy*, no 8, pp 35–83.

HCWPC (House of Commons Work and Pensions Committee) (2008) *Valuing and supporting carers: Vol 1*, London: The Stationery Office.

HRSCFCH&Y (House of Representatives Standing Committee on Family, Community, Housing and Youth) (2009) *Who cares? Report on the inquiry into better support for carers*, Canberra: Parliament of the Commonwealth of Australia.

Jegermalm, M. (2003) 'Support for carers of older people: the roles of the public and voluntary sectors in Sweden', *Social Policy and Administration*, vol 37, no 7, pp 756–71.

Jeppsson Grassman, E., Whitaker, A. and Taghizadeh Larsson, A. (2009) 'Family as failure? The role of informal help-givers to disabled people in Sweden', *Scandinavian Journal of Disability Research*, vol 11, no 1, pp 35–49.

Johansson, L., Sundström, G. and Hassing, L.B. (2003) 'State provision down, offspring's up: the reverse substitution of old-age care in Sweden', *Ageing and Society*, vol 23, no 3, pp 269–80.

Johansson, L., Long, H. and Parker, G. (2011) 'Informal caregiving for elders in Sweden: an analysis of current policy developments', *Journal of Aging and Social Policy*, vol 23, no 4, pp 335–53.

Kikuchi, I. (2010) *Kazokukaigo he no genkin shiharai – Kôreisha kaigo seisaku no tenkan wo megutte* [*Cash payments for family caring – on elderly care policy change*], Tokyo: Kôshokuken.

Kommunal (2011) *Hänger din mammas trygghet på dig? Att kombinera jobb med omsorg om föräldrar* [*Does your mum's safety depend on you? Combining a job and the care of a parent*], Stockholm: Municipal Workers Union.

Kôsei Tôkei Kyôkai (2009) *Zusetsu tôkei de wakaru kaigohoken 2009* [*Databook: the Long-Term Care Insurance scheme in figures 2009*], Tokyo: Kôsei Tôkei Kyôkai.

Kröger, T. (2005) 'Interplay between informal and formal care for older people: the state of the Nordic research', in M. Szebehely (ed) *Äldreomsorgsforskning i Norden: En kunskapsöversikt*, Köpenhamn: Nordisk Ministerråd, pp 243–80.

Kröger, T. and Leinonen, A. (2012) 'Transformation by stealth: the retargeting of home care in Finland', *Health and Social Care in the Community*, vol 20, no 3, pp 319–27.

MHLW (Ministry of Health, Labour and Welfare) (2008) *Basic survey on equal employment*, Tokyo: MHLW.

MHLW (2009) *Introduction to the revised child care and family care leave law*, Tokyo: MHLW.

MHLW (2012) *Act for partial revision of the Long-Term Care Insurance Act in order to strengthen long-term care service infrastructure*, Tokyo: MHLW.

MHSA (Ministry of Health and Social Affairs) (2008) *Stöd till anhöriga som vårdar och stödjer närstående* [*Support to family carers*], Stockholm: MHSA.

MoI (Ministry of Interior) (2012) *Reports of survey analyses: older people, disabled people, youth and citizens*, Taipei: MoI, Department of Statistics. Available at: http://sowf.moi.gov.tw/stat/Survey/list.html

NHHRC (National Health and Hospitals Reform Commission) (2009) *A healthier future for all Australians*, Canberra: Commonwealth of Australia.

OFW (Opportunities for Women) (1990) *Carers at work*, London: Opportunities for Women.

OLL (Omaishoitajat ja Läheiset -Liitto ry) (2011) *Onneksi on omaishoitaja. Yhdistykset toimivat 1991–2011* [*Thank God for carers. Activities of associations 1991–2011*], Helsinki: Omaishoitajat ja Läheiset -Liitto ry.

Phillips, J. and Magarey, K. (2010) *Carer Recognition Bill*, Canberra: Parliament of Australia.

Productivity Commission (2011a) *Caring for older Australians*, Canberra: Productivity Commission.

Productivity Commission (2011b) *Disability care and support*, Canberra: Productivity Commission.

Salanko-Vuorela, M., Purhonen, M., Järnstedt, P. and Korhonen, A. (2006) *Hoitaahan ne joka tapauksessa. Selvitys omaishoidon tilanteesta 2006* [*They care in any case. A report on family care in 2006*], Helsinki: Omaishoitajat ja Läheiset -Liitto ry.

Sand, A.-B. (2010) *Anhöriga som kombinerar förvärvsarbete och anhörigomsorg* [*Family members who combine paid work and family care*], Stockholm: Nationellt kompetenscentrum Anhöriga.

Suda, Y. (2006) 'Devolution and privatization proceed and centralized system maintained: a twisted reality faced by Japanese nonprofit organizations', *Nonprofit and Voluntary Sector Quarterly*, vol 35, no 3, pp 430–52.

Szebehely M. and Trydegård, G.-B. (2012) 'Home care in Sweden: a universal model in transition', *Health and Social Care in the Community*, vol 20, no 3, pp 300–9.

TAFC (Taiwan Association of Family Caregivers) (2011) *History and main tasks*, Taipei: TAFC.

Ulmanen, P. (2013) 'Working daughters: a blind spot in Swedish eldercare policy', *Social Politics*, vol 20, no 1, pp 65–87.

Williams, F. (2001) 'In and beyond New Labour: towards a new political ethic of care', *Critical Social Policy*, vol 21, no 4, pp 467–93.

Yeandle, S. and Buckner, L. (2007) *Carers, employment and services: time for a new social contract?*, London: Carers UK.

Yeandle, S. and Starr, M. (2007) *Action for carers and employment: impact of the ACE partnership 2002–2007*, London: Carers UK.

Yeandle, S. and Wigfield, A. (eds) (2011) *New approaches to supporting carers' health and well-being: evidence from the National Carers' Strategy Demonstrator Sites programme*, Leeds: CIRCLE, University of Leeds.

Yeandle, S. and Wigfield, A. (eds) (2012) *Training and supporting carers: the national evaluation of the Caring with Confidence programme*, Leeds: CIRCLE, University of Leeds.

PART ONE

Working carers of older people

THREE

Family rediscovered? Working carers of older people in Finland and Sweden

Outi Jolanki, Marta Szebehely and Kaisa Kauppinen

Introduction

In this chapter, we draw together knowledge on employment legislation and payments to working carers with studies on family care of older people. The chapter focuses on adult children and other family members who care for older people in Finland and Sweden. As discussed in previous chapters, carers in general and working carers in particular have only recently become a policy issue in the Nordic countries. However, as we have also seen, the lack of political interest does not reflect a lack of actual care provided by family members. The characteristics and situations of working carers are somewhat uncharted territory in both countries. Four central questions are addressed in this chapter: 'Who are the carers?'; 'What kind of support is available for them?'; 'Are their working lives affected by caring responsibilities?'; and 'How do they perceive their everyday lives?'

In Finland and Sweden, the position of carers of older people cannot be understood without addressing the role of public actors, such as the state and municipalities. As discussed in *Chapter Two*, in both countries, municipalities are legally obliged to organise care for older people and a wide variety of social and health care services have been developed to meet the care needs of older people through formal, publicly funded systems.

Nevertheless, family members in both countries provide a great deal of support and help to older people, and their role seems to be growing (Kröger, 2005). In Sweden, family care (in particular, help by daughters) has increased among older people with compulsory – rather than with further – education only (Szebehely and Trydegård, 2012). The reduction of services for older people in Finland and Sweden (see *Chapter Two*) has happened without any significant legislative or policy change at the national level, but was possible because public care services for older people are not legally enforceable rights, and laws and regulations do not clearly define what type of services municipalities should provide. The state can steer and recommend, but municipalities are free to decide the type, eligibility criteria and coverage of the services they offer, including the extent of support for family carers.

While older people's care services vary across municipalities, in most cases, the proportion of older people living in residential care facilities or receiving home care services has been declining and care services have been redirected to those with greater care needs. Since the mid-1990s, the coverage of eldercare services has been lower in Finland and Sweden than in the other Nordic countries (Nososco, 2009). It can be argued that families of older people are not openly 'responsibilised' (Clarke, 2005) as carers, but that the restructuring of public care services has implicitly increased the expectation that family members will provide care.

In the past, comparative policy analysis has stressed the de-familialising potential of Nordic welfare states; however, recent studies have argued that, latterly, reduced public services in Finland and Sweden have increased the pressure on family members to provide care. Saraceno (2010) notes that in countries like Sweden and Finland, publicly funded services are increasingly targeted towards those with greater care needs. She argues that the situation of family members of older people with high-level needs can be characterised as 'supported familialism', whereas 'unsupported familialism' (or 'familialism by default') better depicts the situation of family members of older people with low-level needs.

Despite their similar trends of declining service coverage, there are also important differences between the two countries that probably affect the role family members play in older people's care. Service users pay higher fees in Finland than in Sweden (Kröger and Leinonen, 2012; Szebehely and Trydegård, 2012) and there is evidence that more Swedes than Finns find eldercare services affordable (Eurobarometer, 2007:77). Thus, formal care services may be perceived as more attractive by those who use them in Sweden. In Finland, citizens of all ages see both public care services and next of kin as important sources of help (Siltaniemi et al, 2009). By contrast, Swedish attitude surveys suggest that older people in general prefer to receive public home care services rather than help from their family members (Szebehely and Trydegård, 2012). These different attitudes are reflected in a Eurobarometer survey (Eurobarometer, 2007) that asked respondents about the best option for older people who can no longer live alone because of health problems. In this international comparison, public care services were seen as an important source of support in both countries, but more so in Sweden than in Finland.

Table 3.1: Perception of the best care options for elderly parents among population aged 15 years and above, 2007 (%)

	Live with family, or children should visit and help	Use public or private home care services	Move to a nursing home	Other (it depends, don't know, none)
Finland	32	51	13	4
Sweden	17	60	20	3
EU-27	54	27	10	9

Source: Eurobarometer (2007: 67).

How should the difference between Finland and Sweden in these figures be interpreted? Some suggest that Swedes appreciate their generous public care services and see formal care as a high-quality option (Alber and Köhler, 2004), whereas public discussion in Finland has been dominated in the past decade by news of poor-quality institutional care and inadequate public home care services. From this perspective, the figures in Table 3.1 may say more about trust – or mistrust – in the quality and accessibility of public care services than about family norms. Thus, while it seems evident that the views of Finns and Swedes differ, the explanation for this difference remains a matter for further research.

Employment and care responsibilities

Drawing on available Finnish and Swedish studies of the prevalence of caring and the characteristics of working carers, this part of the chapter outlines what is known about gender divisions and the age and working status of employees with care responsibilities. Unfortunately, most studies do not report the age of those cared for, but as very few older people live with their offspring in the Nordic countries, we focus on care provided outside the carer's own household, which is where most intergenerational care of older people takes place in these countries. In considering this topic, it should be noted that women have participated in paid work almost as much as men in both Finland and Sweden for several decades and that a higher proportion of middle-aged women have paid jobs in the Nordic countries than in the EU as a whole. In addition, as discussed in *Chapter One*, in both Finland and Sweden, more middle-aged women work full-time or long part-time hours than in most countries.

Finland

The Work and Health in Finland 2009 study examined the caring responsibilities of employees aged 45–63, finding that 22% reported looking after someone who needed help due to old age, illness or disability (Kauppinen and Jolanki, 2012: 139).[1] Another study reported even higher numbers of employees with care responsibilities outside their own homes: 45% of employees aged 45–54 helped an adult relative at least monthly and 21% in this group helped for 10 or more hours per month (Lehto and Sutela, 2008: 154). The differences in the figures reported probably arise from different question wording: the Work and Health in Finland study asked respondents if, outside their own work, they look after someone who needs help due to 'old age, illness or disability', while Lehto and Sutela (2008) asked about helping or looking after a parent or spouse's parent or grandchild without specifically mentioning care needs arising from disability or illness.

In the Work and Health in Finland study, 62% of those who provided help were women and 38% were men (Kauppinen and Jolanki, 2012: 133). Women and men differed significantly in their socio-economic circumstances, with caring being most frequent among male manual workers and among female lower-level salaried employees. Respondents mainly gave support to a parent or parent-in-law (79%). Helping was rather intensive, as 74% of carers provided assistance at least two or three times a week (69% of women, 78% of men). Care tasks were noticeably gender-divided: women mostly helped with household chores and personal care while men mainly helped with repairs, gardening and financial matters (Kauppinen and Jolanki, 2012: 142; see also Autio, 2005).

Both carers' and non-carers' preparedness to take care leave to care for their relative seemed very high. About half the respondents (52% of carers, 51% of non-carers) said they would be willing to leave work for a certain period to look after someone who needed constant care, and another quarter said they would do so under certain conditions.[2] The main issues affecting willingness to take care leave were financial – including the likelihood of being compensated for loss of earnings – and work-related, such as the opportunity to return to the same job (Kauppinen and Jolanki, 2012).

Workers with care responsibilities experienced work–family conflict more often than workers without such obligations (Kauppinen and

Jolanki, 2012: 146). Both men and women with caring roles were significantly more likely than other workers to feel that they were neglecting home due to work and to experience their life situation outside work as difficult.[3] Carers reported significantly more difficulty in concentrating at work than non-carers, but caring women reported this more than caring men (21% and 11%, respectively). Compared with workers who had no care responsibilities, carers more often doubted their ability to continue working in their profession until retirement, and had more often considered applying for early retirement. The difference between carers and non-carers is clear, even though the data do not provide information about whether the respondents felt their difficulties were related to care responsibilities. Nevertheless, the study showed that among carers, three factors in particular were related to thoughts of early retirement: (1) caring for a parent or spouse's parent; (2) rating one's own health as poor; and (3) having diminished interest towards work (Kauppinen and Jolanki, 2012). Having care responsibilities does not necessarily mean that they are experienced as a burden. Lehto and Sutela found that the experience of feeling burdened was linked to the number of hours spent caring. Almost a quarter (24%) of workers caring for more than 10 hours per month, and a third (32%) of those caring for 30 or more hours per month, reported problems in combining work and family life (Lehto and Sutela, 2008: 157). These findings suggest that care responsibilities alone do not create work–family conflict, but, as exemplified in the studies cited later in the chapter, result from several different factors.

Sweden

In Sweden too, there is a scarcity of population-based interview studies on working-age carers of parents and other family members. Jeppsson Grassman (2005: 43) found that 22% of those aged 16–84 years regularly helped a sick, disabled or frail older person who lived outside the respondent's own household (for an average of 14 hours per month). A further 5% helped a person within the same household (for an average of 67 hours per month). Caregiving outside the household was most common among those aged 45–59 years, and in this age group, parents were the most frequent recipients of care.

Another study (Szebehely and Ulmanen, 2009) found that 26% of women and 16% of men aged 45–64 reported that a family member or a friend outside their own household depended on their help, for example, with shopping, cleaning, laundry or getting out of the home. Women helped more often than men with all household tasks and with personal care: on average, they provided help almost three times a week, twice as often as men. This study also found that full-time work was less common among carers than among non-carers, although only women with compulsory or only upper secondary education were affected, not men or women with higher education (Szebehely and Ulmanen, 2009).

Similar gender patterns have been identified elsewhere. Based on the large national Living Conditions Survey conducted in 2002/03, Szebehely (2006: 445–8) found that 9% of people in the 55–64 age group provided help to an older, sick or disabled person daily or several times a week. A further 10% provided help once a week, while 11% helped someone less often. Women reported providing care somewhat more often than men, but their working lives were significantly more affected: 44% of the women aged 55–64 who provided care daily or several times a week to a person living in a separate household (often a parent) were outside the labour force, compared with 30% of women in the same age group with lesser or no caring responsibilities. No such relationship between caring and paid work was found for men.

Over the life course, many women in Sweden combine part-time working (mainly long hours, part-time work) with responsibility for children as well as for other family members. Thus, part-time work often precedes taking on a (new) caring responsibility, and it is therefore difficult to identify the precise importance of caring for an older person as a reason for working parttime. However, Szebehely (2006: 449) found that in the 55–74 age group, 4.5% of women and 1.5% of men had either reduced their working hours or stopped working altogether before their normal retirement age as a result of caring for an older, sick or disabled person.

The impact of care on working life is also shown in an earlier study of carers (mainly women) employed by municipalities to provide care to a family member, conducted in the early 1990s (see *Chapter Two* about this option in Sweden). Mossberg Sand (2000) found that before becoming employed as family carers, most respondents had cared without payment, often for a long period. Many had reduced their working hours or stopped working long before becoming an employed family carer. Arguably, employment as a family carer enabled these women to continue caring without unacceptable economic strain. The fact that both formal eldercare services and the number of family carers employed by the municipality have declined since that time suggests that such economic strain has become increasingly common among family carers of working age (Ulmanen, 2013).

Finland and Sweden compared

The review of Finnish and Swedish studies tells us that the majority of family care for older people in both countries is provided by women, in particular by middle-aged women who are also in paid work. These findings are in line with international research showing that most working carers of older people are middle-aged daughters (see *Chapter One*).

Several comparative studies have found that occasional help from adult children to their parents is more common in Northern Europe, whereas intensive caregiving is much more common in Southern Europe, where services are less developed (see, eg, Brandt et al, 2009). The less generous public spending on eldercare and the higher user fees in Finland suggest that family members of older people have to fill in larger gaps in Finland than in Sweden. The only comparative study of working carers that includes both countries supports this hypothesis. The European Working Conditions Survey[4] reports that caring intensively was more common in Finland than in Sweden: 13% of the working population in Finland provided help at least weekly compared with 9% in Sweden. In Denmark, which has the highest coverage of eldercare services in the Nordic countries, this figure was 6%.

International research shows that caring may affect participation in the labour market, causing absenteeism, job-quitting or early retirement. Some studies indicate that care responsibilities may negatively affect carers' income and career development (for a systematic review of this research, see Lilly et al, 2007). Several studies suggest that working-age carers in the Nordic countries are less negatively affected than carers in Southern Europe (see, eg, Kotsadam, 2011).

The studies reported in this chapter do not contradict the international research in this field. But even if it is obvious that the vast majority of working-age carers in both Finland and Sweden manage to combine paid work and care, we have seen that caring intensively for an older family member has an impact on working life in these countries too. The gender pattern seems to be similar in both countries: women's working lives are more affected than those of men. One Swedish study also indicates an important class-related pattern: the working lives of daughters of older people with fewer educational qualifications seem to be most affected.

Employment legislation and payments to working carers

The position of those caring for older people in Finland and Sweden is barely recognised in national employment legislation. By contrast, the situation of working parents caring for young children is a major concern in both countries and addressed in various regulations to facilitate the reconciliation of paid work and childcare. Some older workers caring for parents or other older relatives may use flexible working arrangements to have extra time, or some temporary relief, from their dual responsibilities, but there is almost no information available on the role played by such care responsibilities in workers' decisions to apply for these options.

In Finland, a parliamentary initiative was launched in 2007 to strengthen the options for care leave for employees caring for older parents or another person close to them. The right to be absent from work for 'compelling family reasons' was mentioned in earlier legislation (the Employment Contracts Act 2001), but the initiative to amend the legislation was explicitly linked to a parliamentary debate about whether employed people should have the right to take care leave to look after a sick relative (Kauppinen, 2010). The amendment was opposed on the grounds of the potentially negative consequences for women's participation in the workforce, increased employment costs and a risk to longer working lives. Despite this opposition, in 2010, an amendment was passed in Parliament to give employees the opportunity to take a leave of absence to care for a family member or other person close to the employee (Amendment to Employment Contracts Act 2011). The leave of absence is unpaid, but the employee can return to the same work duties after the caregiving needs are fulfilled. The leave has to be negotiated between the employer and the employee. If the leave is denied, an explanation must be provided. The law came into force only in April 2011, so its impact on working carers is not yet known, although the Ministry of Employment and the Economy plans to evaluate the use and gender impact of the law.

In Sweden, leave to care for an older parent or other adult family member is less developed than in Finland, and no strong voices are raised for the right to leave for caring. In public discussion, such care leaves – especially if they are longer – are usually regarded as 'gender traps' (Sand, 2010). On the other hand, the only legal right for carers in relation to the labour market in Sweden – the allowance for care of close relatives (*Närståendepenning*) – is reimbursed at a more generous level than the Finnish care leave. Introduced in 1989 (see *Chapter Two*), the allowance gives a family member (or friend) of a person with a life-threatening illness the legal right to paid, short-term care leave from work (paid at the same rate as sick leave, normally 80% of salary). A doctor's certificate is required. The length of this leave has been extended several times, from six weeks initially to 20 weeks in 2010. The leave is unrelated to the actual care provided and can also be used if the sick person is in hospital or a nursing home. In 2010, the leave was used by 11,000 people (74% women) for just over two weeks on average (Swedish Social Insurance Agency, 2012).

Apart from this allowance, working carers in Sweden have no rights to leave or reduced hours for caring for an adult family member. For many decades, it has been possible in Sweden for family carers to receive a modest care allowance or to be employed by the municipality to provide care for a family member (see Table 2.1), but these forms of payment for care are at the discretion of each municipality and since the early 1980s, the number of users has declined sharply. Latest statistics, for 2007, show that only 7,000 carers were employed as family carers or received a cash allowance (Sand, 2010). Not all cared for an older person, but in relation to the number aged 65+ in the population, this corresponded to just 0.4%.

The Informal Carer's Allowance in Finland is similar to the Swedish cash allowance but is more widely used, and supports carers caring for 2.6% of the 65+ population (Kröger and Leinonen, 2012: 323; see also *Chapter Two*). As in Sweden, even the highest rate, for demanding care needs considered incompatible with paid work, does not fully compensate for a monthly salary, as the allowance is just €364–€728 per month in Finland and very similar in Sweden (Sand, 2010). In Finland, the allowance is turning into an income support option for retired partner-carers, as the number of working carers receiving it has fallen, but the number of recipients who are retired is rising.

Family care and carers' situations are nevertheless receiving increasing attention in public discussion and politics in Finland. The Finnish Government Programme 2007–10[5] noted the importance of bringing together public care services, the Carer's Allowance and tax deductions for domestic help to ensure that comprehensive and good-quality care is given to older people. Carers were thus implicitly defined as part of the care system, and family care and supporting carers seem to remain as key issues on the political agenda. The new government appointed in 2011 recognised the importance of supporting family carers in its programme[6] and appointed a working group[7] to prepare a national development programme enabling carers to work part-time or take unpaid leave from work for care.

Some Finnish workers take 'job alternation leave', made a permanent arrangement in 2010, in order to give care to their older parents (see *Chapter Two*). While this scheme provides quite good financial compensation and can enable a carer to take leave for up to almost a full year, it requires the employer to agree and to hire an unemployed person in her/his place. As eligibility for the scheme includes a 10-year minimum work history (25 years for maximum benefit), it is used mainly by older workers. Most users are women (71%, average age 43 years), predominantly municipal employees in the social and health care sectors (Nätti et al, 2005). The leave is used for a variety of reasons, and the percentage using it primarily for caregiving has been small but increasing (4% in 1996, 6% in 2003). This may indicate that alternation leave is not especially important for working carers. However, since tiredness and time pressure are commonly experienced by working carers (see the next section in this chapter and *Chapters Eight* and *Nine*), it can be argued that the scheme may be helpful in reconciling work and care, even if caring would not be the primary reason for applying for it.

Everyday life experiences of working carers of older people

Qualitative research on working carers' experiences at work and at home, and on the subjective meanings given to caring and work, is still relatively scarce in both Finland and Sweden. However, the few studies conducted report similar findings to those of research done elsewhere. The defining element of carers' experience is ambivalence.

While previous studies have tended to emphasise the 'burden' of caring, recent studies note both negative and positive aspects of caring. Giving care was experienced as natural, expected and important (Eldh and Carlsson, 2011) and carers felt it important to be there when their parent's life is coming to an end (Dunér, 2010). Managing paid work alongside the care of older parents also contributed to skills and personal development and to a feeling of having a good 'balance' in life (Eldh and Carlsson, 2011). Caring was motivated by love and affection, but also by lack of good-quality public care services or the reluctance of the relative to accept formal help (Dunér, 2010; Leinonen, 2011a). Combining work and care was experienced as having negative effects on carers' health and well-being. In particular, carers report that a constant sense of crisis, lack of leisure time and inadequate rest led to tiredness and exhaustion. This was especially the case for 'lone carers' who had no (or little) help from other people or from formal care workers (Autio, 2005; Dunér, 2010; Eldh and Carlsson, 2010; Leinonen, 2011b; Jolanki, 2013a).

Trying to combine care and work created not just practical problems of time use, but also emotional and moral dilemmas. Carers felt constantly guilty about neglecting work or the rest of the family for care (or vice versa) (Autio, 2005; Dunér, 2010; Eldh and Carlsson, 2011). According to Dunér (2010), adult daughters found managing the situation most difficult and sometimes felt strongly trapped between the needs of the person cared for, the needs of the rest of the family and the demands of work. Working daughters stand out as more burdened than other categories of carers in other studies too (Krevers and Öberg, 2007; Sand, 2010) and the support for family carers provided by social services seems to be geared more towards the needs of older than of working-age carers.

The studies mentioned here show that carers found many different ways of finding a balance and reducing stress in their own lives. For a working carer, paid work can be either a source of strain or a necessary break from the constraints imposed by caring (Mossberg Sand, 2000; Sand, 2010; Leinonen, 2011a). Thus, work served as a balancing factor, offering respite from care demands and an arena for developing other skills (Eldh and Carlsson, 2011), social contacts (Dunér, 2010) and a source of identity (Jolanki, 2013). While support and recognition from managers and co-workers was an important source of 'balance', lack of support at work contributed to exhaustion (Eldh and Carlsson, 2011).

As discussed earlier in this chapter, studies in several countries have shown that caring can affect carers' labour market participation. However, leaving work or reducing working hours is not necessarily the solution carers prefer (Autio, 2005; Kauppinen, 2010; Kauppinen and Jolanki, 2012). An important strategy for maintaining balance in one's life was refusing to give up work (Eldh and Carlsson, 2011; Jolanki, 2013) and part-time work was sometimes sought as a way of continuing caring without having to leave work (Dunér, 2010; Jolanki, 2013). Workers closer to retirement were more likely to view retirement as a way of having time for caring and for oneself, and some have sought part-time retirement with this in mind (Leinonen, 2011b).

Many carers also sought to balance their lives by setting limits to their own involvement and trying to involve other family members or public care services in providing the care needed (Dunér, 2010; Eldh and Carlsson, 2011; Leinonen, 2011b, 2011c). Care services enabled working carers to have time for their own rest and leisure activities and offered relief from constant worry (Leinonen, 2011a, 2011c). It might be expected that in Nordic countries, publicly provided care services play a major role in the lives of carers of older people. However, adequate and suitable services were not always available (Leinonen, 2011a). They were not used if carers did not trust the quality of the care (Dunér 2010; Leinonen, 2011a) or if the person cared for was reluctant to accept formal support (Leinonen, 2011a). Jolanki's (2013b) study of working carers' encounters with paid care workers showed that if family members trust the quality of care and the commitment of care workers, public care services play an important role in their lives, with some carers seeing care workers as co-workers and allies with whom they can share caring tasks and concerns. However, this study also showed that they can be viewed as 'piece-workers', who carry out specific tasks but do not take overall responsibility for the person cared for. In such cases, working carers found that they had to control and supervise the care workers too, which increased their experience of feeling burdened by the situation.

The findings of these Finnish and Swedish studies echo findings in other countries and the studies reported elsewhere in this book. Perhaps a particularly Nordic aspect is that carers in Finland and Sweden very much expect joint responsibility between formal services and family care, rather than seeing themselves self-evidently as the primary carers of those they care about. Carers, mostly adult children, saw their own role as important, but also felt that other options – such as other family members or public care – have to be available to meet the needs of their older relatives. The studies highlighted here focused mainly on women and only a few men participated, but it can cautiously be argued that another common feature for Nordic carers seems to be that for both male and female carers, work has an important independent meaning, in addition to its economic value, as a means of achieving balance in life.

Conclusions

The role of family carers in older people's care has long been important both in Finland and in Sweden, as the figures in this chapter and in *Chapter One* demonstrate. Survey results reported in this chapter show a small difference between Finland and Sweden in people's opinions about caring for older people, with Swedes more strongly favouring public care services. However, in both countries, the role of family members is growing, apparently due at least partly to declining public care services for older people.

As discussed in *Chapter Two*, from the late 1990s and throughout the 2000s, the Swedish state increased its focus on the position of carers, initiating and supporting projects and measures to support municipalities and voluntary organisations. However, the precise form this support should take is not clearly stated and it has focused mostly on supporting retired partner-carers. Practical actions to support working family carers have been rather modest, and employment regulations have not been considered (Sand, 2010). As noted by Ulmanen (2013), working daughters are still a blind spot in Swedish eldercare policy. In Finland, a similar development has taken place over the same time period, although starting a little later than in Sweden. However, in Finland, more financial support is available in the form of a Carer's Allowance, and employment and workplace-related policy measures have recently been introduced. In Finland, carers have also been included in national-level strategies and defined as an essential part of the care system, while in Sweden, their role is still seen in national-level strategies primarily as voluntary helpers.

The few studies of working carers' everyday life experiences indicate that carers experience their situation in rather similar ways to carers in many other countries. Carers try to maintain a balance between different spheres of their lives. They are motivated to care but expect support from the public sector to enable them to continue to work and have time for their own rest. Many struggle with feelings of guilt about neglecting work for care or vice versa. Paid work is a balancing factor for many carers, although trying to manage both work and care may result in problems with time use and exhaustion.

This chapter has also shown that the special situation of working carers is poorly acknowledged in Finnish and Swedish employment policies. Reconciliation of work and care continues to be discussed mainly from the point of view of families with small children. In the 2000s, governments and other societal actors in both countries began to pay more attention to the situation of working carers of older people, but legislation and practical actions to support carers at work are still largely absent, especially in Sweden. Practices supporting working carers mostly depend on the goodwill of employers. The gender equality aspect, so self-evident in care and work policies in relation to carers of small children, is almost non-existent in discussions of working carers of older people. As the figures show, men care too, but women's role is more prominent and women's working lives seem to be more affected by care responsibilities.

The invisibility of working carers of older people in both Finland and Sweden is also reflected in the scarcity of information and research on this topic. It is clear that much more research and information on the circumstances of those who combine work and care of an older relative is needed in both countries.

Returning to the question posed in the title of this chapter, we can conclude that, for a long time, the role of family members received little recognition in policy debates. Recently, supporting carers has become an important topic on the political agenda. In this sense, the family has been 'rediscovered' in older people's care, although public actors have not relinquished all responsibility, as public care services and financial support are still available for older people and their families. However, most support of older people with substantial care needs and their families is 'supported familialism' (Saraceno, 2010). By contrast, in both countries, recent developments have shifted support for other, less needy older people towards what Saraceno (2010) calls 'familialism by default'. Although no new legal demands have been placed on family members to provide such care, the availability of family support is increasingly taken for granted. An implicit consequence of restructured and declining public care services is that family care has become less optional while the effects of care responsibilities on working carers' lives and well-being remain largely unacknowledged. Family is indeed 'rediscovered' in older people's care, but support for working carers remains scarce.

Notes

[1] The study looked at wage-earners' self-reported care responsibilities and, therefore, the self-employed and farmers were excluded from the analysis.

[2] 'Perhaps, depending on the situation'.

[3] 'How has your personal life been outside work during the past six months?' (quite easy or quite hard).

[4] Available at: www.eurofound.europa.eu/ewco/surveys/EWCS2005/4ewcs_01_14.htm#large

[5] Government Programme 2007–10, see: www.vn.fi/tietoarkisto/aiemmat-hallitukset/vanhanenII/hallitusohjelma/en.jsp

[6] Government Programme, see: www.valtioneuvosto.fi/hallitus/hallitusohjelma/pdf/fi.pdf

[7] See: www.stm.fi/vireilla/tyoryhmat/omaishoito

References

Alber, J. and Köhler, U. (2004) *Health and care in an enlarged Europe*, Dublin: European Foundation for the Improvement of Living and Working Conditions.

Autio, T. (2005) 'Tukea ansiotyössä käyville omaishoitajille' ['Support to working carers'], *Työ ja ihminen*, vol 19, no 2, pp 275–8.

Brandt, M., Haberkern, K. and Szydlik, M. (2009) 'Intergenerational help and care in Europe', *European Sociological Review*, vol 25, no 5, pp 585–601.

Clarke, J. (2005) 'New Labour's citizens: activated, empowered, responsibilized, abandoned?', *Critical Social Policy*, vol 25, no 4, pp 447–63.

Dunér, A. (2010) 'Motives, experiences and strategies of next of kin helping older relatives in the Swedish welfare context: a qualitative study', *International Journal of Social Welfare*, vol 19, no 1, pp 54–62.

Eldh, A.C. and Carlsson, E. (2011) 'Seeking balance between employment and the care of an ageing parent', *Scandinavian Journal of Caring Sciences*, vol 25, no 2, pp 285–93.

Eurobarometer (2007) *Health and long-term care in the European Union – report special Eurobarometer 283*, Brussels: European Commission.

Jeppsson Grassman, E. (2005) 'Informella stöd- och hjälpinsatser' ['Informal support and help'], in L.-E. Olsson, L. Svedberg and E. Jeppsson Grassman (eds) *Medborgarnas insatser och engagemang i civilsamhället*, Stockholm: Swedish Ministry of Justice.

Jolanki, O. (2013a) 'To work or to care? Working women's decision-making', unpublished manuscript.

Jolanki, O. (2013b) 'Whose business is it anyway? Distributing responsibilities between family members and formal carers', in J.-Ö. Östman and A. Solin (eds) *Discourse and responsibility in professional settings*, London: Equinox Publishing.

Kauppinen, K. (2010) 'Who cares when grandmother gets sick? Ageing, employment and intergenerational family support in contemporary Europe', in T. Addabbo, M.-P. Arrizabalaga, C. Borderías and A. Owens (eds) *Gender inequalities, households and the production of well-being in modern Europe*, Farnham: Ashgate, pp 163–75.

Kauppinen, K. and Jolanki, O. (2012) 'Työn sekä omais- ja läheishoivan yhdistäminen – työssäjatkamisajatukset' ['Reconciling work and care giving – to continue working or retire?'], in M. Perkiö-Mäkelä and T. Kauppinen (eds) *Työ, terveys ja työssä jatkamisajatukset*, Helsinki: Finnish Institute of Occupational Health, pp 133–56.

Kotsadam, A. (2011) 'Does informal eldercare impede women's employment? The case of European welfare states', *Feminist Economics*, vol 17, no 2, pp 121–44.

Krevers, B. and Öberg, B. (2007) *Närstående till* äldre – *deras behov och användning av stöd* [*Family carers of older people: their needs and use of support*], Linköping: Linköping University.

Kröger, T. (2005) 'Interplay between formal and informal care for older people: the state of the Nordic research', in M. Szebehely (ed) *Äldreomsorgsforskning i Norden*, Copenhagen: Nordic Council of Ministers, pp 243–80.

Kröger, T. and Leinonen, A. (2012) 'Transformation by stealth: the retargeting of home care in Finland', *Health and Social Care in the Community*, vol 20, no 3, pp 319–27.

Lehto, A.-M. and Sutela, H. (2008) *Työolojen kolme vuosikymmentä* [*Three decades of working conditions*], Helsinki: Statistics Finland.

Leinonen, A. (2011a) 'Informal family carers and lack of personal time: descriptions of being outside the sphere of formal help', *Nordic Social Work Research*, vol 1, no 2, pp 91–108.

Leinonen, A. (2011b) 'Masters of their own time? Working carers' visions of retirement', *European Journal of Ageing*, vol 8, no 4, pp 243–53.

Leinonen, A. (2011c) 'Adult children and parental caregiving: making sense of participation patterns among siblings', *Ageing and Society*, vol 31, no 2, pp 308-27.

Lilly, M., Laporte, A. and Coyte, P. (2007) 'Labor market work and home care's unpaid caregivers: a systematic review', *The Milbank Quarterly*, vol 85, no 4, pp 641–90.

Mossberg Sand, A.-B. (2000) *Ansvar, kärlek och försörjning: om anställda anhörigvårdare i Sverige* [*Responsibilities, love and economy: family carers employed by municipalities in Sweden*], Gothenburg: Gothenburg University.

Nätti, J., Manninen, M., Väisänen, M. and Anttila, T. (2005) *Vuorotellen virkeäksi* – *vuorotteluvapaan seurantatutkimus* [*Follow-up study of the use of job alternation leave*], Helsinki: Työministeriö.

Nososco (2009) *Social protection in the Nordic countries*, Copenhagen: Nordic Social Statistical Committee.

Sand, A.-B. (2010) *Anhöriga som kombinerar förvärvsarbete och anhörigomsorg. Kuskapsöversikt* [*Combining gainful employment and family care: a research overview*], Stockholm: Nationellt kompetenscentrum Anhöriga.

Saraceno, C. (2010) 'Social inequalities facing old-age dependency: a bi-generational perspective', *Journal of European Social Policy*, vol 20, no 1, pp 32–44.

Siltaniemi, A., Perälahti, A., Eronen, A., Särkelä, R. and Londén, P. (2009) *Kansalaisbarometri 2009* [*The citizen barometer 2009*], Helsinki: The Finnish Federation for Social Welfare and Health.

Swedish Social Insurance Agency (2012) *Social insurance in figures 2011*, Stockholm: Försäkringskassan.

Szebehely, M. (2006) 'Informella hjälpgivare' ['Informal caregivers'], in J. Vogel (ed) *Äldres levnadsförhållanden*, Stockholm: Statistics Sweden, pp 435–62.

Szebehely, M. and Trydegård, G.B. (2012) 'Home care in Sweden: a universal model in transition', *Health & Social Care in the Community*, vol 20, no 3, pp 300–9.

Szebehely, M. and Ulmanen, P. (2009) 'Att ge omsorg till gamla föräldrar och andra anhöriga: påverkar det relationen till arbetsmarknaden?' ['To give support to parents and other relatives: does it affect the relationship to the labour market?'], unpublished report for the Swedish Ministry of Health and Social Affairs.

Ulmanen, P. (2013) 'Working daughters: a blind spot in Swedish eldercare policy', *Social Politics*, vol 20, no 1, pp 65–87.

FOUR

Working carers of older people: steps towards securing adequate support in Australia and England?

Sue Yeandle and Bettina Cass

Introduction

This chapter focuses on older people who need care in Australia and England, liberal democracies in which the state has long recognised some responsibility for older people's welfare, introducing 'old age' pensions (from 1908) and allocating some public funds to provide residential care, home care and local community services for sick, frail or disabled older people.

The limited public eldercare services developed in England after 1945 were initially delivered by public sector employees: social workers, residential care staff, 'home helps' and community health workers. Services for older people in Australia, developed from the colonial period onwards by voluntary societies and charitable and religious organisations, were later mainly funded by government (Murphy, 2011: 30; Productivity Commission, 2011a: 12–14). Although neither country made providing care or financial support to older relatives a legal obligation for family members, it was assumed in both countries that while they lived at home, older people's care needs would mainly be met by their families.

Australia's national (Commonwealth) government assumed greater responsibility for social services in the decade after 1945, creating what some consider a 'social service' rather than a European-style 'welfare' state (Phillips, 1976: 259; Roe, 1976). Public support for aged care developed at the intersection of pensions, housing and health care policy (Productivity Commission, 2011a: 12): the 1954 Aged Persons Homes Act made capital funding available for residential eldercare and nursing home benefits were introduced in 1963 (Dixon, 1977: 147). Residential care was subsequently expanded within a mixed economy of government-subsidised non-government and commercial providers

(Fine, 2007a: 275). In 1985, responding to escalating expenditure on residential support and older consumers' desire to stay at home, an Aged Care Reform Strategy shifted the emphasis from residential to home care (Howe, 1997: 306–8; Pfeffer and Green, 1997: 282). Since that date, the Home and Community Care (HACC) programme – delivered under the aegis of the states and jointly funded by the Commonwealth, State and Territory governments – has provided domestic assistance, personal care, meals, transport, home maintenance and nursing health care (AIHW, 2011: 187).

After 1945, England introduced a universal entitlement to free health care through the National Health Service (NHS) and obliged local authorities through the National Assistance Act 1948 to provide 'social services' to meet the care needs of older people (and others) who lacked other support: residential homes; domestic help and 'nursing attention' at home; meals-on-wheels for 'housebound' older people; and various community and home-based services, some provided by voluntary organisations (Baugh, 1973). Underpinning this support for older people was the unpaid and often unnoticed care provided by their families – especially middle-aged single daughters (Lewis and Meredith, 1988) – from whose ranks the first call for carer recognition emerged in the 1960s (see *Chapter Two*).

By the 1980s, it was also clear in Australia that much, if not most, eldercare was being provided by family carers, predominantly daughters and daughters-in-law, but also spouses (female and male). Their care was gradually acknowledged and legitimated as women's unpaid family work emerged from its 'hidden' sphere into the public realm, in a context of rising female labour force participation, emerging formal care services and the research and advocacy of feminist scholars (Fine, 2007b: 29–30). These developments influenced the introduction of both Carer Pension and the HACC programme, as carers came to be recognised and relied upon in public policy (Austin, 2005; AIHW, 2009).

In the 1980s, official data in both countries revealed in greater detail the importance of spouses and children in the care of older people. Australia's *Survey of carers of the handicapped at home: Australia 1988* (ABS, 1990), later the *Survey of disability, ageing and carers* (SDAC) (ABS, 1993, 2011), underpinned policymakers' emerging recognition of carers' need for policy support (Schofield et al, 1998; Watson and Mears, 1999), and in England, the employment consequences of caring also began to emerge in survey data and academic studies (Martin and Roberts, 1984; Parker, 1985; Qureshi and Walker, 1989).

The care of older people in Australia and England

The state's approach to the care of older people in both countries changed significantly in the late 20th century, influenced by population ageing, rising female employment and increasing costs (Ungerson and Yeandle, 2007; Hill et al, 2011). Despite policies designed to reduce residential and promote home-based care, both countries struggled to reduce care costs and continued to spend most resources allocated to eldercare on residential support (Yeandle et al, 2012). Nevertheless, by the late 2000s, rather few older people were living in residential establishments: in Australia in 2009, 5% of people aged 65+ and 25% of people aged 85+ (AIHW, 2011); and in England in 2011, 4% of people aged 65+ and 16% of people aged 85+ (Institute of Public Care, 2012). In both countries, people in residential care were becoming older, with increasingly complex needs (CSCI, 2009; AIHW, 2010). Both also promoted 'market mechanisms' in residential aged care in the 1980s and 1990s (Howe and Healy, 2005; Laing & Buisson, 2007; CSCI, 2009; Davidson, 2009), resulting in far fewer care places for older people being provided directly by the state. By 2009/10, only 6% of residential eldercare was provided in Australia's state or local government sectors (DoHA, 2010), and in England in 2007/08, only 6% of care homes remained in council ownership.

Despite this, home care has not become easier to access. England tightened its systems of needs assessment, eligibility criteria and means-testing in the 2000s, and in both countries, most older people now contribute to or cover the costs of any home care they receive (Laing & Buisson, 2010). Although home care packages have become more intensive – especially in England, where the number of households receiving services has been falling – significant familial care is also needed and provided in both countries (Yeandle et al, 2012). 'Substantial unmet demand for Home Care packages' has been recognised in Australia too, with support often fragmented and inconsistent, and plans for improved arrangements, alongside revised means-testing of clients' co-payments, have been announced (Commonwealth of Australia, 2012: 3–4).

Both countries have introduced systems of direct payments, personal budgets and self-directed support for older people. England's social services 'modernisation' policy (1997–2010) emphasised user-centred services, tailored individual support and putting users 'in control' (Davey et al, 2007; DH, 2007). Direct payment schemes were opened to older people from 2000 and all service users are due to be offered 'personal budgets' by 2013 (DH, 2010). In Australia, consumer-directed funding and personalised packages of support are a more recent but growing development (Cass and Thompson, 2008): a National Disability Insurance Scheme, funded on an individualised, person-centred care and planning basis, is being developed (AIHW, 2011: 133; Productivity Commission, 2011c) and planned reforms in aged care services include offering care to all home care recipients on a consumer-directed basis from 2013 (Commonwealth of Australia, 2012: 5).

These developments undoubtedly increase the pressure on family members of working age to support their older parents. Whether or not they identify as 'carers', families play an increasing role, both in arranging and coordinating health and social care for their parents and by providing much of their care themselves.

Carers of older people: characteristics, activities and living arrangements

Prevalence, characteristics and caring tasks

In England, carers of a parent or parent-in-law[1] are among the largest groups of carers. In 2009/10, an official survey of 35,000 carers known to social services departments (NHSIC, 2010a: 5) showed that 29% cared for a parent, while a representative household survey found that 40% were in this category (NHSIC, 2010b: 111). The latter survey showed that carers of a parent were usually middle-aged: 61% of carers aged 45–54 and 53% of those aged 55–64 cared for a parent (NHSIC, 2010b: 112).

For reasons discussed later, much of their care takes place *outside* the carer's household, in marked contrast to the typically co-resident care of a sick or disabled child or partner (see *Chapters Seven* and *Ten*). Some 60% of people caring for someone in a *separate* household care for a parent (48%) or parent-in-law (12%), whereas only 22% of those caring for someone in the *same* household do so (NHSIC, 2010b: 111). Caring for a parent usually involves caring for an older person. Yeandle and Buckner (2007) found that among 425 people caring for a parent, half (49%) supported someone aged 65–84 and 41% someone aged 85 or older.[2] Two thirds of these carers looked after a parent who was frail and had limited mobility (66%), almost half cared for a parent with a specific physical disability (45%) and one third looked after a parent with dementia (31%). The care they gave was often of long duration: many (44%) had been caring for their parent for five years or more and most others (50%) had done so for between six months and five years.

Almost all these carers (95%) gave practical help to their parent (meals, shopping, laundry, housework, repairs and taking them to medical appointments). Many dealt with their parent's bills, letters, banking and form-filling (88%); 87% visited, sat with, read to or provided emotional support for their parent; and 85% took their parent out for walks or drives or to see relatives or friends. Two thirds (66%) checked that their parent took medication, gave injections or changed dressings, and over half provided personal care (52% helped with dressing, bathing, washing, shaving, cutting nails, feeding and using the toilet) or physical help (51% assisted with walking, using stairs or getting in/out of bed). In the same study, although most carers of a parent (55%) supported a relative living separately, most were in regular contact: 74% saw their parent daily and 20% at least weekly. Many lived nearby: 30% in the same street or neighbourhood and 13% within three kilometres. Nearly a third lived at a distance, however: 19% in the region but over eight kilometres away; and 11% further away than this.

Australia had about 2.6 million carers – 12% of the population – assisting someone with a disability, chronic illness or an older person in 2009 (ABS, 2011), including 771,400 'primary carers' (see *Chapter Two*), most of whom were women (ABS, 2011: 52–3). About 350,000 primary carers assisted an older person (aged 65+), most of them (69%) living in the same household as the person they supported (Productivity Commission, 2011b: 326).[3] While most primary carers of an older person supported a partner (69%), a large minority were caring for a parent or parent-in-law (24%) (Productivity Commission, 2011b: 37).

In 2009, the SDAC estimated that 513,000 people aged 60 or older received 'informal assistance' from a daughter (272,000) or son (241,000). However, daughters were much more involved in some aspects of their parents' care than sons, notably, their health care, self-care and meal preparation. They also helped their parents more with mobility, transport, household chores and cognitive or emotional tasks, although sons assisted their parents much more than did daughters with property maintenance (ABS, 2012: Table 26).

Much of the published analysis of the SDAC focuses on Australia's 771,000 'primary' carers, among whom substantial minorities were daughters (129,000) and sons (53,000) caring for their parents. Within this group, the two reasons most often given by children caring for their parents were 'family responsibility' (68% of daughters, 64% of sons) and 'emotional obligation' (40% of daughters, 38% of sons). However, over a third of daughters (37%, compared with 22% of sons) said 'no other family or friends were willing to care'. Some daughters (12%) and slightly more sons (15%) provided care themselves because 'alternative care was too costly', while 12% of daughters and 10% of sons said that they were their parent's primary carer as they had had 'no other choice' (ABS, 2012: Table 38).

Living arrangements and care

Between 1971 and 2001, older people in England became much less likely to live in multi-generation households: among women, the proportion doing so fell from 23% to 11% for women aged 75–9; from 31% to 12% for women aged 80–84; and from 42% to 13% for women aged 85+ (Grundy, 2009). Men's household circumstances changed in a similar way (19% to 12%, 27% to 13% and 38% to 16%, respectively).

Older people were not moving into institutions, however: the main trend was towards ageing in place. The proportion of middle-aged children residing with their elderly parents – already quite low by 1981 – fell further among single, married and widowed/divorced people aged 35–64 years by 1991 (except among single, middle-aged men). By 1991, rates of co-residence with elderly parents for people aged 45–54 were below 3% for married women and below 10% for unmarried women, lower still for married men, although rather higher for unmarried sons (20%) (Grundy, 2000: 197).

In England, it is thus not surprising that co-resident care for older people has for several decades been less common than care in a separate household (Phillips et al, 2002). This change reflects rising living standards and home-ownership, shifting values about independence and autonomy, and societal changes in women's roles. Home-ownership rates in England peaked at 71% in the mid-2000s and were among the highest in the Organisation for Economic Co-operation and Development (OECD) (Andrews and Caldera Sánchez, 2011: 9). Older people are the age group least likely to move home, and by age 75, half live alone (Ball et al, 2011: 14). Most say that they wish to remain in their own homes, with adaptations to accommodate disability if necessary (Croucher, 2008); many are 'very keen not to become dependent on either their family, friends or social services' (Boaz et al, 1999: 27). Nevertheless, an attitude survey of a representative population sample in 2008 found that most respondents (57% of women, 51% of men) felt that the main responsibility for looking after older people needing care lay with family members, although almost a quarter of women (24%) and nearly a third of men (32%) felt that 'the state' or 'local government' should have this role (Elsmore, 2009).

Most older people in Australia lived in private dwellings in 2009, with only 5% in residential care. Most of those in private homes (69%)

lived in single-family households and about one quarter lived alone. Of those aged 85 or older, over half (51%), mostly women, lived alone (AIHW, 2011: 175). Home-ownership among older people is high in Australia too: in 2007/08, mortgage-free home-ownership rates among people aged 65+ were 86% for couples and 69% for single people (ABS, 2009a). Thus, most Australians are 'ageing in place', in a single-family household, usually in private home-ownership. Low-income older people who have not been owner-occupiers in their earlier years are more likely to live in private and public rental housing and are less able to cover any additional costs of home-based aged care (Kendig and Bridge, 2007: 221).

However, the concept 'living independently' does not do justice to older people's needs for assistance, which increase with age. In 2009, 41% of those aged 85 or older who lived in an independent household required assistance with at least one of the 'core activities' of daily living – self-care, mobility or communication – compared with 18% of those aged 75–84 and 10% of those aged 65–74. The proportions requiring assistance with 'non-core' activities (meal preparation, cognitive or emotional tasks, reading or writing tasks, transport, property maintenance, household chores, and health care) were greater and also increased with age: 27% of those aged 65–74; 45% of those aged 75–84; and 72% of those aged 85+ (AIHW, 2011: 185). Most of the 1.3 million older people aged 60+ who required assistance received support from an (unpaid) carer (76%) and many (56%) had help from a formal provider: indeed, most of those requiring assistance got help from both (unpaid) carers and formal providers, indicating that formal services did not meet all of their needs. A few with support needs (7%) received no help. Two thirds of carers assisting older people were women; partners, daughters, other relatives and friends/neighbours (ABS, 2012). Since formal services are also primarily provided by women, older people's support in Australia clearly rests on a gendered infrastructure of care.

Work–care reconciliation issues

Supporting frail older people to live independently at home, caring for elderly parents at a distance and combining parental care with a job, home or family of their own present challenges for carers of working age (Phillips et al, 2002; Yeandle et al, 2007c). The Carers, Employment and Services (CES) study in Great Britain found that carers of older people were more likely than other carers (47%, compared with 41%) to say that those they care for were reluctant to accept home care or other formal services (Yeandle et al, 2007b: 33). Other challenges encountered by carers of older people in this study included: managing acute episodes (which could suddenly disrupt routines and require unscheduled absence from work); end-of-life care (carers sometimes found that previously manageable care became very intensive and incompatible with paid work); and dealing with caring crises, extreme anxiety and excessive tiredness (eg when caring for a parent with dementia) (Yeandle et al, 2007d). Pressure points included: supporting older parents to adapt their homes; helping them move to sheltered housing or residential care; providing post-operative support at home; and supporting one parent while the other was dying. Negotiating with professionals and service providers on their parents' behalf could be difficult too, and some complained that eligibility criteria, charging policies and services were confusing and varied from one place to another (Yeandle et al, 2007a).

The CES study analysed data on 425 people of working age who were caring for an older person, among whom 145 did *not* have paid work; 69% of them had given up their job because of caring. While many (43%) in this group said that they would rather be working, when surveyed, almost half (46%) felt that they had been away from work so long that they would need extra support to return to employment. Of the 131 carers of older people who were working full-time, most (69%) felt 'under a lot of pressure'. About a third of all those with paid jobs (full- or part-time) said that they were considering giving up their job because of their caring responsibilities. Among those in part-time work, most (70%) had chosen to work reduced hours so that they could combine work and care, 42% of them saying that they worked part-time only because 'care services are not effective enough to allow me to work full-time'. Fewer than half of the full-time and part-time employees (40% and 46%, respectively) felt that they had 'adequate services to enable me to work', although most (66% and 71%, respectively) said that they had a 'carer-friendly' employer and 'felt supported' when caring affected their job.

Caring for older people in Australia also poses major challenges with respect to labour force participation. The 2003 SDAC survey found that only 32% of primary carers who were caring for an older person were employed, compared with 59% of other carers (ABS, 2008: 57). Among primary carers who were not employed, only 27% of those caring for an older person (compared with 36% of other carers) had been working immediately before taking on their caring role. This difference is associated with both their caring responsibilities and their average older age, characteristics that exacerbate the employment costs of care.

Many primary carers of older people who had left work just before their caring began (45%) said that they did so in order to commence or increase their care. Many (43%) explained that alternative care was unavailable or too expensive or said that it was impossible to change their working arrangements to accommodate caring. However, 56% spoke of having emotional obligations or said that they preferred to care full-time. Primary carers of younger people, by contrast, were less likely to give the former type of explanation (34%) and more likely (66%) to offer the latter reasons (ABS, 2008: 57).

Australia's Survey of Employment Arrangements, Retirement and Superannuation (ABS, 2009b), focusing on all carers – not only primary carers – showed that in 2007, among people of working age (15–64), carers were less likely than non-carers to be employed (61%, compared with 74%) or to work full-time (62%, compared with 72%) and were more likely to be outside the labour force (35%, compared with 22%). The main reason carers gave for being outside the labour force was that they were caring for at least one person who was ill, disabled or elderly (39%). This figure was higher (46%) among carers aged 45–64, who were also more likely to be caring for a parent (45%, compared with 33% of younger carers) (ABS, 2009b: 2). Those combining caring and employment (especially full-time work) often reported feelings of time pressure. In 2007, 60% of employed carers aged 15–64 said that they always or often felt rushed or pressed for time (compared with 47% of others in work); and one quarter, especially those aged 45–64, said that they would prefer to work fewer hours (ABS, 2009b: 2).

Policy developments in the 2000s

In England, the 'right to request flexible working' (see *Chapter Two*) was the main policy change affecting carers of older people trying to reconcile work and care in the 2000s. Awareness of this new right reached employees slowly: a year after implementation, just 9% of employees knew about it (Elsmore, 2009), although in a separate survey conducted in 2008, most carers (78%) reported working 'flexibly' (BIS, 2010: 29). The work arrangements of the carers in the latter survey included: 'part-time' work (45%); flexi-time (33%); compressed and annualised hours (both 17%); and working from home (13%). An employer survey in the same year found that most employers (69%) were positive about the change in the law (CBI, 2008, cited BIS, 2010: 33): 40% had received at least one request for flexible working, and most had accepted all requests (BIS, 2010). However, a later survey of employers and employees found that 21% of employees with caring responsibilities said that their request had been rejected. This was a more common experience for older employees (45+) and employees in firms with 50–249 employees (Leighton and Gregory, 2011: 66). Flexible working requests were rejected least often in the voluntary sector (6%) and more frequently in the hotels and restaurants (21%) and public administration (18%) sectors (Leighton and Gregory, 2011: 69). Some carers also benefitted from modest improvements in return-to-work support schemes and additional services offering carers breaks, training and support programmes (Yeandle and Wigfield, 2011, 2012; see also *Chapter Two*).

In Australia, the main policy developments relevant to work–care reconciliation in the 2000s were new employment arrangements (personal/carers' leave and compassionate leave), the anti-discrimination protection provided in the Fair Work Act 2009 and additional carer-focused community services, especially respite care (Charlesworth, 2011; see also *Chapter Two*). While Australia's Federal Disability Discrimination Act 1992 had previously outlawed discrimination against a person because they cared for someone with a disability, this had a limited impact on work–care reconciliation because of deficits in the operation and enforcement of the law (Charlesworth, 2011: 93). Other developments in support of carers have been partial and insufficient: while the new National Employment Standards (NES) set out conditions under which parents of young and disabled children up to age 18 may request flexible working arrangements, this entitlement was not made available to employees caring for disabled adults and so does not benefit carers of older people (AGFWO, 2010: 85). Official reports and carers' associations have both recommended extending this entitlement to other carers (HRSCFCH&Y, 2009; Productivity Commission, 2011a, 2011b). The Australian government made a commitment in 2011 to consult with 'stakeholders' on such a change (Australian Government, 2011: 24), but no definite plans have been announced in 2012. This issue is important as international analysis has shown that the intensity of care (defined by the hours of care provided) is clearly associated with carers' reduced working hours (Colombo et al, 2011: 9).

The extension of flexible working arrangements, still an unfinished agenda in Australia, could enable carers to remain in employment and reconcile work and care. This is evident from analysis of the Household Income and Labour Dynamics (HILDA) survey, which shows that access to one or more types of special leave for caring (permanent part-time work, flexible start and finish times, and home-based work) improves the odds of staying in employment (Hill et al, 2008: 31). The analysis also found that employees were more likely to leave employment at the start of caring if they were casual employees, worked part-time, had no supervisory responsibilities, did not belong to a union and/or worked for a smaller firm. Lack of access to any carer-friendly workplace arrangements also increased employees' odds of leaving their jobs when they became carers. Since casual and part-time work is more characteristic of female than male employment, this has evident implications for female carers (Charlesworth, 2011).

Although Australia offers services for carers (see *Chapter Two*), the 2009 SDAC survey found that 86% of son or daughter primary carers never used respite care. Some felt that they did not need the service – about half of son/daughter carers – or that their care recipient did not want it; others said that services were not available in their area or that available respite was unsuitable (AIHW, 2011: 228). Although caring has been shown to impact negatively on carers' health, well-being and labour force participation, carers' associations have recognised that where sufficient, suitable and flexible services are unavailable, respite services will not be used. Nonetheless, they continue to see access to respite care as a priority (HRSCFCH&Y, 2009; AIHW, 2011). Plans to increase funding for respite care were set out in the Commonwealth government's policy statement for aged care reform, and a National Respite for Carers programme is set to expand services to offer carers more choice and flexibility (Commonwealth of Australia, 2012: 7–8). By announcing this within its reformed Home Support Program for older people, the Australian government has recognised both the informal care infrastructure on which its eldercare services rest, and the inadequacy and inflexibility of current provision. Its aged care reform document (*Living longer, living better*) indicates the intention to develop a more extensive and accessible system of flexible respite care services for carers of older people (Commonwealth of Australia, 2012).

The content, sustainability and future prospects of the support, services and employment rights for working-age carers of older people in Australia currently rests upon extending the NES of the right to request flexible working arrangements to employed carers in this group and on widening access to flexible employment and carers' leave so that employees in casual employment or seeking to enter or re-enter employment are included (Charlesworth and Heron, 2011). Current arrangements exclude casual employees who have less than 12 months' continuous service and the 'reasonable expectation' of continuing employment. Such a change would mean developing policies that are not based on a male-breadwinner normative model of continuous full-time employment, but which encompass the varied employment circumstances of women and men with caring responsibilities.

Conclusion

This chapter has shown that among people of working age, caring for an older person – frequently, a parent or parent-in-law – is a relatively common experience, particularly for women in middle age. Alongside well-established and continuing demographic change, trends in public policy towards ageing in place and a shift away from residential services for older people towards consumer-directed care, personal budgets and 'personalised' support mean that reliance upon family members is likely to increase in coming years.

In both countries, trends towards more older people living independently and alone (or in single-family or older couple households) are now well-established, and the incidence of co-resident care for frail or disabled older parents has declined. As shown earlier, there is some evidence that attitudes, values and preferences, as well as changed socio-economic circumstances (particularly greater home-ownership among older people), underpin these developments. Nevertheless, as Australia's detailed evidence base about 'primary carers' shows, co-resident care, particularly by daughters of their older parents or parents-in-law, is still an important feature of overall caring arrangements, despite trends towards greater participation in paid work among women in both countries (see *Chapter One*).

Both countries considered in this chapter have taken some steps in public policy to recognise and support carers, and policy statements at national government level and in state and local policies increasingly acknowledge that support for working carers of older people is needed. This responds to a growing evidence base which shows that caring for older people and elderly parents often has negative effects for employees, reducing their employment rates and well-being and causing them stress and difficulties, many of which could be reduced by greater flexibility at work and better local services and support.

In the 2000s, changes to employment legislation, introducing modest and partial entitlements to request flexible working or to take a period of carers' leave (Australia) or emergency time off to deal with caring emergencies (England), have begun to address the needs of this group of carers. So too have programmes focused on carers' health and well-being, which – strongly advocated by carers' organisations and associations in both countries – remain on the policy agenda in both contexts, albeit reaching only a small minority of carers at present.

Both countries have explored a variety of ways of offering carers of working age access to breaks, respite and support, with the primary aim of making their care sustainable, which has long been central to the operation of eldercare arrangements in each case. If that policy aim is to be met, such support will need to become more comprehensive, accessible and universal, and to link together public policy, new support services and greater responsiveness from employers and managers. This will be critical if carers of older people and of frail elderly parents are to avoid falling out of work, suffering damage to their careers and long-term financial well-being, or coming under intolerable pressure as they struggle to reconcile paid work and unpaid care in the years ahead.

Notes

[1] In this chapter, except where otherwise indicated, the phrase 'carer of a parent' includes those caring for either a parent or a parent-in-law.

[2] In this section, data for England are based on additional analysis specially undertaken for this chapter.

[3] Information linking primary carers with care recipients is available only for co-resident carers. The 2009 ABS survey did not collect data about those receiving care from primary carers not resident with them or from 'non-primary' carers (Productivity Commission, 2011b: 327).

References

ABS (Australian Bureau of Statistics) (1990) *Survey of carers of the handicapped at home: Australia 1988*, Canberra: ABS.

ABS (1993) *Survey of disability, ageing and carers: Australia 1993*, Canberra: ABS.

ABS (2008) *A profile of carers in Australia*, Canberra: ABS.

ABS (2009a) *Household income and income distribution: Australia, 2007–2008*, Canberra: ABS.

ABS (2009b) *Australian social trends*, Canberra: ABS.

ABS (2011) *Caring in the community*, Canberra: ABS.

ABS (2012) *Disability, ageing and carers Australia: summary of findings 2009, consolidated set of tables*, Canberra: ABS. Available at: http://www.abs.gov.au/

AGFWO (Australian Government Fair Work Ombudsman) (2010) *National Employment Standards: the Fair Work Act 2009*, Canberra: AGFWO.

AIHW (Australian Institute of Health and Welfare) (2009) *Australia's welfare 2009*, Canberra: AIHW.

AIHW (2010) *Residential aged care in Australia: a statistical overview 2008–2009*, Canberra: AIHW.

AIHW (2011) *Australia's welfare 2011*, Canberra: AIHW.

Andrews, D. and Caldera Sánchez, A. (2011) *Drivers of homeownership rates in selected OECD countries*, Paris: OECD Publishing.

Austin, J. (2005) *The ageing population: can we rely on informal, unpaid care to provide?*, Canberra: Carers Australia.

Australian Government (2011) *National Carer Strategy*, Canberra: Commonwealth of Australia.

Ball, M., Blanchette, R., Anupam, N. and Wyatt, P. (2011) *Housing markets and independence in old age: expanding the opportunities*, Oxfordshire: Henley Business School.

Baugh, W. (1973) *Introduction to the social services*, Basingstoke: Macmillan.

BIS (Business, Innovation and Skills) (2010) *Work and Families Act 2006: evaluation report*, London: BIS.

Boaz, A., Hayden, C. and Bernard, M. (1999) *Aspirations of older people: a review of the literature*, London: Department of Social Security.

Cass, B. and Thompson, C. (2008) *Approaches to packages of support*, Sydney: SPRC, University of New South Wales.

Charlesworth, S. (2011) 'Law's response to the reconciliation of work and care: the Australian case', in N. Busby and G. James (eds) *Families, care-giving and paid work*, Cheltenham: Edward Elgar, pp 86–104.

Charlesworth, S. and Heron, A. (2011) 'New Australian minimum time standards: reproducing the same old gendered architectures?', *Journal of Industrial Relations*, vol 54, no 2, pp 164–81.

Colombo, F., Llena-Nozal, A., Mercier, J. and Tjadens, F. (2011) *Help wanted? Providing and paying for long-term care*, Paris: OECD Publishing.

Commonwealth of Australia (2012) *Living longer, living better*, Canberra: Commonwealth of Australia.

Croucher, K. (2008) *Housing choices and aspirations of older people*, Wetherby: Communities and Local Government Publications.

CSCI (Commission for Social Care Inspection) (2009) *State of social care in England, 2007–2008*, London: Commission for Social Care Inspection.

Davey, V., Fernandez, J.L., Knapp, M., Vick, N., Jolly, D. and Swift, P. (2007) *Direct payments: a national survey of research into direct payments policy and practice*, London: PSSRU.

Davidson, B. (2009) 'For-profit organisations in managed markets for human services', in D. King and G. Meagher (eds) *Paid care in Australia: politics, profits, practices*, Sydney: University of Sydney Press, pp 43–80.

DH (Department of Health) (2007) *Carers and personalisation: improving outcomes*, London: DH.

DH (2010) *Recognised, valued and supported: next steps for the Carers' Strategy*, London: DH.

Dixon, J. (1977) *Australia's policy towards the aged: 1890–1972*, Canberra: Canberra College of Advanced Education.

DoHA (Department of Health and Ageing) (2010) *Report on the operation of the Aged Care Act 1997*, Canberra: Australian Government Department of Health and Ageing.

Elsmore, K. (2009) *Caring and flexible working: research summary*, London: Department for Work and Pensions.

Fine, M. (2007a) 'Uncertain prospects: aged care policy for a long-lived society', in A. Borowski, S. Encel and E. Ozanne (eds) *Longevity and social change in Australia*, Sydney: UNSW Press, pp 265–95.

Fine, M. (2007b) *A caring society? Care and the dilemmas of human service in the 21st century*, Basingstoke: Palgrave Macmillan.

Grundy, E. (2000) 'Co-residence of mid-life children with their elderly parents in England and Wales: changes between 1981 and 1991', *Population Studies*, vol 54, no 2, pp 193–206.

Grundy, E. (2009) 'Changing times and changing lives: investigating age related change using the Office for National Statistics Longitudinal Study of England and Wales', presentation to 'Longview Conference', 22 September, Cambridge. Available at: www.longviewuk.com/pages/documents/EmilyGrundy.pdf

Hill, T., Thomson, C.M., Bittman, M. and Griffiths, M. (2008) 'What kinds of jobs help carers combine care and employment?', *Family Matters*, no 80, pp 27–32.

Hill, T., Thomson, C. and Cass, B. (2011) *The costs of caring and the living standards of carers*, Canberra: Department of Families, Housing, Community Services and Indigenous Affairs.

Howe, A. (1997) 'The aged care reform strategy', in A. Borowski, S. Encel and E. Ozanne (eds) *Ageing and social policy in Australia*, Cambridge: Cambridge University Press, pp 301–26.

Howe, A. and Healy, K. (2005) 'Generational justice in aged care policy in Australia and the UK', *Australasian Journal on Ageing*, vol 24, no 2, pp S12–S18.

HRSCFCH&Y (House of Representatives Standing Committee on Family, Community, Housing and Youth) (2009) *Who cares? Report on the inquiry into better support for carers*, Canberra: Parliament of the Commonwealth of Australia.

Institute of Public Care (2012) 'Projecting older people population information system', Tables 'Population by age' and 'Living in a care home'. Available at: www.poppi.org.uk/

Kendig, H. and Bridge, C. (2007) 'Housing policy for a long-lived society', in A. Borowski, S. Encel and E. Ozanne (eds) *Longevity and social change in Australia*, Sydney: UNSW Press, pp 219–38.

Laing & Buisson (2007) *Care of elderly people market survey: summary report*, London: Laing & Buisson.

Laing & Buisson (2010) 'Councils set to shunt social care costs to the NHS and service users as cuts take effect', press release, 29 October. Available at: http://www.laingbuisson.co.uk/LinkClick.aspx?filetick et=7NqbssCOgKA%3d&tabid=558&mid=1888

Leighton, D. and Gregory, T. (2011) *Reinventing the workplace*, London: Demos.

Lewis, J. and Meredith, B. (1988) *Daughters who care: daughters caring for mothers at home*, London: Routledge.

Martin, J. and Roberts, C. (1984) *Women and employment: a lifetime perspective*, London HMSO.

Murphy, J. (2011) *A decent provision: Australian welfare policy, 1870–1949*, Surrey: Ashgate.

NHSIC (NHS Information Centre, Social Care) (2010a) 'Personal Social Services Survey of Adult Carers – England, 2009–10', The NHS Information Centre, Social Care. Available at: http://www. ic.nhs.uk/pubs/psscarersurvey0910

NHSIC (2010b) 'Survey of carers in households – England, 2009–10', The NHS Information Centre, Social Care. Available at: http://www. ic.nhs.uk/pubs/carersurvey0910

Parker, G. (1985) *With due care and attention: a review of research on informal care*, London: Family Policy Studies Centre.

Pfeffer, M. and Green, D. (1997) 'The making of policies for the aged', in A. Borowski, S. Encel and E. Ozanne (eds) *Ageing and social policy in Australia*, Cambridge: Cambridge University Press, pp 276–300.

Phillips, J., Bernard, M. and Chittenden, M. (2002) *Juggling work and care: the experiences of working carers of older adults*, Bristol: The Policy Press.

Phillips, P.D. (1976) 'Federalism and the provision of social services', in J. Roe (ed) *Social policy in Australia: some perspectives 1901–1975*, Sydney: Cassell, pp 228–45.

Productivity Commission (2011a) *Caring for older Australians: draft report*, Canberra: Australian Government Productivity Commission.

Productivity Commission (2011b) *Caring for older Australians: final inquiry report*, Canberra: Productivity Commission.

Productivity Commission (2011c) *Disability care and support: final inquiry report*, Canberra: Productivity Commission.

Qureshi, H. and Walker, A. (1989) *The caring relationship*, Basingstoke: Macmillan.

Roe, J. (1976) 'Never again? 1939–1949', in J. Roe (ed) *Social policy in Australia: some perspectives 1901–1975*, Sydney: Cassell, pp 217–27.

Schofield, H., Bloch, S., Herrman, H., Murphy, B., Nankervis, J. and Singh, B. (eds) (1998) *Family caregivers: disability, illness and ageing*, Sydney: Allen and Unwin and the Victorian Health Promotion Foundation.

Ungerson, C. and Yeandle, S. (eds) (2007) *Cash for care in developed welfare states*, Basingstoke: Palgrave Macmillan.

Watson, E. and Mears, J. (1999) *Women, work and care of the elderly*, Aldershot: Ashgate.

Yeandle, S. and Buckner, L. (2007) *Carers, employment and services: time for a new social contract?*, CES Report Series No 6, London: Carers UK.

Yeandle, S. and Wigfield, A. (eds) (2011) *New approaches to supporting carers' health and well-being: evidence from the National Carers' Strategy Demonstrator Sites programme*, Leeds: CIRCLE, University of Leeds.

Yeandle, S. and Wigfield, A. (eds) (2012) *Training and supporting carers: the national evaluation of the Caring with Confidence programme*, Leeds: CIRCLE, University of Leeds.

Yeandle, S., Bennett, C. and Buckner, L. (2007a) *Carers, employment and services in their local context*, CES Report Series No 4, London: Carers UK.

Yeandle, S., Bennett, C., Buckner, L., Fry, G. and Price, C. (2007b) *Diversity in caring: towards equality for carers*, CES Report Series No 3, London: Carers UK.

Yeandle, S., Bennett, C., Buckner, L., Fry, G. and Price, C. (2007c) *Managing caring and employment*, CES Report Series No 2, London: Carers UK.

Yeandle, S., Bennett, C., Buckner, L., Fry, G. and Price, C. (2007d) *Stages and transitions in the experience of caring*, CES Report Series No 1, London: Carers UK.

Yeandle, S., Kröger, T. and Cass, B. (2012) 'Voice and choice for users and carers? Developments in patterns of care for older people in Australia, England and Finland', *European Journal of Social Policy*, vol 22, no 4, pp 432–45.

FIVE

Struggling for recognition: working carers of older people in Japan and Taiwan

Frank T.Y. Wang, Masaya Shimmei, Yoshiko Yamada and Machiko Osawa

Introduction

This chapter considers the situation of working carers of older parents in Taiwan and Japan. Both countries are deeply influenced by Confucian thinking, which views the care of older people as a family responsibility and frames care as an invisible, private and family issue rather than a public matter. The chapter explores similarities and differences in these countries' changing systems of care for older people and analyses the processes involved in securing carers' rights through a struggle between the state and the women's movement in which shifting carer subjectivities are shaped by discourses of rights and duties.

These countries' similar demography, ageing populations, shrinking family structures and rising female employment were described in *Chapter Two*. In Japan, among the world's most rapidly ageing societies, traditional family-based eldercare is often no longer viable. Living apart from their extended families, many older people either live alone or rely for support on their aged spouse (Cabinet Office, 2010). Changing residential patterns and an increasing number of women working outside the home have made caring for older family members a social issue. Taiwan's demographic circumstances are very similar: its population is still younger than Japan's, but in barely two decades, it has moved from an ageing to an aged society and in 10 years' time, it will be a 'super-aged' state (CEPD, 2011). Ageing faster even than Japan, it has had very little time to establish the infrastructure needed to cope with these changes. As discussed later, Taiwan looks to Japan as a reference point for public policy on eldercare, particularly its policy on Long Term Care Insurance (LTCI).

Definitions and support for working carers of older people

In line with the Confucian values of filial piety and respect for elders, the Civil Codes of both countries define care as a family responsibility. Thus, under Taiwan's Welfare of Older People Act 2009, adult children can be penalised for abuse, neglect or leaving an elderly resident in a nursing home without paying fees, and in both countries, governments tend to view the family as the natural source of care for older people. This has the effect of rendering caring invisible and of constraining the development of carer support. This section considers how carers of older people are defined and the support they can access in the health and social care systems and in employment in both countries.

In practice, policies and societal norms that emphasise familial responsibility for the old often mean that women provide unpaid care (Hu, 1995). Indeed, 'carer' often means the 'daughter-in-law of the eldest son' in Confucian thinking, the relative designated with care responsibility. Because care responsibility is naturalised through family relations, carers tend to see themselves as mothers, daughters and/or daughters-in-law, and few think of themselves as 'carers'. To do so in the East Asian context is a political move, through which carers lay claim to recognition and rights. Making caring a public issue – including defining and conceptualising 'carers' – has been a long struggle for the women's movement in both Taiwan and Japan, where the assumption of family responsibility still permeates public policies and reinforces gender inequality.

Japan has a more developed welfare state than Taiwan and increasingly its arrangements for care depart from the assumption of family obligation, reshaping it as a 'quasi-rights' regime in contrast to the 'obligation' regime still extant in Taiwan. This is especially apparent in assessment of long-term care needs, as eligibility for long-term care in Japan is based on the older person's functional status without reference to the availability of informal support. This 'family-free' principle – a major triumph of the Japanese feminist movement's attempt to de-familialise care work in the household – has affected who does the caring. The proportion of daughters-in-law who are the main carers of their elderly in-laws has decreased, with older people in Japan increasingly identifying a 'home helper' as their primary caregiver (MHLW, 2008a). Japan's LTCI scheme and rising female employment are gradually transforming attitudes to the use of formal care services. Japan's Childcare and Family Care Leave Act 2010 is a further feature of its 'quasi-rights' regime and has been important in defining and conceptualising carers (see *Chapter Two*).

Taiwan's welfare system has the disciplinary function of ensuring that family members, as defined in the Civil Code, fulfil their 'proper' caring roles (see *Chapter Two*). The assumption that family care is available permeates all welfare practices, with carers viewed as a taken-for-granted 'resource' rather than 'potential clients' (Wang, 1998). To be eligible for social assistance, a family's average monthly income must fall below the poverty line, with 'family' defined so broadly that it even includes the husband of a married daughter living in a separate household. The history of Carer Allowance for Older People (CAOP) illustrates the prevailing discourse, in which carers are seen as unworthy of state financial support. Although CAOP was originally designed as a universal benefit, the government soon introduced means-testing and limited the target population to low-income households. Eligibility criteria for CAOP are extremely restrictive: recipients must be on a 'low income' and be in the social assistance system, aged under 65, and have no form of paid employment. Although recipients must be of working age and caring full-time, the level of payment is not intended to ensure minimum living standards or compensate for loss of income: it is a symbolic recognition of the carer's situation and less than 30% of the minimum wage (just NT$5,000/€125 per month). The central government initially funded Taiwan's local authorities (LAs) for one year to cover the costs of CAOP, but passed financial responsibility, and discretion, to the LAs in 2001. Furthermore, receiving CAOP makes families ineligible for home care, day care or respite care services: in 2011, fewer than 1,500 carers received CAOP, less than 0.25% of all estimated carers (MIA, 2011).

Work–care reconciliation in the Japanese and Taiwanese employment systems

Since 1995, many Japanese employees who care for older people have been eligible for unpaid care leave (up to 93 days for each family member needing care) and are protected from long working hours (see *Chapter Two*). Their employers must also offer support such as shorter working hours, flexible working or subsidising the cost of eldercare services (MHLW, 2009a). By 2008, 62% of employers with five or more regular employees had such policies (up from 40% in 1999): almost all large companies (500+ employees), but only 57% of Japan's smaller firms (5–29 employees), offered carers support (MHLW, 2009b). This leaves many workers in small companies without the option of family care leave. Less than 2% of workers providing care have actually taken family care leave (JILPT, 2006). Many working carers in Japan say that they did not take care leave because they had help from family members, used formal services or used their vacation days (JILPT, 2006). However, other common reasons included: not knowing the policy existed; having no department they could turn to to talk about family care; having no information on the leave because no one had used it in their workplace; hesitancy to use it because they were worried about putting a burden on their colleagues; losing income through taking leave; and a feeling that no one else could do their job (JILPT, 2006; MHLW, 2010). This suggests that having a policy is not sufficient: disseminating relevant information and providing both human and financial support are also essential to enable workers to take advantage of it.

In Taiwan, working carers received official recognition in 2002, when an amendment to the Gender Equality in Employment Act 2002 made family care leave available to carers of elderly parents (among others with caring responsibility). Companies with 30 or more employees must allow seven days' (unpaid) family care leave, alongside other recommended measures (see *Chapter Two*); however, this counts as part of annual leave, so working carers of older people do not get 'extra' leave days but simply a legitimate reason to take (annual) leave. In this context of minimal support in the employment and welfare system, working carers need to find substitute care. Migrant care workers have become an important and practical way of negotiating the tension between work and care. Taiwan began recruiting migrant domestic care workers in 1992, and since then, they have offered the least expensive form of eldercare and are now the primary providers of care at home (Lo et al, 2007). Coming mostly from South-east Asian countries, migrant care workers have become a way of easing Taiwan's 'care deficit', demonstrating that Hochschild's (2000) 'global chain of care' has indeed been formed in Taiwan. Migrant care workers care for between 40% (Lo et al, 2007) and 60% (Wang, 2010) of older people needing long-term care in Taiwan. The government presents recruiting migrant care workers as a cost-saving way of meeting the growing demand for paid eldercare and sees it as a form of welfare: welfare provided not by the state, but by the market, with the state merely giving families the right to access the market.

In Japan, care for older people – until recently viewed as a family problem best dealt with at the household level – has become a major public policy issue. The emphasis on home care and the relative neglect of assisted living and nursing home options mean that older people who really need institutional care face limited options and shortages of space. Many end up as long-term patients in relatively expensive hospitals even when they do not need 24-hour care, although such 'warehousing' of older people in hospitals without medical reasons is recognised as a misuse of resources (Mizuguchi, 2008).

Japan adopted its LTCI system (*Kaigo Hoken Seido*) in 2000 to help families and to control the costs of eldercare. Japanese people over 40 years of age must pay premiums that make them eligible for nursing and day care services, as discussed in *Chapter Two*. The system includes options for home care and local service facilities, determined in consultation with local care managers applying national criteria. A guiding principle is to encourage older people to remain at home and maximise their independence for as long as possible, with an emphasis on home and community-based care (Cabinet Office, 2001). The system has been swamped by demand and there are acute shortages of care workers: by 2008, 1.2 million older people were enrolled in community-based adult day care programmes and demand for nursing care at home is surging, from 4.1 million in 2004 to a projected 6.4 million by 2014 (MHLW, 2008b). Both trends raise questions about the sustainability of services and the overall system. Within LTCI, family members still serve as primary carers and receive only limited help from professional care workers. As norms and employment patterns change, future generations of women may not accept the tasks of primary care as their mothers and grandmothers did, however. Assisted living arrangements may prove a more appealing option, although there is a shortage of such facilities at present.

In its support for carers, Taiwan has adopted a traditional 'burnout' model. Public care is provided only when carers cannot, or can no longer, care. Since the 1980s, state subsidies for older people's care at home have been available, targeted towards low-income older people and those lacking family support. This has provided a residual home care service, consistent with the government's position and with familial ideology on older people's care. From 2003, publicly subsidised home care became available to all, with services provided according to an older person's assessed needs and family income. The 30% co-payment required makes home care less attractive than employing a migrant domestic care worker, however. Publicly subsidised home care meets a very small proportion of the need for eldercare and is used by just 0.5% of older people (DGBAS, 2011). Most older people needing care still receive this help from family members, whose contribution far outweighs other types of support (see Table 5.1). Figures suggest that formal care in Taiwan is highly marketised, globally organised and strongly oriented towards consumers' capacity to pay.

Table 5.1: Supply of long-term care for older people in Taiwan (%)

Type of help	All types of care	Formal care
Family care	75	–
Private nursing assistant	4	15
Home care worker	<1	2
Private institutional care	8	31
Migrant care worker	13	52
Total	*100*	*100*

Source: DGBAS (2011: 57).

The growth of the care market in Taiwan is related to both limited public provision and the preference of older people and their families for care at home, in line with cultural expectations of filial piety. A live-in migrant care worker is the cheapest option, and explains the popularity of this choice, which Lan (2002: 812) refers to as 'subcontracting filial piety'.

Like many other countries, Taiwan is introducing and expanding its policies to address the need for long-term care (Colombo et al, 2011). It is on the verge of completing its own comprehensive social safety net, comprising national insurance arrangements for health, retirement pensions, unemployment and long-term care. The LTCI scheme, to be implemented in three to five years' time, is expected to cover all citizens on a social insurance basis. Whether it will enable Taiwan to move towards a 'quasi-rights' regime for carers – like Japan – remains to be seen.

Real-life experiences of working carers of older people

In this section, qualitative data collected from 10 working carers in a study by the Japan Institute for Labour Policy and Training (JILPT, 2006) reveals the real-life experiences of combining work and care in Japan. Data drawn from Hsieh's (2006) study of working carers in Taiwan is then presented, offering similar insights into everyday work–care reconciliation practices there.

The JILPT study shows that working carers in Japan negotiate flexibility at work at various levels: with supervisors, they mainly negotiate days off, family care leave or plan their general work schedules; and with colleagues, they tend to arrange more detailed work schedules to support one another. Thus, Mrs Fujita, a part-time English instructor, took a week off when her father-in-law was hospitalised some distance from her own home. Her supervisor let her take days off when necessary:

> "I told my supervisor about my parent's condition and that I might not be able to continue my work if things get worse. Since my work was part-time, my supervisor said it would be better if I did not quit. My supervisor said it would be OK if I needed to take days off."

Ms Abe, a part-time social worker, took regular paid days off when she needed to take care of her mother, and was able to arrange these in advance with her colleagues:

> "We make a schedule for the next month. Since we are a team of three people, it is possible that only one of us will be available at work. When it happens, it happens. But we all agree that any one of us can be the only one on duty."

The study showed that crises of different types arise at different stages of caring. At first, working carers of older people often needed to deal with transitions – such as moving their aged parents from one place (their own home or hospital) to another (to a working carer's home or another institution) – and applying for LTCI benefits. While these initial transitional tasks faded out over time, working carers still needed to deal with changes in their aged parents' circumstances. These can be unexpected, such as hospitalisation or refusing to go to a day care centre for unknown reasons. Crisis situations are especially hard for working carers to plan for and often require them to take regular paid days off or miss work hours or days.

Working carers in the Japanese study used a wide range of support to reconcile care and work. While workplace support is sometimes provided through company policies, supervisors and/or colleagues, carers also use other help, including informal support networks and formal long-term care services. Thus, when Mrs Fujita was caring for her father living far away, she was helped by many of his friends in the neighbourhood, who provided him with daily support, and exchanged contact details with them in case of emergency. In her case, the combination of support from her supervisor at work and her father's friends seemed to work well.

Some working carers also use formal services, including day care centres, meals-on-wheels and home helps. However, most day care centres are open only until late afternoon, and many working carers are still at work at the time those they care for come home. In such cases, some working carers use home-help services to provide care before their relative leaves the house and returns home. Nonetheless, most working carers provide care before and after work as well as at weekends. Sometimes, they need to give care late at night and still go to work the next day. The study found that lack of sleep is a serious issue among working carers.

In Taiwan, Hsieh's (2006) study of eight working carers found that, in a culture that emphasises filial piety, becoming a carer is seen as natural by both the carer and others. Ms Bo saw caring for her elderly mother with dementia as a way of repaying her mother's care: "My mother cared for me once, so to care for her in the same way is what I should do". However, cultural perspectives on family care can also place unwelcome social pressure on the carer to leave her job. As Mrs Chang stated, "people around me kept telling me that 'Your husband has been ill, so you should give up your work to care for him'".

Since working carers in Taiwan have no legal right to support at work, negotiating employment flexibility is heavily dependent on a boss's personal attitudes. Some are lucky and have a good boss, like Ms Ding, an administrative assistant whose manager knew her situation and was willing to offer her care leave so that she could concentrate on caring for her father with cancer. Other carers do not even tell their supervisors they have family care responsibilities, fearing being labelled as incompetent workers. Mrs Yi explained:

> "I dared not let my boss know what was happening at home.
> I try my best to cover it up. I was concerned that if my
> supervisor knew, he would think that 'This is your family
> business' or even have negative views about me."

Depending on the nature of the job, working carers found different ways of adjusting to the situation. Some changed to a part-time position or contracted worker role to increase their flexibility at work and reduce their workload, trading this off against lower pay. Ms Ding was able to negotiate a new contracted worker role enabling her to work at home, paid on a piece rate system.

Carers who could not negotiate flexibility at work tried to find another job that could accommodate their caring tasks. Thus, Mr Fang changed his job to an internet-based role so that he could work at home with flexible working hours. Similarly, Ms Bo, a full-time nurse in a nursing home, was able, perhaps unusually, to negotiate with her boss to take her mother with dementia to the adult day care centre in the nursing home each day. She could work and care for her mother at the same time: "This job allows me to bring my mother with me to work because this is a nursing home. She feels safe here, can make friends, and go home with me after work".

In five of the eight cases in Hsieh's study, a migrant care worker was used as a substitute carer when a caring crisis arose: such workers were seen as the most affordable, accessible and available type of paid care. After caring for her mother with dementia for 10 years, Ms Bo applied for a migrant care worker because she felt that she could no longer care for her mother alone. Carers nevertheless need to ensure that the migrant care worker will provide care of the right quality before they can go to work and, even while at work, feel that they need to manage the migrant care worker from a distance, as Mr Fang said: "When I saw my mother was getting along with the Filipina worker, I felt relieved and started to think about my work". It took Ms Bo a while to make that transition:

> "I had to make sure she was well taken care of. I still worry about her when I work. I need to act as a bridge between my mother and the Filipina care worker. I even lied to her, saying the care worker is my friend, so she can gradually get used to the worker. Only when the Filipina worker gets to know her completely, I will be able to go to work."

Although family members and neighbours are helpful in providing support to working carers, their contribution is not enough to relieve carers of their care responsibility, and a migrant care worker is the most popular way of reconciling work and care for Taiwanese working carers. This arrangement does not entirely relieve their situation; rather, it transforms their role from direct care provider to indirect care manager, and managing the migrant care worker becomes another task to be carried out alongside their own paid work.

Caring for older people in East Asian contexts: unfinished reforms?

Common to both Taiwan and Japan is the influence of Confucian thinking on family ethics, which defines family care as an obligation rather than as a right, allowing choice for both carer and care recipient. What is distinctive in the two states is that Japan has been moving away from an 'obligation' regime towards a 'quasi-rights' regime, while in its social policies, Taiwan still maintains the rhetoric of family care.

The shift in Japan is evident in three aspects. First, eligibility for care in the LTCI system is defined at the 'intake' and 'evaluation' phases in relation only to individual functional status and takes no account of informal or family support. Through this 'carer-free' principle, the Japanese government recognises that family support is no longer available to all. Second, after Japan introduced its Childcare and Family Leave Act 2010 to support working carers, the interplay of cultural and institutional change became evident. A cultural expectation of family care still exists, and the wife of the first son remains the main source of care, but this practice is decreasing and older people increasingly report that a 'home helper' is their primary carer. Third, paying LTCI premiums seems to be changing people's attitudes by identifying care services as a commodity that people have a right to use.

A similar trend can be anticipated in Taiwan. Despite the prevalence of the market in care provision, Taiwan's still-to-be-implemented LTCI offers a chance to expand public provision for older people and transform its 'burnout' model into a 'quasi-rights' one, as in Japan. Democracy plays a key role in the process. In Taiwan, a lack of progress towards established and widely embraced goals – such as long-term care reform – can quickly be turned into political capital by the opposition party. Taiwan's President needs to deliver on his campaign promise to implement LTCI, even though Taiwan's older population (11%) is still smaller than Japan's was (17%) when its LTCI scheme became effective in 2000 (Colombo et al, 2011). However, LTCI premiums are likely to be set low, with only modest initial impact. Taiwan's demographic and labour market circumstances have pushed the 'obligation' regime to its limits and proved it to be impractical. The disjuncture between cultural expectation and demography has become the driving force in making care of older people a public responsibility. Both states have chosen social insurance as the means of dealing with this issue, effectively changing cultural expectations by transforming daughters-in-law into citizens who can claim their rights from the state.

LTCI has thus become a contested site for defining private and public responsibilities. The move away from family care as obligation is by no means complete: returning responsibility for care to the family still remains an option for East Asian policymakers, especially at times of financial crisis. This was evident in 2005 when, to improve the financial sustainability of the scheme, the Japanese Ministry of Health, Labour and Welfare (MHLW) proposed a reduction in scheme benefits for older people with light to moderate disabilities. To prevent bogus claims, a regularisation policy with strict guidelines for providers was also introduced, instructing care managers to limit the use of home-help services by eligible older people living with a carer. This provoked such debate in Parliament that the Ministry was forced to backtrack and issue new directions to local government. However, the 2005 reform reduced the benefits established in 2000 even though the pressures of caring on carers had not reduced (Sugihara et al, 2009).

Women remain over-represented as primary carers of older family members, and in both countries, the issue of care remains a central concern of the feminist movement. Japanese women's groups have chosen to reject a cash benefit in the LTCI scheme, seeing it as reinforcing women's caring responsibilities in a society where women are seeking to break out of such roles (Campbell and Ikegami, 2003) and arguing that a formal delivery system needs to be built. In Taiwan, women's groups are divided on this issue: those against a cash benefit, using Japan as their example, argue that it would reinforce women's role as family carers, encourage families to hire migrant care workers and reduce job opportunities for local women. Proponents of the cash benefit offer two different rationales. As long-term care is not well-established in Taiwan, a cash benefit is seen as a cheaper way of providing services. The Taiwanese government proposed setting cash benefits at 30–40% of the value of the in-kind benefit (mirroring similarly structured arrangements in Germany). This sparked opposition from the Taiwanese Association of Family Caregivers (TAFC), which has argued that cash benefits should be equal in value to in-kind benefits. It emphasises that a cash benefit would provide choice and income security for carers, enabling them to be treated as employees of the state and paid as home care workers with regular breaks. Carers' groups thus support a cash benefit, although critics of their proposals suggest that it is too costly to implement (Nadash and Shih, 2013).

As has been shown, work–care reconciliation has gained visibility and become a political issue in both countries, although there are differences in terms of which care responsibilities each country recognises among workers. In Taiwan, the only caregivers identified as needing support at work are mothers with a child under three, whereas in Japan, carers are more broadly defined and include carers of older people. While both countries have laws requiring employers to provide support for carers, the impact in Taiwan is mainly symbolic. In both cases, the country's economic structure affects how measures to support working carers operate. Japan's economy comprises many large corporates (27% of companies have 500+ employees), which have greater capacity to support working carers, whereas almost all (98% of) Taiwanese companies have fewer than 100 employees (MOEA, 2011). Caring for an elderly family member tends to be seen as a 'family matter' at work, rather than something an employer has the responsibility to share. In an era of global capital fluidity, Taiwan's government is unwilling to impose strict carer support regulations, fearing that capital may relocate to China.

Another distinction between Taiwan and Japan is their choice of migrant care worker policy. For policymakers – and many families in Taiwan – importing migrant care workers seems an easy and immediate solution to the care deficit. Policymakers in Japan, however, aim to regulate and limit incoming migration. Taiwan's migration regime is dominated by a market of private brokers who mediate between families in Taiwan and migrant workers in sending countries. Caring takes place in a largely private and informal space and the cost of migration is shouldered by both the migrant and the employer. It is situated in the private sphere through the strong three-generation family ideology, which is used to justify minimal state involvement. Migration flows are dominated by the logic of the market, which does not always pay attention to migrants' human rights, and locates migrant workers at the bottom of the care market as affordable and flexible labour. Migrant workers are incorporated into the care regime as 'guest workers' who cannot stay longer than 12 years and they are kept outside the plans for a publicly subsidised long-term care system.

By contrast, Japan's migration arrangements for care workers are state-led, sponsored and covered by an Economic Partnership Agreement (EPA) (Ogawa et al, 2010). Through the EPA, Japan takes in 1,000 Indonesian nurse trainees annually, expecting them to learn Japanese and to obtain the official care worker qualification within four years. Government institutions in both the sending and receiving countries are heavily involved in the recruitment, matching, deployment and training of migrants. The cost of migration is covered by the government and host institutions, and because the cost of training one Indonesian or Filipino care worker exceeds the annual salary of a Japanese care worker, migrant care workers are not cheap labour. The EPA states that migrants can only work in institutions, not in private households. Their working conditions, including salaries and benefits, are covered by labour standard law and are the same as for Japanese workers. Migrant workers in Japan's long-term care system are thus expensive, inflexible and formal. Employers must support their studies for the (difficult) national exam (in Japanese), which provides an opportunity to incorporate migrants into Japan's single long-term care system. The scheme has been less successful than expected and was initially opposed by both the MHLW and the Japanese Nursing Association. Both are slowly changing their stance, reflecting the anxieties of an ageing society where the public is deeply concerned about the deteriorating pension system and lack of human resources to provide eldercare (Asato, 2009: 395).

The use of migrant workers in the care systems of Taiwan and Japan represents two opposing cases: one market-dominated, the other state-dominated. Neither seems sustainable in the long run: the former raises concerns about migrants' human rights and the latter is too costly for the state. Hochschild (2000) notes the tension between the state and the market regarding migration, arguing that classical liberalism has two precepts: (1) that markets function most smoothly in the absence of constraining regulations; and (2) that labour is a commodity to be bought and sold in the market. Even the most liberal states seek to control immigration, seeing it as a critical element of state sovereignty. The contradictory logic between the state and the market with regard to the economic and political dimension of migration presents a 'liberal paradox'. In Taiwan, the market-dominated model emphasises the economic dimension of migration, while the political dimension is likely to be addressed by confining migrants to guest worker status. In Japan, the state-dominated model plays down the economic dimension, but controls the political dimension through a quota system and the imposition of a national exam.

Facing similar demographic challenges, low fertility and population ageing, both countries are attempting to cope with a common care deficit crisis. This chapter is written at the historical juncture of the collapse of the old and the emergence of a new welfare state model in which the configuration of the care regime is highly contested. Carers in both states are socially marginalised and excluded by the cultural expectation of Confucian family ethics, which is nevertheless gradually being undermined. Williams (2003) proposed that care as a policy analysis framework provides a focal point for examining three intersecting forces in a country: (1) welfare state regimes; (2) social movements; and (3) levels of globalisation. Japan, the most advanced welfare state in Asia, has implemented a LTCI policy that has subsequently become a contested site for the feminist movement. Similar developments are occurring in Taiwan. Taiwan is a 'latecomer and student of East Asian welfare states' (Lue, 2012), in which the Taiwanese implicitly face the challenge of 'catching up' with their peers.

Part of the motive behind the push to welfare reform is Taiwan's emergence as a newly democratised and industrialised nation. Social movements, including the carers' movement, play an important role in shaping both countries' policies. These, in turn, reshape the everyday conceptualisation of carers. However, as the debate on cash benefits demonstrates, other countries' approaches to gender equality offer no easy or simple answers. The formation of a global care chain, as in Taiwan, further complicates the policy debate. The paradox – that the liberation of women from the family care culture depends on the exploitation of women from another country – is one of the most difficult ethical choices facing carers' rights activists. Taiwan has looked not only to Japan to learn from its experiences in implementing LTCI, but also to the UK and Germany (Finer, 2001; Chen, 2005; Ho and Kao, 2010; Huang et al, 2010). Its carer support framework remains limited and incomplete, but working carers are beginning to be recognised in public debate, as in Japan, creating perhaps the best opportunity yet for the possibility of change in public policy.

References

Asato, W. (2009) 'Rondan: Gaikokujin kaigo rôdosha wa naniga tokubetsuka' ['What is special about migrant care workers?'], *Japanese Journal of Gerontology*, vol 31, no 3, pp 390–6.

Cabinet Office (2001) *National survey of lifestyle preferences*, Tokyo: Cabinet Office.

Cabinet Office (2010) *Annual report on the aging society 2010: summary*, Tokyo: Cabinet Office.

Campbell, J.C. and Ikegami, N. (2003) 'Japan's radical reform of long-term care', *Social Policy and Administration*, vol 37, no 1, pp 21–34.

CEPD (Council for Economic Planning and Development) (2011) *Population projections for Taiwan: 2010–2060*, Taipei: Executive Yuan. Available at: www.cepd.gov.tw/encontent/m1.aspx?sNo=0001457

Chen, C.F. (2005) 'Long-term care policies in Germany, Japan and Canada: a lesson for Taiwan', *Taiwanese Journal of Social Welfare*, vol 5, no 1, pp 49–69 (in Chinese).

Colombo, F., Llena-Nozal, A., Mercier, J. and Tjadens, F. (2011) *Help wanted? Providing and paying for long-term care*, Paris: OECD Publishing.

DGBAS (Directorate-General of Budget, Accounting and Statistics) (2011) *2010 census on population and living arrangements*, Taipei: Directorate-General of Budget, Accounting and Statistics.

Finer, C.J. (2001) *Comparing the social policy experience of Britain and Taiwan*, Aldershot: Ashgate.

Ho, E. and Kao, Y.L. (2010) 'Visiting Japanese official offers advice on long term care system', *The China Post*, 2 March. Available at: www.chinapost. com.tw/taiwan/foreign-community/2010/03/02/246594/Visiting-Japanese.htm

Hochschild, A.R. (2000) 'Global care chains and emotional surplus value', in W. Hutton and A. Giddens (eds) *On the edge: living with global capitalism*, London: Jonathan Cape, pp 130–46.

Hsieh, Y.-Y. (2006) 'Exploratory research of the transition processes for family caregivers' labor roles', Master's thesis, Department of Social Work, National Taipei University, Taipei.

Hu, Y.H. (1995) *Three-generation-family: myths and traps*, Taipei: Chui-Liu Publishing.

Huang, H.W., Liu, S.H. and Pai, Y.C. (2010) 'Taiwan long-term care insurance and the evolution of long-term care in Japan', *The Journal of Nursing*, vol 57, no 4, pp 77–82.

JILPT (Japan Institute for Labour Policy and Training) (2006) *Promoting usage of family care leave policy*, Tokyo: JILPT.

Lan, P. (2002) 'Subcontracting filial piety: elder care in ethnic Chinese immigrant families in California', *Journal of Family Issues*, vol 23, no 7, pp 812–35.

Lo, J.C., Suchuan Y. and Wu, S.-F. (2007) 'An exploratory investigation on the care takers cared by foreign workers', in J.C. Lo (ed) *The study of foreign workers in Taiwan*, Taipei: Academia Sinica and Taipei Institute of Economics, pp 129–54 (in Chinese).

Lue, J.-D. (2012) 'Welfare regime, social protection and poverty reduction: the case of Taiwan', paper presented at the International Conference on Social Inequality and Mobility in Chinese Societies, 16–17 December, Hong Kong.

MHLW (Ministry of Health, Labour and Welfare) (2008a) *Comprehensive survey of living conditions of the people on health and welfare*, Tokyo: MHLW.

MHLW (2008b) 'Fuzoku shiryô 1. Heisei 20 nendo, dai ikkai kaigo rôdosha no kakuho – teichaku to ni kansuru kenkyûkai' (Handout 4), 1st Meeting on Securement and Settlement of Care Workers, MHLW, Tokyo. Available at: www.mhlw.go.jp/shingi/2008/04/dl/s0418-3h.pdf

MHLW (2009a) *Introduction to the revised Child Care and Family Care Leave Law*, Tokyo: MHLW.

MHLW (2009b) *Basic survey of gender equity in employment management 2008*, Tokyo: MHLW.

MHLW (2010) *A study to understand the actual conditions of reconciliation between work and care*, Tokyo: MHLW.

MIA (Ministry of the Interior) (2011) *Monthly statistics of the Ministry of the Interior*, Taipei: MIA.

Mizuguchi, Y. (2008) Shakaiteki nyûin ni kansuru sôgoteki rebyû to sono yôin moderu no kôchiku' ['A literature review on 'social' hospitalisation in Japan and a development of an explanatory model on its causes'], *Keio SFC Journal*, vol 8, no 2, pp 1–16.

MOEA (Ministry of Economic Affairs) (2011) *Survey on middle and small sized company*, Taipei: MOEA.

Nadash, P. and Shih, Y.-C. (2013) 'Introducing social insurance for long-term care in Taiwan: key issues', *International Journal of Social Welfare*, vol 22, no 1, pp 69-79.

Ogawa, R., Wang, F. and Lui, H. (2010) *Transnational migration from Southeast Asia to East Asia and the transformation of reproductive labor: comparative study between Korea, Taiwan and Japan*, Kyushu: Kitakyushu Forum on Asian Women.

Sugihara, Y., Sugisawa, H., Shimmei, M., Kikuchi, K. and Takahashi, R. (2009) 'Yôshien-ninteisha ni okeru kaigohokenseidokaitei no eikyôhyôka: Sâbisu sakugen he no taisho to sono shinriteki eikyô' ['Impact of reformed Long-term Care Insurance System on those certified for support: coping with service cutbacks and the psychological impact'], *Japanese Journal of Social Welfare*, vol 50, no 2, pp 56–67.

Wang, F.T.Y. (1998) 'Disciplining Taiwanese families: a study of family ideology and home care practices', PhD thesis, University of Toronto, Toronto.

Wang, F.T.Y. (2010) 'From undutiful daughter-in-law to cold-blood migrant household worker', in K. Scheiwe and J. Krawietz (eds) *Transnationale Sorgearbeit: Rechtliche Rahmenbedingungen und gesellschaftliche Praxis*, Wiesbaden: VS Verlag, pp 309–28.

Williams, F. (2003) 'Rethinking care in social policy', keynote presentation at the Finnish Social Policy Association Annual Conference, 24 October, Joensuu.

PART TWO

Working parent-carers of disabled children

Parent-carers of disabled children in Finland and Sweden: socially excluded by a labour of love?

Sonja Miettinen, Kristina Engwall and Antti Teittinen

Introduction

One feminist definition of care is 'a labour of love' (Graham, 1983: 13). This nicely captures the nature of caring as work that is both infused with and concealed by the emotional bond that exists between those in a care relationship, especially when that care is given to a disabled son or daughter. In this chapter, we shed light on the lived realities of being a parent-carer,[1] in which care is experienced as gratifying yet demanding work, and explore how this work affects parents' employment careers and lives in Finland and Sweden.

Who performs care work and on what terms are matters of social organisation. Finland and Sweden each have a dual-earner employment and social system in which women and men are expected to have paid work, and extensive public care services have been established to facilitate women's entrance into the labour market (Anttonen and Sipilä, 1996). In recent years, however, public care services have been dominated by a new development in the policy agenda, especially in Finland, which has encouraged and supported unpaid family care (see *Chapter Two*). This policy agenda has been counterbalanced by ambitious developments in disability policy, particularly in Sweden. The state's support for people with disabilities affects the care responsibilities of parents of disabled children in important ways, and before examining parents' experiences of reconciling care and paid work, we first review developments in disability policy in Finland and Sweden, indicating how these have shaped the conditions in which parent-carers attempt this.

Current trends in Finnish and Swedish disability policy

Disability policy has undergone similar kinds of ideological change in both Finland and Sweden in recent decades, under the influence of various factors: the principle of 'normalisation' (Nirje, 1969); the growth of the independent living movement (DeJong, 1979); and the development of the concept of human rights. These can be summarised as:

- *Normalisation* – The core statement of the normalisation principle is that disabled people should have access to living conditions and lifestyles that are common in their societies. It includes the idea that people with disabilities should have the same opportunity to experience life-course transitions as others: living with their parents in childhood and moving away from home and starting a life of their own in adulthood.
- *Self-determination* – This is a central concept both in the original Nordic formulation of the normalisation principle and for the independent living movement. The demand for the right to make decisions about one's life and to have control over the support received has led to the development of personal assistance[2] in many countries.
- *Rights* – As a rights-based approach to disability has taken root, the social inclusion of people with disabilities and responding to their needs have been framed as basic human and civil rights. This approach is epitomised in the 2006 UN Convention on the Rights of Persons with Disabilities (UN, 2006).

While these concepts – normalisation, self-determination and rights – have reshaped disability policy in both Finland and Sweden, in practice, services for people with disabilities have not always developed in ways entirely consistent with them.

Developments in disability policy in Finland

Finland's Special Care for the Mentally Handicapped Act 1977 heralded a transformation in services for people with disabilities, from long-term institutional care to community-based services. It prioritised mainstream services, and emphasised the importance of community-based provision. Today, the latter has all but replaced institutional care in Finland (Vesala, 2003): by 2010, just 1,800 of the estimated population of 40,000 people with intellectual disabilities remained in institutions (Sotkanet, 2012).

In 2004, 27,000 people used special care services for people with intellectual disabilities, of whom, about half lived with family members, one third in community-based housing services, just over 10% independently in their own homes, 10% in institutions and a small minority in foster families (Kumpulainen, 2007). Of those who were children, almost all lived with their parents; however, about half of those living with family members were adults (Kumpulainen, 2007). There are also estimated to be a further 13,000 persons with intellectual disabilities – living either with their families or independently – who do not use special care services (Niemelä and Brandt, 2007: 50, 114).

Because the 1977 Act applied in practice only to people with intellectual disabilities, additional legislation was needed on services for people with physical disabilities. This was addressed in the Services and Assistance for the Disabled Act 1987, now the primary legislation on disability services in Finland. This offers a legally enforceable right to services to those with the most severe disabilities, while the 1977 Act provides a right to services to all people with intellectual disabilities. Community-based services provided under the 1977 Act include housing services, day and work activities, and supported employment. The 1987 Act provides transportation, interpreters, housing and personal assistance services, and enables municipalities to reimburse the cost of home adaptations and technical support. People with disabilities in Finland are also entitled to general health care services and to education, either in mainstream or special educational institutions. In addition, they and their families are entitled to financial support (Disability Allowance and Disability Pension). Employed parents of disabled children get the same parental leaves, benefits and day care services as parents of non-disabled children and the same support as other carers, but they also have the right to work part-time until their disabled child is 18 (see *Chapter Two*).

Exact information about the prevalence of disability is not available in Finland, but the number of people receiving disability benefits provides one indicator: in 2010, 33,300 people received Disability Allowance for under 16s, 10,400 received it in respect of persons aged 16 and over, and 165,700 people received a Disability Pension (KELA, 2011: 97, 117).[3]

Although community-based services have increased, they do not fully meet needs due to financial constraints on municipalities (Harjajärvi, 2009). During the 1990s' recession in Finland, state subsidies to municipalities were cut back sharply – and not subsequently reversed – and since then, municipalities have been preoccupied with cost-containment. Reductions in welfare spending continued in the 1990s and 2000s, accompanied by tax cuts, which reduced state revenues and favoured the wealthiest (Jutila, 2011). Some Finnish researchers have noted a profound ideological change in Finnish politics, as neoliberal principles have been adopted (Julkunen, 2001; Patomäki, 2007; Jutila, 2010, 2011). The neoliberal turn in economic policies, evident in some form in most countries, has implications for disabled people and their families as it often involves reducing publicly funded services and expecting family members, particularly women, to provide informal care alongside their participation in paid work (Roulstone and Prideaux, 2012).

Developments in disability policy in Sweden

In Sweden, the dismantling of institutional care has already been accomplished. Large institutions have been replaced by group homes comprising private apartments with access to community rooms and staff, or by separate apartments with support. Disability policy underwent further substantial change in the 1990s with new legislation, which still regulates policy: the Support and Service for Persons with Certain Disabilities Act 1993 (the LSS) and the Assistance Benefit Act 1993 (LASS).

The LSS defines three different categories of people (adults and children) entitled to help. They are people with: (1) a development disorder, autism or a related disability; (2) substantial and permanent intellectual impairments arising from brain damage in adulthood; and (3) other permanent physical or mental disabilities (except those caused by normal ageing). Ten types of support can be provided, including: advisory services; personal assistance; short stays away from home; out-of-school and holiday support for disabled schoolchildren aged 12 or over; residential support for those needing to spend time away from the parental home; escorting services; contact persons; home-based respite services; housing with special services; and day services for those not in training or gainful employment. Other needs are met through the Social Services Act 2001. The LSS and the Social Services Act aim to achieve different outcomes, however: the LSS aspires to secure 'good living conditions', the Social Services Act 'a reasonable level of living'. In 2011, 63,300 people received help through the LSS, among whom, 20,100 were children aged under 22 (Socialstyrelsen, 2012).

The LASS improved opportunities for independent living through personal assistance, giving users rights and choices about their support (Askheim, 2008). Thus, both care users and care providers have considerable influence, with limited state control (Lindqvist, 2009: 136). The emphasis on choice also means that users can employ who they wish as personal assistants (PAs), including relatives.

Sweden has an explicit policy aim of making the reconciliation of paid work and parenthood possible. This is realised through parental rights granted to parents of children under eight years old that include: parental leave (480 days); Temporary Parental Benefit, paid when a child needs care because of illness (maximum 120 days per year); and the right to work part-time. These rights are also accorded to parents of disabled children, for whom the age limit for Temporary Parental Benefit is 21 years. Parents of disabled children also have the right to the specific Childcare Allowance (see *Chapter Two*), which is paid to parents with a disabled child who needs special care for at least six months, or who have extra costs due to the child's impairments. In 2009, 46,000 children aged 19 received this (Försäkringskassan, 2011). It is based on the child's needs, and is not meant to provide a regular salary.

Despite the aims and aspirations of Swedish disability policy, severe problems exist, which Ringsby Jansson and Olsson (2006: 34) have identified as a 'retreat of the welfare state'. Lewin and colleagues (2008) also note geographical differences, which persist despite the LSS's aim of offering equal rights nationwide, and difficulties with individualisation and choice, which require knowledge and persistence (abilities that, because of impairments, may be lacking).

Parent-carers' experiences of combining work and care in Finland and Sweden

In this section, evidence collected using a variety of research methods is brought together to highlight the experiences of parent-carers in Finland and Sweden. The Finnish data are drawn from semi-structured, biographical interviews with parents who care for an adult child with intellectual disabilities who lives at home. They were collected as part of the 'Working Carers and Caring Workers' (WoCaWo) project (see *Chapter One*) in 2008/09 and comprise interviews with 14 families[4] conducted either with the parent with primary care responsibility (usually the mother) or, where they wished to participate, both parents. One case from this Finnish research material is described in detail. The account focuses on the interplay between care responsibilities and paid work in this interviewee's life – from the birth of her disabled son until the time of the interview – illustrating the difficulties carers of severely disabled people face in combining work and care, and showing how being a lone parent further complicates the situation.

The situations of Swedish parent-carers are explored through LSS applications written by municipal administrators.[5] These applications were initiated by parents of disabled children and the material includes the administrators' investigation of the families' situation, the decisions made and the rationales given for these. The material comprises 60 documents collected from eight Swedish municipalities in 2011. The LSS applications reveal different perspectives on the need for support. Negotiation takes place between the parents' felt need for assistance, the child's opinion and the administrators' consideration of the legal position, regulations and finances (cf Gundersen, 2011). Here, the material is used mainly to illustrate the everyday lives of families with disabled children: it also elucidates the ongoing negotiations between parents and professionals and their occasionally divergent views. The analysis was informed by earlier reports, based on qualitative data, on the living conditions of families with disabled children, including information on the availability of support and parents' ability to participate in the labour market (RFV, 2002; Socialstyrelsen, 2005) and by two studies based on statistical information on parents of children with disabilities (Socialstyrelsen, 2008; RiR, 2011).

Experiences of Finnish parents: care responsibilities limiting participation in paid work

Kaarina[6] is a middle-aged mother of two adult children. Her son Teemu, now in his 20s, has intellectual disabilities and lives at home. He can move and talk a little, but needs help with all other activities and has challenging behaviour. Her daughter, who is a little older than Teemu, has no disabilities. Kaarina stayed at home caring for her two children for many years, but when her marriage fell apart, she suddenly needed to find a way of supporting her family and decided to begin occupational training. This was possible at the time because Teemu was at school, with after-school care at the end of the day. She also had help from her daughter, who was able to put her brother into a taxi in the mornings. Kaarina came home in the afternoon to be there when Teemu arrived home and stayed with him in the evenings and at weekends. The municipality provided Kaarina with home-help services for about 70 hours a year. With the help she received from her daughter, Kaarina had enough free time to continue her regular activities and interests.

On completing her training, Kaarina obtained a job in the occupation for which she had studied. However, needing to be at home at 3pm to receive her son meant that she could not work full-time or do evening shifts, and she was unable to keep the job. After this, she took a part-time job in her brother's enterprise and worked there for several years before it went out of business and she again needed to reorganise her own and her son's lives. Kaarina was offered a job in another town, and decided to move there.

For the first few months, everything seemed to go well. Teemu completed school in the new town and Kaarina then felt that it was time for him to move away from home. The municipality offered him a place in a group home, but it quickly became clear that this was not suitable for him. Kaarina was told that there was no option but to transfer Teemu to an institution. She agreed at first, but had second thoughts when she found out how he was treated: placed in a closed ward and given heavy medication to keep him calm and restrict his drooling. Kaarina took Teemu out of the institution, quit her job and returned to her previous hometown.

When interviewed, Kaarina was still waiting for the municipality to provide housing services for Teemu. She did not know when a place would become available or whether it would be suitable. She felt that she had no choice but to care for him at home, although she did not like the fact that he, an adult man, had to live with his mother. Kaarina no longer had any career expectations for herself. She felt that she had neither the energy nor any real opportunity to work outside the home. To make ends meet, she now did some paperwork at home for her former employer and also had her niece, who also has intellectual disabilities, living with her, which doubled the monthly Carer's Allowance the municipality paid her.

The municipality had reduced Kaarina's home-help hours to 20 per year, however, and her daughter had now moved to another town where she was busy with her own studies and work. The only free time Kaarina had was the four hours on weekdays when her son was in a day centre and her niece was at school. Because of these changes, Kaarina had given up all her own previous activities and interests. She was able to take about a month's holiday once a year, but only by saving all the monthly days off that she was entitled to throughout the year.

Kaarina's story depicts the current situation in which most children with disabilities in Finland are cared for at home by their parents, primarily by their mothers. It also illustrates how care responsibilities are shared between the family and public services. Community-based services for people with disabilities provide indirect support for parents, freeing them from care responsibility for certain periods of time. Nevertheless, these services do not remove the need for support from informal networks: for example, Kaarina needed her daughter's help to be able to study and continue her activities and interests. Informal support also played a significant role in the lives of other parent-carers interviewed, although in these cases, it was only members of the immediate family who provided regular help: friends and relatives could be relied on only occasionally. Kaarina's case also shows that informal support is sometimes not available: when her daughter moved away from home, she became dependent on public services, and more tightly tied to home.

The availability and quality of public services influences the duration of caring responsibilities (Miettinen, 2012). Kaarina continued to care for her son at home because she could see no alternative to family care. The solutions offered by the municipality seemed to offer alternatives, but were not satisfactory in practice. Consequently, there was no *real* chance for her son to move away from home. Other interviews showed that if an adult child with disabilities succeeds in moving away from the parental home into a group home, the lives of the parents change too: care responsibilities do not necessarily end altogether, but they change substantially, releasing time and energy for other activities in the parents' lives (Miettinen, 2012).

Several of the parent-carers interviewed had at some stage in their lives made the same decision as Kaarina, relinquishing paid work to stay at home to care for a child with disabilities. All except one were mothers. Their children's care needs were extensive, and they considered caring a demanding task that left little time or energy for paid work. Where the child's disability was severe, caring often required constant presence and watchfulness (see Brannen, 2005). Kaarina felt that working outside the home meant working simultaneously in two spheres – in her workplace and at home – with limits on her personal time that she found intolerable. In the end, she chose to give up her career to preserve at least some personal time.

Although caring for a child with disabilities can be a work-like activity, it is not a job in the sense of being a properly paid role. In Finland, the Carer's Allowance (see *Chapter Two*) is not high enough for carers to live on, so those who stay at home become dependent on their partner's incomes. Lone parents face contradictory pressures: their opportunity to work outside the home is severely restricted, yet doing so is economically necessary. Kaarina's case shows that getting by without working outside the home requires creative, exceptional solutions from lone parents of children with disabilities.

Although Kaarina eventually felt that she had to give up her career, there were periods in her life when she managed to work outside the home. This was much more complicated for her than for parents whose children have milder disabilities, however. While they could work full-time and did not require longer breaks from work due to their care responsibilities, Kaarina and other parents caring for children with severe disabilities could only work outside the home on a part-time basis. Their ability to work was both enabled and restricted by the services provided to their children. The difficulty with these services was that they were provided in a standardised manner that did not take into account the individual needs of parent-carers. Those like Kaarina who cannot turn to informal solutions – such as having another family member look after the disabled child – have to adapt to the schedules of public services. This means that they cannot work full-time, as in Finland, services for children with disabilities do not cover a full eight-hour working day, let alone overtime hours, and such parents are unable to work shifts or at night.

Other interviews indicated that carers of severely disabled children want to work shorter days not only because of service restrictions, but also because caring takes up so much energy. However, Kaarina's case shows that the needs of carers and employers can clash. Even though parent-carers have a formal right to part-time work, opportunities for part-time employment are in reality very limited in Finland as the labour market is structured on the basis of full-time work. Pressures in the workplace also complicate the situation: parent-carers spoke about feeling that they were expected to be efficient and flexible, an additional source of stress for parents with heavy care responsibilities.

Due to the stresses at work and home, even a shortened working day may prove harmful to the health of working parent-carers. Kaarina anticipated this, and another single parent-carer, who had worked part-time but had to take sick leave because of exhaustion, experienced it directly. The loss of personal time and space and the exhaustion that ensues seem to be major problems for working carers of severely disabled children.

Experiences of Swedish parents: the significance of PAs in reconciling family care and paid work

In Sweden, the LSS aims to support children with disabilities and their families to live the same kind of life as other children and families. This includes the opportunity for parents to keep their jobs, social life and social interests, as well as making it possible for disabled children to have good living conditions.

An example of how the LSS can work is provided by Sara, a 17-year-old girl with an intellectual disability and behavioural problems. Her everyday life is described in an LSS application in which her parents argue for more support. Sara needs attention *all* the time: she cannot travel by bus alone, has no insights about time or money, and cannot control her eating. During the day, she attends a special school. Because she cannot handle being in a large group with many teenagers, she has individual after-school support for two hours daily. She also has individual support between 8am and 5.30pm on weekdays in school holidays, and each week receives 10 hours of individual support to facilitate her leisure activities (horse-riding and swimming) and 10 hours of home-based respite support.

Compared to Teemu's case in Finland, Sara's parents seem to have more opportunity to continue working, as Sara's supervision covers whole days and is more individualised, taking Sara's interests into account. Sara's parents nevertheless feel that they need more help. The administrator agrees: Sara 'needs more supervision in her everyday life than teenagers without disabilities. This need consists of ... extra supervision and support to carry out activities, not become too passive and practice independence'. As a result of the application, Sara is allowed more hours per week.

In Sara's case, the negotiation between parents and the administrator seems to work reasonably well. Nevertheless, there are many examples of the system failing to meet the needs of parent-carers (Socialstyrelsen, 2005). Parents experience various obstacles to receiving the kind of assistance they and their children need and want. Parents argue that the municipalities do not inform parents of existing forms of support, say that the handling of applications is a bureaucratic, drawn-out process, and report that positive decisions are not always implemented due to a lack of resources (Socialstyrelsen, 2005: 22–38).

In general, parents feel that they have to be very knowledgeable, 'up-front' and strong to get their needs recognised and addressed (RFV, 2002: 14–19). These experiences represent the much-criticised process of 'individualisation' in the Swedish system of services for people with disabilities, which requires competence and persistence from users or their parents (Lindqvist, 2009: 139). The loss of paid work may also affect a family's financial well-being. Parent-carers are usually entitled to Childcare Allowance, which helps the family 'get by', but this is low and not pensionable (RFV, 2002: 21; Socialstyrelsen, 2005: 49).

Although the policy aim is for parent-carers to have the chance to work if they want, in practice, the chance of both parents – or of lone parents – of a disabled child working full-time is limited (RFV, 2002: 20; Socialstyrelsen, 2005: 48). Many reduce their working hours, while others cannot work at all due to their child's extensive care needs. Those who do work often rely on employers with flexible attitudes, muddle along as hourly paid employees or establish their own business to have control over their working hours and conditions (Socialstyrelsen, 2005: 49). Earlier studies also indicate gender differences in reconciling care and work: to develop and maintain a career in an occupation is difficult, especially for mothers, who usually carry the main responsibility for the care of a disabled child and reduce their working hours or quit their jobs if the child's care requires it (RFV, 2002: 21; Socialstyrelsen, 2005: 49). Mothers in these families also take more sick leave than fathers (Socialstyrelsen, 2005: 16).

The toll that combining family care and paid work takes on the parents' health is visible in a study based on interviews with 80 parents of disabled children: 15% of participants were on sick leave, two thirds of them mothers (Socialstyrelsen, 2005: 16). High levels of sickness absence among Swedish parent-carers were also clearly evident in a study that compared parents receiving Childcare Allowance, parents with PA compensation and parents of non-disabled children (RiR, 2011). This showed that parents with Childcare Allowance – that is, with children with high support needs – fall ill more often and have on average 14 more sick leave days per year than parents of non-disabled children. They are also worse off than parents with PA compensation (RiR, 2011: 44–5). In another study, parents interviewed identified constant watchfulness, a lack of recreation and the expectation that they would both work and care as the main reasons for their sickness absence (RFV, 2002: 22).

In many respects, parents whose children have PA compensation are better off than parents who care for their disabled children relying on other kinds of support. They are more likely to have paid jobs, have higher gross and disposable incomes, and need housing allowance or financial support less often (Socialstyrelsen, 2008: 59).[7] Having personal assistance also improves the situation of families in other ways: parents have more time for themselves and for other children in the family. The rhythm of everyday life becomes more relaxed. Continuity in support increases and, as a result, children feel more secure and develop better. Children and young people are also able to do things more independently from their parents. The health of the whole family improves and personal assistance also helps grown-up children to move away from home (Socialstyrelsen, 2008: 50–6).

Getting PA assistance for a child can be difficult, however. In 2009, only about 4,000 children aged 0–19 years had PA compensation, and it is much more common for disabled children to have home-based respite or short stays away from home (Socialstyrelsen, 2012). Parents whose children are entitled to PA compensation can choose to work as their child's PA and be paid a salary comparable to that of a nursing assistant or childminder. There are negative sides to being a parent and PA, however. Teenagers have less opportunity to become independent: it may not feel right to go out with your friends accompanied by your mother as your PA, and some fear that relatives may become financially dependent on the PA job, limiting the disabled person's freedom to choose their own PA (Hugemark and Wahlström, 2002).

In Sweden, most adults with disabilities live separately from their parents. Adult social status is very much symbolised by living alone or with a partner in one's own apartment, even though one may need assistance and support. This was emphasised in the LSS, where living independently is seen as important for identity and as the platform from which one develops relations to other people and takes part in society.

The process of leaving the parental home and moving into one's own place is also emphasised in practice. The transition is facilitated by granting disabled children places in short-term living or youth camps. An example of the high status of independence and self-management is seen in an LSS application by 19-year-old Ulrika, who wants to participate in activities on her own. Her application was approved with this explanation:

> At Ulrika's age there is a natural process of separation from parents and, taking account of this, the decision should focus on Ulrika's need for independence. Ulrika should be given the best opportunities to develop this and to prepare for her adult life. This means creating a social network outside the family and feeling that you can manage without Mum and Dad.

Adults with disabilities covered by the LSS have the right to live their own lives and to work. Although adult children live in their own apartments with supervision and support, many parents report that they continue to have a never-ending 'back-up' role, and that no one else takes 'total responsibility' for their child (Whitaker, 2008). Some parents, contrary to the prevailing ideology, keep their adult disabled children at home. No national statistics exist, but two regional studies of people with intellectual disabilities suggest that this applies to between 10% and 20% (Tideman, 2004; Umb-Carlsson and Sonnander, 2005). A lack of group homes and a view of people with intellectual disabilities as 'child-like' have both been offered as possible explanations (Umb-Carlsson and Sonnander, 2005: 246).

Regardless of the housing arrangement, parents often help and support their grown-up disabled children. This covers everything from practical help with cleaning to appointments with dentists and contacts with officials. One study (Gustafsson et al, 2011: 31) of the support adults with neuropsychiatric diagnoses receive from their relatives indicated that parents sometimes feel that the assistance they give is unhelpful to the child–parent relationship: "She should have somebody who takes care of all that which I do today, so we can have a mother–daughter relationship" (mother of a daughter with attention deficit hyperactivity disorder [ADHD], aged 23).

Parents' desire to have an adult relationship with their disabled child that is not dominated by caregiving underlines the strong emphasis in Sweden on independence and autonomy. The focus within the prevailing ideology on disabled adults managing on their own or with public support has led to ignorance about how much support relatives of disabled adults actually provide. One of the few studies to explore how much help is provided by relatives concludes: 'family as carer and help-giver is seen as an expression of "failure" within the disability field, in policy as well as in research' (Jeppsson Grassman et al, 2009: 46).

Discussion

There are both similarities and differences in the situations of Swedish and Finnish parents of children with disabilities. In both countries, it is common for disabled children to live with their parents. Some continue to do so even in adulthood, this being much more usual in Finland than in Sweden. In both countries, parents have wide-ranging responsibilities for the care of their children with disabilities.

In cases where the child's disability is severe, caring can demand much time and energy. This reduces a parent's ability to participate in the labour market, which – in the absence of adequate compensation schemes – affects their financial position. The Swedish system of personal assistance is a rather ingenious way of countering this risk. By allowing parents to work as their child's PA, this scheme enables them to care for them and be paid for doing so (at least as long as children are small, and do not need to act independently of their parents). On the other hand, having a PA who comes from outside the family helps parents to work outside the home. It also responds to the child's need for independence and self-determination, and is positive for the whole family in many other ways.

Services provided directly to people with disabilities are crucial for their own and their family members' ability to live normally. In both countries, a range of public services are available to people with disabilities, but it seems that it is in Sweden where they receive more support and where support is more often offered in a flexible and individual way, making it possible to combine paid work with the care or ongoing support of a disabled son or daughter. This also means that Sweden offers more opportunities for disabled people to move away from the parental home and start a life of their own when they grow up. By contrast, ongoing daily care responsibility, with all its consequences for parents, is more common in Finland than in Sweden.

In both countries, welfare state retrenchment is a visible trend affecting disability services, particularly in Finland. The experiences of the Finnish parents studied imply a tougher climate also in the labour market. These trends are detrimental to parents of children with disabilities, especially those whose children are most severely disabled. For them, the combination of increasing demands on employees and tightening support provision creates an exclusionary mechanism, making it more difficult to participate in paid work and make a living.

Notes

[1] As explained in *Chapter One*, 'parent-carer' is used in this book to refer to people who provide care or support to a son or daughter, of whatever age, who requires additional help because of a serious long-term illness or a disability, which may be physical, mental or intellectual. It is most often mothers who are parent-carers, but many fathers take part in caring for their ill and disabled children, as well.

[2] As explained in *Chapter Two*, in Sweden and Finland, a group of disabled people have a right to employ personal assistants to cover assistance needs and have the costs compensated from public funds. Such assistance is often experienced as more user-centred and empowering than traditional social and health care services.

[3] A person can only receive one of these benefits, so figures represent different individuals. Eligibility is based on functional abilities, medically assessed to have declined significantly due to prolonged illness, injury or impairment.

[4] Families were identified through an advertisement published in the magazine of a non-governmental organisation (NGO) that supports people with intellectual disabilities and their families.

[5] As explained in *Chapter One*, the international network of the WoCaWo project drew together researchers working in the same field, but did not fund parallel studies in each country.

[6] All names used here are pseudonyms.

[7] Differences are also because the median age for disabled children with PA compensation was 26, whereas for those with other kinds of support it was 15. Parents were thus older, with higher salaries and no longer caring for young children alongside part-time work. Some increase their salaries by working as PAs during weekends/evenings (Socialstyrelsen, 2008: 60).

References

Anttonen, A. and Sipilä, J. (1996) 'European social care services: is it possible to identify models?', *Journal of European Social Policy*, vol 6, no 2, pp 87–100.

Askheim, O.P. (2008) 'Personal assistance in Sweden and Norway: from difference to convergence?', *Scandinavian Journal of Disability Research*, vol 10, no 3, pp 179–90.

Brannen, J. (2005) 'Time and the negotiation of work–family boundaries: autonomy or illusion?', *Time and Society*, vol 14, no 1, pp 113–31.

DeJong, G. (1979) *The movement for independent living: origins, ideology and implications for disability research*, East Lansing, MI: Michigan State University.

Försäkringskassan (2011) *Socialförsäkringen i siffror 2011* [*Social services in figures*], Stockholm: Försäkringskassan.

Graham, H. (1983) 'Caring: a labour of love', in J. Finch and D. Groves (eds) *A labour of love: women, work and caring*, London: Routledge and Kegan Paul, pp 13–30.

Gundersen, T. (2011) 'Human dignity at stake: how parents of disabled children experience the welfare system', *Scandinavian Journal of Disability Research*, iFirst edition, pp 1–16.

Gustafsson, H., Nordquist, K. and Engwall, K. (2011) *Behov i vardagen hos personer med neuropsykiatriska funktionsnedsättningar* [*Needs in everyday life among indivduals with neuropsychiatric diagnoses*], Tullinge: FoU-Södertörn.

Harjajärvi, M. (2009) 'Kuntien näkemyksiä kehitysvammaisten ja mielenterveyskuntoutujien asumispalvelujen kysynnästä ja tarjonnasta sekä kehittämishaasteista' ['The views of municipalities on demand, provision and challenges in housing services for persons with intellectual disabilities and persons with mental health problems'], in M. Harjajärvi, T. Kairi, K. Kuusterä and S. Miettinen, *Toimivatko kehitysvammaisten ja mielenterveyskuntoutujien asumispalvelut?*, Helsinki: Finnish Association on Intellectual and Developmental Disabilities, pp 8–55.

Hugemark, A. and Wahlström, K. (2002) *Personlig assistans i olika former* [*Personal assistance in different ways*], Stockholm: FoU-rapport 2002: 4.

Jeppsson Grassman, E., Whitaker, A. and Taghizadeh Larsson, A. (2009) 'Family as failure? The role of informal help-givers to disabled people in Sweden', *Scandinavian Journal of Disability Research*, vol 11, no 1, pp 35–49.

Julkunen, R. (2001) *Suunnanmuutos: 1990-luvun sosiaalipoliittinen reformi Suomessa* [*Change of course: social policy reform in Finland in the 1990s*], Tampere: Vastapaino.

Jutila, M. (2010) 'Enter neoliberalism: transformation of the Finnish welfare state, 1991–2007', dissertation submitted to the Graduate Faculty in Political Science, City University of New York.

Jutila, M. (2011) 'Narrowing of public responsibility in Finland 1990–2010', *Social Policy and Administration*, vol 45, no 2, pp 194–205.

KELA (Kansaneläkelaitos, The Social Insurance Institution of Finland) (2011) *Statistical yearbook of the social insurance institution*, Helsinki: KELA.

Kumpulainen, A. (2007) *Kehitysvammapalvelut vuonna 2004* [*Services for people with intellectual disabilities in 2004*], Helsinki: Ministry of Social Affairs and Health.

Lewin, B., Westin, L. and Lewin, L. (2008) 'Needs and ambitions in Swedish disability care', *Scandinavian Journal of Disability Research*, vol 10, no 4, pp 237–57.

Lindqvist, R. (2009) *Funktionshindrade i välfärdssamhället* [*Disabled people in the welfare state*], Malmö: Gleerup.

Miettinen, S. (2012) 'Family care of adults with intellectual disabilities: analysis of Finnish policies and practices', *Journal of Policy and Practice in Intellectual Disabilities*, vol 9, no 1, pp 1–9.

Niemelä, M. and Brandt, K. (2007) *Kehitysvammaisten yksilöllinen asuminen* [*Individual housing for persons with intellectual disabilities*], Helsinki: Ministry of Social Affairs and Health.

Nirje, B. (1969) 'The normalization principle and its human management implications', in R.B. Kugel and W. Wolfensberger (eds) *Changing patterns in residential services for the mentally retarded*, Washington, DC: President's Committee on Mental Retardation, pp 179–95.

Patomäki, H. (2007) *Uusliberalismi Suomessa. Lyhyt historia ja tulevaisuuden vaihtoehdot* [*Neoliberalism in Finland: a brief history and future alternatives*], Helsinki: WSOY.

RFV (Riksförsäkringsverket) (2002) *För barnets* bästa: *en studie över hur föräldrar till barn med funktionshinder upplever det offentliga stödsystemet* [*For the best of the child: a study on parents of disabled children and their experiences of the formal support system*], Stockholm: Riksförsäkringsverket.

Ringsby Jansson, B. and Olsson, S. (2006) 'Outside the system: life patterns of young adults with intellectual disabilities', *Scandinavian Journal of Disability Research*, vol 8, no 1, pp 22–37.

RiR (Riksrevisionen, The Swedish National Audit Office) (2011) *Samordning av stöd till barn och unga med funktionsnedsättning – Ett (o)lösligt problem?* [*Coordination of support to children and young persons with disabilites: an (in)soluble problem?*], Stockholm: Riksrevisionen.

Roulstone, A. and Prideaux, S. (2012) *Understanding disability policy*, Bristol: The Policy Press.

Socialstyrelsen (2005) *Kompetenta föräldrar, beroende av socialtjänstens stöd* [*Competent parents, dependent on social welfare support*], Stockholm: Socialstyrelsen.

Socialstyrelsen (2008) *Personlig assistans enligt LASS ur ett samhällsekonomiskt perspektiv* [*Personal assistance according to LASS from an economic perspective*], Stockholm: Socialstyrelsen.

Socialstyrelsen (2012) *Personer med funktionsnedsättning – insatser enligt LSS 2011* [*Disabled persons – support according to LSS in 2011*], Stockholm: Socialstyrelsen.

Sotkanet (Statistic and Indicator Bank of National Institute for Health and Welfare) (2012) 'Statistical information on health and welfare in Finland'. Available at: http://uusi.sotkanet.fi/portal/page/portal/etusivu

Tideman, M. (2004) 'Socialt eller isolerat integrerad? Om institutionsavveckling och integrering' ['Socially integrated or isolated? The development of institutions and integration'], in J. Tøssebro (ed) *Integrering och inkludering*, Lund: Studentlitteratur, pp 121–40.

Umb-Carlsson, Ö. and Sonnander, K. (2005) 'Comparison of the living conditions of adults with disabilities in a Swedish county and in the general population', *Journal of Policy and Practice in Intellectual Disabilities*, vol 2, nos 3/4, pp 240–8.

UN (United Nations) (2006) *Convention on the Rights of Persons with Disabilities and Optional Protocol*, New York: UN.

Vesala, H.T. (2003) *Palvelujen käyttäjäurat kehitysvammaisilla henkilöillä* [*The service user careers of people with intellectual disabilities*], Helsinki: Finnish Association on Mental Retardation.

Whitaker, A. (2008) 'Ett liv aldrig mer som andras – föräldraskap, funktionshinder och åldrande' ['A life never again similar to others: parenthood, disability and ageing'], in E. Jeppsson Grassman (ed) *Att åldras med funktionshinder*, Lund: Studentlitteratur, pp 125–63.

SEVEN

Reconciling work and care for parent-carers of disabled children in Australia and England: uncertain progress

Sue Yeandle and kylie valentine

Introduction

In both Australia and England, the needs of families with a sick or disabled child are recognised and addressed in legislation and in national health, care and education systems. Relevant policy frameworks and support measures, which continue to develop and change, have been put in place over several decades (HMT and DES, 2007; Broach et al, 2010) and both countries have made disability discrimination illegal (including in education and social support systems). Each has policies designed to meet the additional educational needs of children with a disability, and offers financial support that parent-carers may claim. Yet, in both countries, many parent-carers feel unsupported, their health and financial circumstances are poor compared with those of other parents and carers, and their employment rates are low (Audit Commission, 2003; Burchardt, 2006; Yeandle et al, 2007; FaHCSIA, 2008).

What help do parent-carers get in these countries to enable them to reconcile work and care? Why are outcomes for them so often unsatisfactory? Is policy adaptation and change addressing these problems? This chapter begins by outlining the context for these issues, focusing first on the prevalence of sickness and disability among children in Australia and England and the services and support available to their families.

Prevalence of disability among children and their families' financial circumstances

In Australia in 2009, an estimated 288,300 children aged 0–14 had a disability: over 3% of 0–4 year olds, and almost 9% of 5–14 year olds (ABS, 2011). Of these, 166,700 had a severe or profound 'core activity limitation', meaning that they need assistance with regular communication, mobility or self-care tasks (AIHW, 2009a; ABS, 2011). Estimates suggest that about half of all disabled children aged 0–14 have two or more disabilities and that almost 7% have four or five (AIHW, 2009b). The type of disability a child has can be important to his or her care needs. A review of payments to primary parent-carers in Australia found intellectual and learning disabilities (4.3% of all children) and physical/diverse[1] disabilities (4.2%) to be most prevalent (FaHCSIA, 2007: 4), while analysis of the primary disability of service users found that this was 'intellectual' for about 30% of people, 'physical' for almost 17% and 'autism' for about 6% (SCRGSP, 2011: Table 14A.13).

Since the introduction of deinstitutionalisation in the 1980s, most policies are designed to support parents to raise their children at home, and such care is usual for most disabled children in Australia (AIHW, 2004), although some parents of children with profound disabilities express frustration that high-quality residential placements are not available (Ombudsman, 2004; Eyler, 2005; SCCA, 2005). There is a tension between these expressed wishes of some carers for residential placements and the policy goal – driven by disabled people – that disabled people live in the community. Parent-carers of disabled children therefore have a political 'voice' in Australia that carers of other people do not have, but often live in disadvantaged circumstances. Their incomes are often lower than those of other families: in 2003, 50% of primary carers of disabled children were in the bottom two income quintiles, compared with 34% of non-carers (FaHCSIA, 2007: 13). Primary carers of children with severe disabilities were much more likely (67%) than non-carers (24%) to have a government pension or allowance as their primary source of income (FaHCSIA, 2007: 13).

In England in 2009, 7% of boys and 6% of girls aged 0–15 years had a 'limiting longstanding illness', while 21% and 16%, respectively, had a 'longstanding illness' (NHSIC, 2010: Table 9). Of children, 11% (1.4 million) lived in households containing one or more disabled[2] children in 2008/09 (Adams et al, 2011: 98) and official data record that in 2011, 335,000 children under 18 (plus 130,000 aged 18–24) received Disability Living Allowance (DLA) (DWP, 2012).

Many parent-carers in England live in difficult financial circumstances. In 2009/10, 53% of children in households with a disabled child – and no disabled adult – lived in 'low-income' households, that is, in the bottom 40% of the income distribution after housing costs, compared with 46% of children in households unaffected by disability (Adams et al, 2011: 83). The figure was 67% for households containing a disabled child *and* a disabled adult. Almost all sick or disabled children under 17 (99% in the 2001 Census of Population) live in family households (Buckner and Yeandle, 2006: 3), with their parents providing most of their regular care: the financial pressures these parents face are further exacerbated if they cannot remain in paid work (Preston, 2005; Buckner and Yeandle, 2006).

Households containing a sick or disabled child are more likely than other households with children to: lack access to a private car (23% versus 17%); have no adult in paid work (34% versus 18%); live in social housing (34% versus 21%) or overcrowded housing (16% versus 10%); and be lone-parent households (32% versus 25%) (Buckner and Yeandle, 2006: 3). Parents living with a sick or disabled child had poorer health (11% of fathers and 12% of mothers reported 'poor health' in the past year, compared with 5% of other parents) and more often 'limiting long-term illness' (20% of fathers and 19% of mothers, compared with 9% of other parents) (Buckner and Yeandle, 2006: 6).

Most parent-carers who cannot fully support themselves through paid work can claim financial support through the social security system. If their disabled child receives DLA (paid at different rates, with 'care' and 'mobility' components), they may be eligible for Carer's Allowance (CA) (see *Chapter Two*).[3] Over one third of CA claimants care for a disabled child and 13% work part-time (Fry et al, 2011: 52). Parent-carers outside the labour market through sickness, disability or unemployment are eligible for means-tested income support and may receive a small 'carer premium' supplement.

Services and support for families with sick or disabled children

Support systems in Australia

In Australia, Commonwealth and state/territory governments have developed a number of initiatives to support all carers (see *Chapter Two*), which include initiatives to support children and young people with disabilities and their parents. These have focused on access to services for disabled children, particularly young children, and support for parents to care for their children. A variety of programmes and support packages exist. Three examples indicate the kind of approaches developed. In Queensland, the Building Bright Futures Action Plan (2010–13) for children with a disability was developed to prioritise access to early intervention services, build evidence-based support and strengthen the disability services workforce. In New South Wales, the Stronger Together Plan (2006–16) is designed to enable children with a disability to grow up in a family and participate in the community, and to support adults with a disability to live in and be part of the community (with services such as respite, therapy, innovative care and family and sibling support). Nationally, the Commonwealth Helping Children with Autism package (from 2009) provides funding for early intervention services, including: access to advisors who provide information on eligibility, funding and services; supported playgroups; new items on the Medicare Benefits Schedule (MBS);[4] and professional development for school staff.

This emphasis on early intervention and access to services – characteristic of state/territory and national policies in Australia – is part of an overall policy framework to support families to care for their children at home, and for children to attend schools. Early intervention is designed to reduce the impact of disability by improving outcomes in the immediate and long term for individuals and by lowering the cost associated with disability for the wider community. It is considered the best solution to address the deficiencies of current systems of disability services (Productivity Commission, 2011). Early intervention does not necessarily mean early in the life course. The policy intent is that it should also mean intervening early after diagnosis or identification of a need, irrespective of age, although many recent initiatives are targeted towards young children with disabilities and their families.

Initiatives specifically for carers, rather than those designed to assist carers to support their children, include the Carer Recognition Act 2010 and the 2011 Carer Strategy; the Fair Work Act 2009 and 2010 National Employment Standards also have provisions for carers (see *Chapter Two*). The Fair Work Act provides parent-carers with the right to request flexible working arrangements until their disabled child is 18. The national Outside School Hours Care for Teenagers with Disability programme is also designed to support parent-carers to resume or take up employment (Australian Government, 2011). This aims to address the high unmet need for before- and after-school and vacation care programmes for children with disabilities aged 12–18. It commenced in 2008 and has around 2,000 participants nationally (FaHCSIA, 2011). It was introduced because mainstream programmes often do not cater for children with disabilities, which can severely curtail their parents' opportunities for paid employment.

A range of financial supports for parent-carers has developed in Australia (see Table 7.1). It includes an income support payment to parent-carers who experience difficulty supporting their families through paid employment, as well as supplementary payments to offset the extra costs of caring for their child. In 2008, an independent taskforce was appointed by the Commonwealth government to conduct a major review of Carer Payment (child), paid at that time to less than 4,000 parent-carers. Its membership included representatives of families of disabled children, carers, non-governmental organisations, academics and clinicians. The review found that because their children did not meet the definition of 'profoundly disabled', many parents were ineligible for Carer Payment. It led to a broadening of the eligibility criteria, with 19,000 parent-carers subsequently expected to be newly eligible for the payment (FaHCSIA, 2009).

Support systems in England

The services and support available to families with sick or disabled children in England are the responsibility of both local authorities (LAs) and central government departments.[5] LAs commission services for disabled children, enacting statutory responsibilities and responding to national guidance. They are responsible for disabled children's education, including necessary specialist services, and any support parent-carers are identified to need. LAs may fund a Disabled Facilities Grant – not means-tested if the disabled child is under 19 – to help with assistive technology or housing adaptations. Like other carers, parent-carers also have the right to an assessment of their own needs, and may be offered services or a carer Direct Payment to meet these (see *Chapter Two*).

Most disabled children's education (until age 19) is provided through LAs, which, under the Childcare Act 2006, must provide 'sufficient' childcare 'suitable for disabled children'. The Act was intended to improve pre-school and out-of-school services for disabled children, which are important for working parent-carers. Despite this and other policies implemented in the 2000s,[6] parent-carers continue to report that services for their school-age disabled children are inadequate and difficult to access (Yeandle et al, 2007; Campbell-Hall et al, 2009).

Parent-carers in paid work in England have modest employment rights through the legislation of 2002, 2006 and 2010 outlined in *Chapter Two*. Those caring for a disabled child under 19 gained these rights a little earlier than other carers, through legislation initially aimed

Table 7.1: Financial support available to parent-carers in Australia

Support	Dates	Type of benefit	Eligibility
Carer Payment (caring for child under 16)	1988	Income support payment	For carers who, because of caring responsibilities for a child under 16 with severe disability or medical conditions, are unable to support themselves through substantial workforce participation. Can be paid either to the primary carer or to both carers in a shared care arrangement (eg if the parents of the child do not live together but both care for the child). Subject to an income and assets test. Maximum payment rate of AUS$671 (approximately €510) per fortnight (about 30% average full-time female earnings). Entitles recipient to Carer Allowance. Aims: (1) to allow parents to provide the care their child needs; and (2) to provide income support, as their caring responsibilities preclude them from paid work; *not* designed to compensate the carer/care recipient for the disability, nor to cover the costs of treatment or caring.
Carer Allowance (originally Handicapped Child Allowance)	1974	Supplementary payment	For carers who live with and are looking after a child with a physical, intellectual or psychiatric disability who needs additional care and attention on a daily basis. AUS$110 (approximately €85) per fortnight; not subject to an income and assets test. Designed to assist in the purchase of support for the disabled child.
Child Disability Assistance Payment	2007	Supplementary payment	152,400 recipients of Carer Allowance (June 2010; up from 142,100 in June 2009). AUS$1,000 (approximately €760), paid annually (2012). Aims to assist in purchasing support for the disabled child (eg continence aids, house and vehicle modifications, therapeutic services).
Other payments	Varied	Pensioner Concession Card, Health Care Card	For recipients of Carer Payment (caring for a child under 16). Reduces cost of medicines, refunds extra medical expenses, free doctors' appointments.

at working parents. Their rights at work remain limited, however: they have no paid parental leave beyond that offered to other parents, and the flexible working arrangements they can request are both contingent upon employer consent and available mainly through widespread use of part-time employment. While part-time jobs help many parent-carers combine work and care, they are mainly found in low-paid, low-status work (Yeandle et al, 2009).

Australia and England both have initiatives in place to help parents meet the additional costs of disabilities, and to provide support and services for disabled children and their parents. Historically, these have been targeted at parents outside paid employment, with policymakers assuming that at least one parent will not be working in order to care for their child. This is now changing as the policy emphasis in both countries shifts towards supporting (or mandating) lone parents' participation in paid employment, and in Australia, is also evident in policies for parents of disabled children (Lane et al, 2011; Summerfield et al, 2010).

Reconciliation of paid work and family life

Reconciling paid work and family life is challenging for most parents, and both countries have policies designed to address this. Parents of disabled children face the same dilemmas of balancing care and employment as other parents, but for them, the difficulties are more numerous and intense. Like other parents, parent-carers need to find schools, recreational activities and out-of-school hours programmes that suit them and their children and fit their working hours. However, these services are generally much scarcer for disabled than for non-disabled children, limiting parent-carers' availability for paid work, working hours/locations and sometimes their occupational choices. In addition, many disabled children receive therapies and services, and parents are almost always responsible for transporting their children to these appointments. These factors impact on parents' capacity to participate in paid work, yet research in both countries shows that parent-carers outside the labour market would often like to have paid employment, while, as discussed later, many of those in jobs would like to work different and sometimes additional hours.

Challenges for parents reconciling employment and care in Australia

In Australia, parents are encouraged to play an active role in therapies and support for young children, especially those with behavioural disabilities such as autism (valentine, 2010). Mothers usually take primary responsibility for this. Its impact on their capacity to undertake employment is affected by the age and care needs of their children. Babies and very young children, whether or not they have disabilities, need more care from their parents, usually their mothers, than older children. To undertake their parenting responsibilities, most mothers of very young children do not work full-time in Australia (del Carmen Huerta et al, 2011), so the impact on employment of caring for disabled children is less evident when children are very young, as many mothers at that stage would not in any case work full-time. Support for the provision of therapy to young disabled children, and the role parents are expected to play in this, is meant to ensure that they receive intensive therapies/treatment before starting school and should mean that they can later participate in mainstream school and other activities, with their parents able to continue (or enter) paid employment. However, as discussed later, the experience of many families indicates that disabled children require intensive care beyond the very early years, reducing their mothers' capacity for employment.

While there has been little quantitative research on the employment of mothers of disabled children in Australia, one study using a representative sample found that mothers of children with disabilities were more likely than other mothers (53% versus 41%) to be outside the workforce (Gordon et al, 2007: 239). Mothers of children with severe/profound activity limitations were also significantly more likely to be outside the workforce compared with mothers of children with less severe disabilities. Among working mothers, mothers of children with disabilities were more likely to work part-time (74%) than other mothers (59%), and much more likely to work very short hours (under 15 hours weekly) (Gordon et al, 2007: 241). The study found that non-employed mothers of disabled children wanted to work, and that 'the desire to work is greater among those mothers whose workforce participation is most constrained' (Gordon et al, 2007: 244).

As noted earlier, Australian policy is directed towards the participation of disabled children in schools: mainstream or special needs classes in mainstream schools, or special needs schools. Most disabled children *do* go to school, but research shows that this does not mean that parents are free to take up paid employment. Parents often need to spend a great deal of time at school responding to crises, advocating for their children's needs or providing care-related assistance. They report high rates of suspension and exclusion from school, and some resort to home-schooling (valentine et al, 2011). They also find that vacation and out-of-school hours care is difficult to secure (FaHCSIA, 2008; George et al, 2008).

Support for parents of older children, including adult children, is just as pressing, but has arguably been a much lower policy priority than support for families with young children. Studies have shown that families' capacity to care for a child with high support needs declines over time, and that parents of older children with disabilities are much more likely to seek out-of-home care placements than parents of younger children (Llewellyn et al, 1999, 2003). The relative lack of supported employment and residential placement options presents particularly acute challenges for families with disabled children who have left school. A study of parents caring for adult children with multiple disabilities found that even where supported employment and day care services are available, these often have shorter hours than school hours, severely limiting their carers' capacity to work outside the home (Cuskelly, 2006).

Australian studies have also found that care for sick and disabled children is intensive and demanding, and that carers often feel that they do not receive sufficient support. Most primary carers of children with severe or profound core activity limitations provide over 40 hours of care per week (FaHCSIA, 2007: 9) and almost half of these carers reported needing more support, compared with one quarter of carers of adults (Ganley, 2009: 53). Mothers of children with autism report extremely high levels of time pressure due to their care responsibilities. A recent study found that mothers of children aged 6–17 with autism experienced an even higher level of time pressure than mothers of pre-school children in the general population, otherwise the most time-pressured group (Sawyer et al, 2010). While some parents in paid work have flexible working arrangements and understanding employers, many do not, reporting unsympathetic employers and difficulty securing leave. The extent to which workplaces accommodate carers' needs depends partly on the attitude of individual employers, although public sector employers may, in general, be more flexible than those in the private sector (George et al, 2008).

Despite the difficulties of combining care and work, many parents of disabled children would like to do more paid work. Two thirds of surveyed working parents indicated that there were difficulties in combining the two, but most wanted to increase their working hours (Ganley, 2009: 54). This is probably due partly to the significant financial costs associated with their child's disability or illness (FaHCSIA, 2008; George et al, 2008). Work is also valued by parents for reasons other than income, providing them with a sense of adult identity and respite from care responsibilities.

Reconciliation under pressure for parent-carers in England

Studies of the experiences of employed parents with sick or disabled children in England have shown that they frequently encounter difficulties (Glendinning, 1983; Lewis et al, 2000; Mearns and Swan, 2006; Stiell et al, 2006). Many report that their care responsibility has an adverse impact on their career, their reputation or their relationships with colleagues. Some find that they have to change jobs or seek another type of work to get 'carer-friendly' or shorter working hours. Many say combining work and care leaves them extremely tired and stressed. Few have regular alternative care services and many are not in touch with their local social services department. Some say accessing basic services for their child has been difficult or distressing, while some others feel that they are 'expected' to stay at home. Difficulties in dealings with schools and with social and health care services are commonly reported, and some parents say that their child's frequent medical appointments 'in working hours' adversely affect their ability to fulfil work obligations. Many use (paid) annual leave to cover their child's needs, leaving them with no breaks or opportunity to rest. Unpaid leave and flexible working can be difficult as employment is often essential for these households' financial management, and reduced or flexible hours usually mean lower pay. Nevertheless, in most studies, parents of disabled children highlight the social benefits of working and many emphasise the desirability of having a 'life outside' the home and of keeping a work-based adult identity. While some display scepticism about the existence of 'family-friendly' employment, those with a supportive or trusting manager or able to access flexible working greatly value these arrangements.

Most research on working parent-carers in England pre-dates the implementation of the new legislation enacted in the 2000s. Data on its early impact suggest that the changes are beneficial for significant numbers of working parents, with increasing uptake of flexible working options and a wider acceptance of non-standard working arrangements by employers (Camp, 2004; Kersley et al, 2005; Hooker et al, 2007). Charities supporting families with disabled children champion this new direction in policy and offer parent-carers advice on using their new entitlements to maintain a 'work–life balance' and negotiate flexibility at work (Mearns and Swan, 2006).

Yeandle et al's (2007) study of over 1,600 carers of working age included responses from 700 parent-carers who were asked in 2006/07 about reconciling work and care. In general, parent-carers were more dissatisfied with available support than other carers and many said that they had inadequate or no formal support or services (Yeandle and Buckner, 2007). Only a quarter (26%) received respite services, although a further 28% would have liked such help, and only 8% had a 'sitting service' and 'community transport' (services that a further 30% and 15%, respectively, said they needed).[7] Of the 700 parent-carers in the study, 444 cared for a disabled child aged 0–19 years and 256 for a disabled son or daughter aged 20 or older. Compared with other carers, they were more likely to be women (86% of those caring for an adult disabled child, 92% of those caring for a younger disabled child), less likely to live with a partner, more likely to have been caring for 10+ years and more likely to provide care for 50+ hours per week. They were much less likely to be in full-time employment, but those caring for a disabled child under 20 more often had a part-time job.

Those in paid work (307 parent-carers) included 38% working full-time, 56% part-time and 6% who were self-employed. Most, especially those working part-time, reported that informal support from family and friends was important for work–care reconciliation; over 60% also said that when caring responsibilities affected their job, their employer was 'supportive'. Two thirds of parent-carers in full-time jobs felt 'under a lot of pressure' however, and only 29% felt that they had adequate services to enable them to work.

Among the 381 parent-carers outside the labour market, over two thirds said that their caring situation had caused them to leave paid work. Most (67%) described themselves as 'looking after home and family full-time' and 15% as 'retired'; a few were sick or disabled themselves (10%), unemployed (8%) or studying (4%). The overwhelming majority felt that finding a job compatible with their caring role would be difficult. Only a third of those caring for a disabled child under 20, and about half of those caring for an adult disabled child, said that not being in paid work was their preference. Two thirds of those caring for a child under 20 (and more than half of those with an older disabled son or daughter) felt that 'the services available to those I care for do not make a job possible for me'.

Future directions for parent-carers in Australia and England

This chapter has shown that in two liberal-democratic welfare systems, parent-carers have gradually become a focus of policy attention. This has happened in part because professionals, academics and voluntary organisations have documented their needs and drawn attention to the difficulties they face. Some services, financial supports and work–care reconciliation measures are in place in both countries, and governments in each have indicated that it is desirable, for individual parent-carers and for wider society, for this group of carers to be able to combine caring with paid work.

Two significant policy developments are likely to affect parents of disabled and severely disabled children in Australia in the future, although their impact on reconciling care and employment responsibilities is uncertain. The 2011 Carer Strategy, as noted earlier, includes provisions that are especially relevant for parent-carers. The elements of the strategy most directly relevant to employment are the Outside School Hours Care for Teenagers with Disability Program and the Day Respite Pilot. The latter is a demonstration programme; the former has sites across Australia, although its coverage is far from universal. The right to request flexible working hours is also particularly relevant for parents of disabled children, as most are of working age, although it is too early to assess its impact. Other initiatives planned in the strategy are less directly relevant to employment but may address the need for better services for parents and their children, thereby creating more opportunities for parents to maintain their employment. These include initiatives to provide coordinated care and flexible funding for people with complex multi-agency care needs, peer support and advice programmes for parents of young children, and new early intervention services for children with certain disabilities (Australian Government, 2011). However, the strategy places much greater emphasis on support services to address the well-being of carers and their families, and to address their needs as carers, than on reconciling employment and care.

Australia's National Disability Insurance Scheme (NDIS) is likely to be a much more significant policy change and to have more substantial effects than any other recent initiative, although it is less directly targeted at carers. It will introduce a universal social insurance scheme to fund care and support for people with disabilities. It is likely to mean that many more parent-carers receive individualised funding to purchase support than currently and aims to provide guaranteed funding based on need and a much greater choice of service providers (Productivity Commission, 2011). As many parents are constrained in their opportunities for employment because available services are insufficient and inflexibly delivered, this could give them greater capacity to take up paid work or extend their working hours. It would require, however, that the intention to provide better services, and greater choice and flexibility, is fulfilled. Both these initiatives currently have bipartisan support. However, the federal election of 2013 may result in a change of government and, as both the Carer Strategy and NDIS are Labor initiatives, it is difficult to know how they would be implemented under a Liberal–National government.

In England, the needs of parent-carers continue to feature on the state's policy agenda, both at the national and often also at the local level. Pressure is maintained by voluntary action, including the Every Disabled Child Matters Campaign, a consortium of organisations working with disabled children and their families, established in 2006. In 2010, national policy became the responsibility of the

Conservative–Liberal Democrat Coalition government, following three Labour administrations (1997–2010). The new government quickly made its position on carers clear and encouraged the formation of a national network of Parent-Carer Forums to 'champion parent-carer participation' in shaping local services (DH, 2010: 11). It also allocated funds for short breaks services and palliative care for disabled children and their families (DH, 2010: 30) and made a commitment to extend flexible working and place greater emphasis on early intervention services. In 2011, the government issued a consultation document on special educational needs and disability, announcing in 2012 that legislation introducing a 'Local Offer' of education, health and social care services for disabled children would follow in 2013 (DfE, 2011, 2012). While this has been welcomed by campaigners, its focus on school-age children has attracted some criticism (EDCM, 2012) and the document does not explicitly address the needs of parent-carers who wish to work.

However, other planned policy changes cause parent-carers and the groups advocating on their behalf concern. The new government announced major changes to national disability and welfare benefits that have worrying implications for some parent-carers. Some whose children receive DLA will lose out financially if planned changes in the Child Tax Credit (a linked benefit) are implemented. More generally, the government's austerity programme – announced in autumn 2010 and due to last until 2017/18 – has substantially reduced LA budgets, leading to a range of cuts in public sector employment, grants to local not-for-profit service providers and council services. Rising unemployment, a freeze on public sector pay and recruitment, and challenging business conditions create a difficult environment for carer-friendly employment. Parent-carers in England are unlikely to see any major changes in their employment rights in the near future, although new workplace protection from discrimination 'in association with a disabled person' – from the Equality Act 2010 – may benefit parent-carers.

The countries studied here have marked similarities, both in their policy arrangements and support for families with disabled children, and in the disadvantaged circumstances of most parent-carers and their households. Both have active voluntary advocacy groups whose campaigning has been important in producing innovations in parent-carer support and a strategic focus encompassing modest legislative measures designed to improve carer well-being. Each also has a complex system of financial support and uneven provision of local services for disabled children and their families, which many parent-carers find frustrating and difficult to access.

Both Australia and England have recently begun to provide support for parent-carers who wish to work, doing so primarily through 'light-touch' legislation. This facilitates flexible working but provides no earnings compensation for those who need to work part-time or take time away from work. In future, more differences may emerge if Australia's policies on labour market activation extend to lone parents caring for disabled children or if austerity measures in England significantly reduce the financial support and services available to families caring for a disabled son or daughter. In both cases, progress on support for parent-carers currently owes more to policies and legislation on the rights and entitlements of their disabled children than on the rights of carers, which remain slight in English law and weaker still in Australia.

Notes

[1] This category describes an impairment which 'may have diverse effects within and among individuals, including effects on physical activities such as mobility' (AIHW, 2007: 158).

[2] The Family Resources Survey defines disability as 'any long-standing illness, disability or impairment that leads to a substantial difficulty with one or more areas of the individual's life'. Those so defined would also be classified as disabled under the Disability Discrimination Act 1995 in the UK. The category cited includes children in households with one or more disabled children, both with and without an adult with disability also in the household.

[3] The care and mobility components of DLA can be paid from birth and age three, respectively, if a child's needs are substantially more than those of a non-disabled child of the same age. Children aged 16+ will be ineligible for DLA after April 2013 but eligible for a new benefit, the Personal Independence Payment. For more information, see the DWP website at: www.dwp.gov.uk

[4] The MBS is the listing of services subsidised by the Australian government. The inclusion of new items on the MBS reduces the costs consumers have to pay for these services.

[5] Health and social care and education are matters devolved to the national administrations in Northern Ireland, Scotland and Wales. Discussion here relates to developments in England. Policy on employment and social security is governed from Westminster for the whole of the UK.

[6] The National Service Framework Standard for Disabled Children (2004, guidance issued by the Department of Health and the Department for Education and Skills) and the *Aiming high for disabled children: better support for families* (HMT and DES, 2007) programme, monitored during 2008–11 by the Every Disabled Child Matters Campaign, see: www.edcm.org.uk

[7] In this section, data for England are based on additional analysis of the Carers, Employment and Services survey, specially undertaken for this chapter.

References

ABS (Australian Bureau of Statistics) (2011) *Disability, ageing and carers Australia: summary of findings 2009*, Canberra: ABS.

Adams, N., Barton, A., Johnson, G. and Matejic, P. (2011) *Households below average income: an analysis of the income distribution 1994/95–2009/2010*, London: DWP.

AIHW (Australian Institute of Health and Welfare) (2004) *Children with disabilities in Australia*, Canberra: AIHW.

AIHW (2007) *Australia's welfare 2007*, Canberra, AIHW.

AIHW (2009a) *A picture of Australia's children 2009*, Canberra: AIHW.

AIHW (2009b) *Disability in Australia: multiple disabilities and need for assistance*, Canberra: AIHW.

Audit Commission (2003) *Services for disabled children: a review of services for disabled children and their families*, London: Audit Commission.

Australian Government (2011) *National Carer Strategy*, Canberra: Commonwealth of Australia.

Broach, S., Clements, L. and Read, J. (2010) *Disabled children: a legal handbook*, London: Council for Disabled Children.

Buckner, L. and Yeandle, S. (2006) *Managing more than most: a statistical analysis of families with sick or disabled children*, London: Carers UK.

Burchardt, T. (2006) 'Changing weights and measures: disability and child poverty', *Poverty*, no 123, Winter, pp 6–9.

Camp, C. (2004) *Right to request flexible working: review of impact in first year of legislation*, London: Working Families.

Campbell-Hall, V., Coulter, A. and Joyce, L. (2009) *Parental experiences of services for disabled children*, London: Department for Children, Schools and Families.

Cuskelly, M. (2006) 'Parents of adults with an intellectual disability', *Family Matters*, no 74, pp 20–5.

Del Carmen Huerta, M., Adema, W., Baxter, J., Corak, M., Deding, M., Gray, M.C., Han, W.J. and Waldfogel, J. (2011) *Early maternal employment and child development in five OECD countries*, Paris: OECD Publishing.

DfE (Department for Education) (2011) *Support and aspiration: a new approach to special educational needs and disability: a consultation*, London: DfE.

DfE (2012) *Support and aspiration: a new approach to special educational needs and disability: progress and next steps*, London: DfE.

DH (Department of Health) (2010) *Recognised, valued and supported: next steps for the Carers' Strategy*, London: DH.

DH/DfES (Department form Education and Skills) (2004) www.dh.gov.uk/en/Publicationsandstatistics/Publications/ PublicationsPolicyAndGuidance/DH_4089112

DWP (Department for Work and Pensions) (2012) 'Disability Living Allowance: cases in payment'. Available at: http://83.244.183.180/100pc/ dla/cnage/ccsex/a_carate_r_cnage_c_ccsex_nov11.html

EDCM (Every Disabled Child Matters Campaign) (2012) 'Government denies 'single plan' to disabled children with health and social care needs', EDCM press release, 15 May. Available at: http://www.edcm. org.uk/news/news-archive/2012/may-2012/send.aspx

Eyler, P. (2005) *Out-of-home – not out of the family: rethinking the care of children with profound disabilities*, Newcastle, Australia: Hunter (DASH) Inc.

FaHCSIA (Department of Families, Housing, Community Services and Indigenous Affairs) (2007) *Review of Carer Payment (child): statistical compendium*, Canberra: FaHCSIA, Commonwealth of Australia.

FaHCSIA (2008) *Carer Payment (child): a new approach*, Canberra: FaHCSIA, Commonwealth of Australia.

FaHCSIA (2009) 'Key reform for carers of children with disability starts tomorrow', media release. Available at: http://jennymacklin. fahcsia.gov.au/node/507

FaHCSIA (2011) *Outside school hours care for teenagers with disability*, Canberra: FaHCSIA.

Fry, G., Singleton, B., Yeandle, S. and Buckner, L. (2011) *Developing a clearer understanding of the Carer's Allowance claimant group*, London: DWP.

Ganley, R. (2009) 'Carer Payment recipients and workforce participation', *Australian Social Policy*, no 8, pp 35–84.

George, A., Vickers, M.H., Wilkes, L. and Barton, B. (2008) 'Working and caring for a child with chronic illness: barriers in achieving work–family balance', *Journal of Management and Organization*, vol 14, no 1, pp 59–72.

Glendinning, C. (1983) *Unshared care: parents and their disabled children*, London: Routledge and Kegan Paul.

Gordon, M., Rosenman, L. and Cuskelly, M. (2007) 'Constrained labour: maternal employment when children have disabilities', *Journal of Applied Research in Intellectual Disabilities*, vol 20, no 3, pp 236–46.

HMT (HM Treasury) and DES (Department for Education and Skills) (2007) *Aiming high for disabled children: better support for families*, London: HMT/DES.

Hooker, H., Neathey, F., Casebourne, J. and Munro, M. (2007) *The third work–life balance employee survey: main findings*, London: DTI.

Kersley, B., Alpin, C., Forth, J., Bryson, A., Bewley, H., Dix, G. and Oxenbridge, S. (2005) *Inside the workplace: first findings from the 2004 Workplace Employment Relations Survey*, London: Routledge.

Lane, P., Casebourne, J., Lanceley, L. and Davies, M. (2011) *Lone parent obligations: work, childcare and the Jobseeker's Allowance regime*, London: DWP.

Lewis, S., Kagan, C. and Heaton, P. (2000) 'Managing work–family diversity for parents of disabled children: beyond policy to practice and partnership', *Personnel Review*, vol 29, no 3, pp 417–30.

Llewellyn, G., Dunn, P., Fante, M., Turnbull, L. and Grace, R. (1999) 'Family factors influencing out-of-home placement decisions', *Journal of Intellectual Disability Research*, vol 43, no 3, pp 219–33.

Llewellyn, G., Thompson, K., Whybrow, S., McConnell, D., Bratel, J., Coles, D. and Wearing, C. (2003) *Supporting families: family well-being and children with disabilities*, Sydney: University of Sydney.

Mearns, J. and Swan, J. (2006) *Make it work for you! A guide for parents trying to combine paid work and caring for disabled children*, London: Working Families.

NHSIC (NHS Information Centre) (2010) *Health survey for England 2009: children trend tables*, London: The NHS Information Centre for health and social care. Available at: http://www.ic.nhs.uk/pubs/hse09trends

Ombudsman (2004) *DADHC (Department of Ageing, Disability and Home Care): the need to improve services for children, young people and their families*, Sydney: NSW Ombudsman.

Preston, G. (2005) *Hard-working families: caring for two or more disabled children*, London: Disability Alliance.

Productivity Commission (2011) *Disability care and support: Productivity Commission inquiry report* (2 vols), Canberra: Commonwealth of Australia.

Sawyer, M.G., Bittman, M., La Greca, A.M., Crettenden, A.D., Harchak, T.F. and Martin, J. (2010) 'Time demands of caring for children with autism: what are the implications for maternal mental health?', *Journal of Autism and Developmental disorders*, vol 40, no 5, pp 620–8.

SCCA (Senate Standing Committee on Community Affairs) (2005) *Protecting vulnerable children: a national challenge*, Canberra: Parliament of Australia, SCCA.

SCRGSP (Steering Committee for the Review of Government Service Provision) (2011) *Report on government services 2011*, Canberra: SCRGSP.

Stiell, B., Shipton, L. and Yeandle, S. (2006) *Caring for sick or disabled children: parents' experiences of combining work and care*, London: Carers UK.

Summerfield, T., Young, L., Harman, J. and Flatau, P. (2010) 'Child support and welfare to work reforms: the economic consequences for single-parent families', *Family Matters*, no 84, pp 68–78.

valentine, k. (2010) 'A consideration of medicalisation: choice, engagement and other responsibilities of parents of children with autism spectrum disorder', *Social Science and Medicine*, vol 71, no 5, pp 950–7.

valentine, k., Rajkovic, M. and Thompson, D. (2011) *Post-diagnosis support for children with autism spectrum disorder, their families and carers: older children and young people*, Canberra: FaHCSIA.

Yeandle, S. and Buckner, L. (2007) *Carers, employment and services: time for a new social contract?*, CES Report Series No 6, London: Carers UK.

Yeandle, S., Bennett, C., Buckner, L., Fry, G. and Price, C. (2007) *Diversity in caring: towards equality for carers*, London: Carers UK.

Yeandle, S., Bennett, C., Buckner, L., Escott, K. and Grant, L. (2009) 'Women's labour market situation: myths, puzzles and problems', in S. Yeandle (ed) *Policy for a change: local labour market analysis and gender equality*, Bristol: The Policy Press, pp 35–56.

EIGHT

Parent-carers in Taiwan and Japan: lifelong caring responsibilities within a familistic welfare system

Yueh-Ching Chou, Toshiko Nakano, Heng-Hao Chang and Li-Fang Liang

Introduction

In East Asia, caring for children, frail older people and people with disabilities has long been seen primarily as a family responsibility. As discussed in *Chapter Two*, however, Japan and Taiwan are currently experiencing extremely low birth rates and both countries have initiated paid parental leave policies as one measure to address this. In addition, Japan has the highest percentage of older people in the world (23% of its population), while in Taiwan, the percentage of older people is also set to rise dramatically, from 11% in 2010 to an anticipated 24% by 2030 (see *Chapter One*). In both countries, Long-Term Care Insurance (LTCI) schemes are seen as the policy solution: Japan launched its LTCI scheme in 2000 and Taiwan is set to follow suit in the near future. With the employment rate of women rising in both countries – in 2010, reaching 60% in Japan and 54% in Taiwan (see *Chapter One*) – how to assist women to reconcile care and work has become an important issue in both societies. The extent to which lifelong parent-carers of disabled children, particularly mothers, are juggling care and work is nevertheless a novel topic in all East Asian countries, including Taiwan and Japan.

This chapter focuses on the reconciliation of work and care for parent-carers, especially mothers, in Taiwan and Japan. It starts with an overview of the prevalence of disability, revealing the extent to which disabled people are cared for at home by their parents. This is followed by a brief summary of the rights and entitlements of disabled people and their families, as set out in the welfare systems of these two countries (see also *Chapter Two*). Detailed case material from interviews with mothers of children with disabilities is then presented to explore how women in each country reconcile paid work with caring for a disabled child. In conclusion, the chapter considers contemporary policy developments and debates affecting parent-carers in Taiwan and Japan and reflects on the effectiveness of reconciliation policies and the implications of the policy changes planned in the two countries.

Family care responsibilities in Taiwan and Japan

As noted in *Chapter Two*, Taiwan's Civil Code places responsibility for the care of people with disabilities – both children and adults – on lineal family members: parents, siblings and children. The Disability Act 1980 nevertheless entitles some disabled people to receive welfare benefits. To be eligible, they and their families must be officially registered through a process that includes a medical assessment and a means test that takes family income into account. In all, the Taiwanese system recognises 16 types of disability as entitling disabled people and their families to welfare benefits (including income tax rebates), with disability categorised at four different levels: profound, severe, moderate and mild.[1]

In 2011, 1.1 million people in Taiwan were classified as disabled; just under 5% of the total population (see Table 8.1). A national survey in 2006 found that 93% of disabled people of all ages lived with their families, while only 7% used residential services (DSMI, 2007). Almost all disabled children under 15 years of age[2] lived with their families (98%), their primary carers being their parents (80%) or other relatives (14%). Most were cared for mainly by their mothers (75%). Very few used residential services (2%) or the services of live-in migrant care workers (1%). On average, the time spent caring for these disabled children was 12 hours per day.

The Japanese Civil Code also states that lineal kin (blood relatives and siblings) have a duty to support each other, and this includes caring for people with disabilities. In 2009, however, the Japanese Cabinet Office established a Committee for Disability Policy Reform, tasking the committee with producing regulations on the rights of disabled people. The measures it proposed focused primarily on providing needs-led services for disabled people and their families. In fact, in 2010, the government revised the Services and Supports for Persons with Disabilities Act 2005, even before the committee reported its findings. The changes made placed most care and support services for disabled children within the remit of child welfare law in Japan, the state thereby acknowledging that disabled children are 'children first' (Cabinet Office, 2010a).

Table 8.1: People with disabilities: number, living arrangements and use of services in Taiwan and Japan

	Age/type of disability	Taiwan	Japan
Number and % of total population	All with disabilities	1,080,000 5%	7,443,000 6%
	All with IDs	96,565 0.4%	547,000 0.4%
% living either with family or independently	All with disabilities	93%	93%
	All under age 18 with disabilities[a]	97%	94% 98%
	All with IDs	93%	77%
% using residential services	All with disabilities	7%	7%
	All under 18 with disabilities[a]	3%	6% 2%
	All with IDs	7%	23%
% employing a live-in migrant care worker	All with disabilities	11%	–
	All under 18 with disabilities	1%	–
	All with IDs	0.7%	–

Notes: [a] For Japan, first figure is for persons under 18 with physical and intellectual disabilities; second figure is for persons under 20 with 'mental disorder'.
IDs – intellectual disabilities.

Sources: Figures for Taiwan: Chou et al (2007, 2010) and DSMI (2007, 2011). Figures for Japan: Cabinet Office (2010b), MHLW (2005, 2006, 2009) and JILPT (2011).

Under Japanese law, people with four broad types of disability – physical disabilities, intellectual disabilities, mental disorders and developmental disorders – are entitled to welfare benefits and disability services. To receive these, they have to apply to be assessed: a medical assessment, a means test or a grant decision assessment may be needed, with the results determining the amount and type of services provided in each case. Each form of assessment is based on different laws and regulations. These include: the Welfare of Persons with Physical Disabilities Act 1954; the Welfare of Persons with Intellectual Disabilities Act 1960 (which introduced the medical rehabilitation handbook system); the Persons with Mental Disorders, Mental Health and Welfare Act 1995; the Act on Support for Persons with Developmental Disorders 2004; and the Services and Supports for Persons with Disabilities Act 2005.

As Table 8.1 shows, Japan's 7.4 million people with disabilities – nearly 6% of the population in 2005 – include 3.7 million people with physical disabilities[3] or severe multiple disabilities. Over half a million people have intellectual disabilities and 3.2 million people have mental health needs.[4] In all, 93% of disabled people live at home: 98% of those with physical disabilities and 76% of those with intellectual disabilities. Two thirds (66%) of adults over age 18 live with their parents or siblings (MHLW, 2005), while 7% of all disabled adults – 23% of those with intellectual disabilities – use residential services (Cabinet Office, 2010b).

In general, then, caring for disabled children is treated as a family responsibility in both Taiwan and Japan. In both countries, welfare benefits for disabled children are allocated through a process of registration and diagnosis. In Taiwan, a single law covers people with physical and mental disabilities, while in Japan, four different laws govern arrangements for people with physical, mental, intellectual and developmental disabilities.

Social services available for disabled children in Taiwan and Japan

Welfare support for people with disabilities in Taiwan includes both services and financial entitlements, based on both the degree of disability and family income. Local authorities in Taiwan may provide a monthly family subsidy and a range of social services, such as respite care, day care, day services (including vocational and educational services), home care and residential services. These can be highly beneficial to the disabled person and their family, especially the primary carer. The family subsidy, for families with a disabled family member who lives at home, is available only to low-income families (defined through an official means test as either 'poor' or 'near poor'). The value of this subsidy is based on both the family's poverty status and the severity of the disability. According to a national survey, 37% of all persons with disabilities received this cash benefit in 2006 (DSMI, 2007). However, families who claim this financial support thereby become ineligible to use social services. Disabled people who use social services (with the exception of those in low-income families) must make co-payments, determined through means-testing, for the support they receive. Given these arrangements, it is unsurprising that very few of those eligible are aware of the support provided by social services in Taiwan (DSMI, 2007).

In Japan, the support available to disabled people also includes both services and cash benefits. Here, too, access to these is based on both the degree of disability and family income, and disabled people or their families need to make co-payments when using services. In Japan, the state provides, via local authorities (LAs), two welfare benefits for families caring at home for a disabled child under 20 years of age: Special Child Rearing Allowance, available to families caring for disabled children; and Welfare Allowance for Children with Severe Disabilities, available if the child needs round-the-clock care. The state and LAs also provide services for disabled children who live at home. They may also get Independence Support, which can include nursing care at home and specialist medical care and equipment. Some participate in regional 'life enhancement' projects and, from 2012, LAs are obliged to provide after-school day care for disabled children who attend school.

In contrast to the universal arrangements in place in the Nordic states and the disability services offered in the liberal-democratic countries described in this book, the social services available in Taiwan and Japan to families with disabled children are based on a selectivist ideology. Furthermore, means-testing is based on total family income – that is, the income of all household members *plus* all income of lineal relatives – instead of on the individual financial circumstances of the disabled person.

How do mothers reconcile paid work with caring for a disabled child?

In this part of the chapter, two examples have been selected from each country to illustrate how mothers of children with intellectual disabilities combine working and caring. Although they live in the same state and are affected by the same welfare system, the two Taiwanese mothers – Mrs Lin and Mrs Kou – give very different accounts of their social context and reconciliation outcomes. The Japanese cases – mothers Mrs Takahashi and Mrs Sasaki – highlight some of the measures needed to reconcile paid work with the care of children with disabilities.

Experiences of Taiwanese mothers: variations in access to support

Mrs Lin

When interviewed, Mrs Lin was working as a government official in the income tax bureau and her husband held a managerial position in a private company. Mrs Lin was also the chair of a parents' organisation. Their only daughter, Jen, has moderate intellectual disabilities. She is 23 years old and regularly attends a day care service. The family also makes occasional use of respite care services. Throughout Jen's life, Mrs Lin has been her primary carer. In the interview, Mrs Lin displayed a very positive attitude towards her caring work, referring to herself as "a mother who cannot be substituted". Mrs Lin mentioned that she was "lucky" to have plenty of resources available through her social networks. As she explained:

> "My mother takes a great interest in my daughter and my sister looks after my daughter a lot. My sister and I are very close. That's why I can continue my work…. Earlier, the principal of the kindergarten was very kind to us; now the staff at the day care centre are very helpful, too. Sometimes, if I am unable to fetch my daughter, I just make a phone call and I have lots of support – lots of people who are able to help me, including my colleagues, my friends and my sister. My colleague's brother-in-law is a physician and he also has become a good friend of my family."

Unlike people working in private companies, government officials like Mrs Lin have a stable salary and a system in place that offers leave for personal matters and leisure, childcare leave and a retirement pension. Women who work in the public sector are more likely to combine work and care, as Mrs Lin does. Mrs Lin pointed out that since she fulfils her job responsibilities, no one can fire her, as public sector jobs in Taiwan offer better job security than private sector positions.

Mrs Kou

Mrs Kou is 54-year-old self-employed hairdresser who works from home. She graduated from elementary school but had no other education apart from her hairdresser's training. When the interview was conducted, her husband was unemployed. Their daughter, Yen, is 27 years old and has 'profound' intellectual disabilities, diagnosed when she was just five months old. Each week, Mrs Kou uses a respite care service for two hours to care for Yen. The couple also have two adult sons who now live outside the family home.

Mrs Kou works almost every day from morning until late in the evening. Sometimes, depending on her customers' needs, her work continues until 11pm. She is Yen's primary carer and Yen usually spends her time in the living room where Mrs Kou works. Combining her work and care in this way means that Mrs Kou is constantly busy. She has some problems with her leg (varicose veins), which she attributes to standing for many hours each day while she works: "Last night I did not go to bed until 3am. I did not sleep well because I had to get up every two or three hours to check if Yen was OK. I did not have time to rest."

In the past, Yen attended a special school and received special home education provided by the LA's education service. However, the family no longer uses the latter service as Mrs Kou became very dissatisfied with her interaction with the service workers. She described her experiences of the time Yen attended the special school:

> "When I was working for my customers, the teachers [at the special school] might call me at any time to respond to my daughter's needs. I had to get on my motorbike and travel there straightaway, even though I was working…. Sometimes, I almost crashed on the way…. The teachers were not friendly, they only gave me extra work…. I have never felt supported by the government…. The more you expect, the more you are disappointed."

During the interview, Yen was with the respite care service worker at home, another mother who had a child with intellectual disabilities. Over the past 20 years, she had become Mrs Kou's close friend.

Both Mrs Lin and Mrs Kou had paid jobs – Mrs Lin in the public sector while Mrs Kou was self-employed – and both were also the primary carers of their adult daughters with intellectual disabilities. Each had been responding to their daughter's demanding care needs for over two decades. Mrs Lin's higher social status and her work as a government official gave her access to better social support and resources. She also had a strong personal network and a good relationship with service providers. In contrast, Mrs Kou was not only her disabled daughter's primary carer, but also the main earner in her family. Both her informal and formal sources of support were rather limited and inaccessible.

The accounts of these two Taiwanese mothers illustrate how parent-carers' social and demographic circumstances can affect their ability to reconcile work and care satisfactorily. In many ways, these women's experiences of motherhood and of caring for a disabled child were similar. Neither complained that their husband did not make an equal contribution to the caregiving and both saw taking care of their disabled child as their own responsibility *because* they were the child's mother.

Mrs Lin and Mrs Kou's stories also show that informal support is as critical for Taiwanese mother-carers as formal support. The availability and use of formal support depends on the LA where the family lives and is also affected by the mother's social status. 'Residual' welfare systems – where social policy relies on family solidarity as the main source of care – deepen social inequality, as has been observed elsewhere (see Knijn and Komter, 2004).

Experiences of Japanese mothers: flexible working conditions and use of private services

Mrs Takahashi

Mrs Takahashi is 48 years old and a care manager working full-time in a community care centre for older persons. She has worked there for over 15 years, ever since her husband became ill. Five years ago, she decided to improve her career and moved from a part-time job to full-time employment in a position using her professional qualifications. Mrs Takahashi lives with her son, Ryota, aged 22, who has a mild intellectual disability, another son, her husband and her mother-in-law. Ryota has a full-time job in a small company where he cleans the offices and sometimes helps with the company's events and entertainment activities. He does not use any care services. All his life, Mrs Takahashi has been Ryota's primary carer, offering him supportive surroundings. She has established an informal network of carers for him using voluntary support in their community. This has enabled him to make friends in the community and to spend time with some of them after work or at the weekend. Mrs Takahashi remarked:

> "Ryota attended a class for children with additional needs in a mainstream school. Because he was frequently in poor health, I regularly had to take him to appointments with doctors. Fortunately, I worked in a job with a flexitime system, and I always did my best to fit these appointments for Ryota in with those arrangements. I was also fortunate to have various supportive social networks, including my colleagues."

She added: "Of course, it is probably true that I will never in my life escape from caring for my son as a parent."

Here, three factors seem to be important in understanding how this mother manages her dual roles of work and care: (1) the flexible working time system in her occupation; (2) having a workplace that is near her home; and (3) her many acquaintances with positive attitudes towards children with disabilities living in the community. Parent-carers of a child with mild disabilities find that they have to make the effort to find private or informal care resources as there is a lack of publicly funded support for these children. Sustaining informal support and developing appropriate services are emerging as key issues for carers' work–care reconciliation in Japan.

Mrs Sasaki

Mrs Sasaki is a self-employed, freelance editor and writer carrying out contract work for publishers. Aged 40, she lives with her husband and two sons. Her husband, also a freelance writer, has a positive attitude towards caring for the children. One of their sons, Taro, aged eight, has severe intellectual and physical disabilities through cerebral palsy and attends a school for children with additional needs.

Mrs Sasaki works from morning till night and sometimes during the night. Her working hours depend on the schedules offered by the publishers. Taro has various kinds of social support and services in his daily life. These include after-school care, respite care and supported transport. Occasionally, he is also hospitalised for short periods. The family also uses private care services (at ¥800–¥1,000/€7.50–€9.50 per hour). This helps Mrs Sasaki to be flexible, to respond to Taro's care needs and to reconcile her work and caring roles. Mrs Sasaki described their approach:

> "First of all, I would like to say that working is the reason for being who I am to me. Keeping Taro's daily life safe and secure is important because this enables us to meet the various individual needs of other family members, including me. We have supported our son to guide him towards independent living in the future, and we have managed all the risks in our lives ourselves, including those of caring for relatives."

Mrs Sasaki also explained that "sharing information, keeping in touch with society and having standing in the community are the best ways of developing a supportive network for my son".

In addition to welfare services, Mrs Sasaki identified other factors that may be important in enabling parent-carers to reconcile work and care for a child with disabilities. These include: the parents' strengths; positive and cooperative attitudes towards rearing their son; management skills enabling them to use both social and private care services; their clear vision for their son's independent life in the future; and, last but not least, financial stability.

Combining work and care for these two Japanese mothers means thinking about how to maximise the independence of each family member: the father, the mother, the child with disabilities, other children and others. Their accounts also highlight that the family needs knowledge and ability to access appropriate social services or social workers who can assist them in managing the challenges they face.

The intertwining of policy, culture and society in Taiwan and Japan

Parent-carers usually face a lifelong care responsibility. In Taiwan, they are affected not only by the long-term strain of caring, but also by the need to cope with the social difficulties that often arise: the prejudices of others and a feeling of being devalued by society (Chou and Palley, 1998; Chou et al, 2009). Most people with disabilities in Taiwan (over 90%) continue to live with their families, usually with their parents (DSMI, 2011). This means that, for their parents, negotiating their work and care responsibilities continues throughout their entire adult life course.

Although social services for people with disabilities would in most cases be very useful for parent-carers, they are often not used simply because people are unaware that they exist (Chou et al, 2008). Most service users are parent-carers who: (1) have a higher level of education (like Mrs Lin, described earlier); (2) live in urban areas; and (3) are involved in voluntary associations (as Mrs Lin is) (see also Chou et al, 2008).

The percentage of women employed in the labour force in Taiwan rose from 47% in 1990 to 54% in 2010 (see *Chapter One*). So far, however, reconciling paid work with family caregiving has not been identified in Taiwan as a social issue in public discourse, by employers or by the state. Paid care leave (to look after a sick or disabled relative) and access to flexible or part-time working hours to accommodate care responsibilities are not yet available. Taiwan's welfare policies and services are still based on the view that a disabled person's care is a family matter, rather than a significant state responsibility or a question of individual rights. In this chapter, the situations of the two Taiwanese mothers – Mrs Lin and Mrs Kou – have been used to exemplify the circumstances of parent-carers who have a child with disabilities. To make paid work and caregiving responsibilities compatible, these mothers have had to develop their own strategies, which include building supportive social networks.

From a gender equality perspective, helping mothers of disabled children to care for them alongside participation in the labour force has not (yet) become an advocacy issue for women's groups in Taiwan. With no specific welfare or employment policies in place, parent-carers have both lower rates of employment and a poorer quality of life than other citizens of working age (Chou et al, 2007). This is especially true for mothers from low socio-economic backgrounds (Chou et al, 2010).

Since 1992, families with a relative needing regular assistance in daily life have been eligible to hire a live-in migrant care worker. However, parent-carers need high incomes to afford this expense. A national survey in 2006 showed that only 1.2% of families with a disabled child aged under 20 employed a live-in migrant care worker, a much lower figure than in families with a frail older family member (18%; see also *Chapter Five*) (DSMI, 2007). This suggests that having a live-in migrant care worker to share the work of caring for a disabled child is possible only for well-off families. The cost of hiring a migrant care worker to care for older people, by contrast, is usually shared between all the older person's adult children.

In Japan, child-rearing arrangements are strongly influenced by societal values. Although new family support measures have been introduced, the value placed on parental care is so deeply embedded that it is very hard for parents bringing up a disabled child to feel free of social norms. This often makes turning to social care services a 'last resort' for parent-carers. Those who try to use such services need to commit a lot of time and effort to finding suitable support and may discover that none exists in their community. There are also complicated procedures to negotiate in terms of eligibility (Nakano et al, 1995). These barriers to service use for parents and their disabled children contribute to their social exclusion.

A recent study of mothers of children with disabilities (Yokohama City, 2007) showed that only 30% were in paid work, barely half the figure for all women in Japan. Of these, 60% held a part-time job and worked to cover their living costs or contribute to the fees charged for using disability services. The non-employed mothers of disabled children in this study were just as keen to have paid work. Similar patterns were also found in another study of parent-carers in which many participants said that they wished or needed to increase the hours they worked (Group YOU, 2010).

Japan's 'work–life balance' policy (see *Chapter Two*) involves some new services, which should, in the future, cover some parent-carers' needs and help them reconcile work and care. Paid care leave could be a useful option for mothers of disabled children as it should give those combining work and care greater choice.

As noted by Fujiwara (2006), it is also important to take gender into account when considering policy on parent-carers. In general, caring for a disabled child involves a lifelong care responsibility (Nakano et al, 1999). This means that even if mothers have access to paid care leave, it may not be an adequate response to their needs as parent-carers. Care services for their children, provided within the community, are also needed. However, regardless of social status and background and whether or not they are in paid work, mothers are still almost always the primary carers of the disabled child, an arrangement exemplified by all four mothers discussed in this chapter.

Discussion: comparative analysis and policy significance

In both Taiwan and Japan, care policy for disabled people does not involve a past history of institutionalisation to the same extent as in some Western countries. Today, over 90% of people with disabilities in Taiwan and Japan are cared for by family members or live in the community, and under 10% use residential services (DSMI, 2011). Historically, families have provided this care for centuries, primarily by mothers or other female family members. Care in these two countries remains a private responsibility and a family obligation. Financial support and services have developed, but their accessibility has been limited by decisions to impose professional needs assessments and means-testing, and most parent-carers have to make co-payments when using disability services. Familial ideas – filial piety, patriarchal authority, strict gender role separation, female subordination and a fear of bringing shame on the family – remain strong values in East Asia, especially in Taiwan, where only low-level social security and social services are provided (Esping-Andersen, 1996; Sung, 2001; Maeda, 2004; Park and Chesla, 2007; Chen, 2008). In many social policy analyses, these states are seen to be distinctive through their lack of worker participation and in having a laissez-faire but not liberal social organisation and solidarity but not equality (Doling and Finer, 2001: 297–8). Nevertheless, compared with other East Asian countries – like South Korea, Singapore, Hong Kong and Taiwan – Japan is more advanced in terms of its welfare system, while welfare policy in Taiwan is less institutionalised (Goodman and Peng, 1996). These factors are relevant in understanding why welfare and employment policies related to work–care reconciliation, such as flexible working hours and part-time employment, have been included in Japanese legislation since 2009, but are issues barely visible in Taiwan. In Japan, the low birth rate and the idea that support for child-rearing is critical as a means of investing in the future have come together in a new generation in which far more people have higher education (50% in 2009) and have been exposed to experiences of 'gender equality'. Younger Japanese people today have an interest in a good work–life balance for fathers and an accessible childcare leave system. To draw public attention to the new legislation, the government launched the Ikumen Project in 2010, which focuses on men who enjoy childcare and develop themselves through it.

The four individual accounts presented in this chapter illustrate some significant differences between Taiwanese and Japanese societies. Unlike the trend identified in the Nordic welfare states described in this book, care responsibilities in Japan are moving away from the family and shifting towards the state. In Taiwan, by contrast, a weak state welfare system is still tolerated, seen by Preston (2001) as an outcome of Taiwan's traditional Chinese familial culture. In Taiwan, building informal support is thus a crucial strategy for parents and mothers with care responsibilities. However, whether Taiwanese families can cope with having only limited formal social support available remains to be seen.

Work–care reconciliation is related not only to welfare arrangements, but also to gender and culture, which affect carers in different societies and families in different ways. The four accounts presented show that some Taiwanese and Japanese mothers undertake paid work alongside the primary care of disabled children. In understanding this, Fraser's (2000) 'universal breadwinner' and 'caregiver parity' models may be useful. Japan has begun to move towards a universal breadwinner model, but Taiwan's system does not fit either mould because Taiwan's welfare state benefits are so limited. Both models have their problems in terms of gender equality (Duncan and Williams, 2002). While Japan has moved towards universal breadwinner status in terms of paternal and maternal labour force participation, there is little evidence of movement towards universal caregiving. In both countries, women's roles increasingly combine both paid and domestic work. As a consequence, policies designed to incentivise men to share care work are needed to improve gender equality and to make paid work and unpaid care equally valued.

Japan has made legislative progress in developing policies that help parents reconcile care and work. However, the fundamental task of developing policies capable of promoting the well-being of parents in both lone-parent and two-parent families, especially those containing a child with disabilities, remains to be done. In Japan, measures are also needed to develop positive attitudes towards parent-carers in the workplace, and parents of disabled children need access to better advocacy services. While Taiwan's planned LTCI scheme aims to meet the care needs of older and disabled people, debates about it have not addressed work–care reconciliation issues, implying that parent-carers' right to work is of less concern than other social rights (see Knijn and Kremer, 1997). Japan's approach to parental leave has encompassed parent-carers since 2009, but similar policies are still lacking in Taiwan. All in all, how to strengthen 'family solidarity' (Knijn and Komter, 2004) – that is, how to encourage fathers to become more involved in care and move towards a dual earner–dual carer model, offering the prospect of gender equality – is a question still unanswered in both countries.

Finally, we note that policymakers in Taiwan need to become aware of the needs and well-being of parent-carers and to build social services capable of supporting these families' economic and caregiving needs. Supporting parents, especially mothers, to undertake paid work and to reconcile their paid work and care responsibilities, particularly when these include the care of a disabled child, should be placed on the agenda and embedded in labour and social welfare policy arrangements. This means including paid care leave for parents in the Employment Insurance Act 2002 (amended in 2011), and reducing the cost of day care for parents to encourage mothers of disabled children to enter the workplace. Finally, the family subsidy should be universal and available for all parents.

In Japan, where the care of children with disabilities is concerned, we make several recommendations to policymakers. First, to formulate new policies emphasising the need for positive attitudes to flexibility in the workplace and raising disabled children. Second, policies need to support children's independent lives in the community, with formal or informal resources available to them and their families. Finally, parent-carers need the chance to choose a working style that suits their caring circumstances, which means providing a special subsidy for children with disabilities to ensure their financial security.

Notes

[1] This is likely to be replaced in the future by a new classification system based on the 'International Classification of Functioning, Disability and Health' (ICF) (WHO, 2002) in compliance with Taiwan's Disability Act (Amended) 2007.

[2] In Taiwan, compulsory education ends at the age of 15 (the Elementary and Secondary Education Act 1979); consequently, official surveys differentiate between children and adults at age 15.

[3] Visual, hearing and speech impairments, mobility disabilities, and illnesses that affect daily living (including cardiac, respiratory and immune system disorders).

[4] Including epilepsy, dementia, Alzheimer's disease, autism and behavioural disabilities.

References

Cabinet Office (2010a) *White Paper for persons with disabilities*, Tokyo: Cabinet Office (in Japanese).

Cabinet Office (2010b) *Annual report on government measures for persons with disabilities (summary)*, Tokyo: Cabinet Office (in Japanese).

Chen, Y.J. (2008) 'Strength perspective: an analysis of ageing in place care model in Taiwan based on traditional filial piety', *Ageing International*, vol 32, no 3, pp 183–204.

Chou, Y.C. and Palley, H.A. (1998) 'The impact of having a child with developmental disabilities on the family in Taiwan: cultural context review', *Social Development Issues*, vol 20, no 3, pp 35–52.

Chou, Y.C., Lin, L.C., Chang, A.L. and Schalock, R.L. (2007) 'The quality of life of family caregivers of adults with intellectual disabilities in Taiwan', *Journal of Applied Research in Intellectual Disabilities*, vol 20, no 3, pp 200–10.

Chou, Y.C., Lee, Y.C., Lin, L.C., Chang, A.L. and Huang, W.Y. (2008) 'Social services utilization by adults with intellectual disabilities and their families', *Social Science and Medicine*, vol 66, no 12, pp 2474–85.

Chou, Y.C., Pu, C.Y., Lee, Y.C., Lin, L.C. and Kröger, T. (2009) 'Effect of perceived stigmatization on the quality of life among ageing female family carers: a comparison of carers of adults with intellectual disability and carers of adults with mental illness', *Journal of Intellectual Disability Research*, vol 53, no 7, pp 654–64.

Chou, Y.C., Pu, C.Y., Kröger, T. and Fu, L.Y. (2010) 'Caring, employment and quality of life: a comparison of employed and non-employed mothers of adults with ID', *American Journal on Intellectual and Developmental Disabilities*, vol 115, no 5, pp 406–20.

Doling, J. and Finer, C.J. (2001) 'Looking east, looking west: trends in orientalism and occidentalism amongst applied social scientists', in C.J. Finer (ed) *Comparing the social policy experience of Britain and Taiwan*, Aldershot: Ashgate, pp 293–306.

DSMI (Department of Statistics, Ministry of Interior, Taiwan) (2007) *National survey of life needs among people with disabilities: summary report*, Taiwan: Ministry of Interior (in Chinese).

DSMI (2011) *Statistical data on people with disabilities*, Taiwan: Ministry of Interior (in Chinese).

Duncan, S. and Williams, F. (2002) 'Universal breadwinner model, the caregiver parity model and the universal caregiver model', *Critical Social Policy*, vol 22, no 1, pp 5–11.

Esping-Andersen, G. (1996) 'Positive-sum solutions in a world of trade-offs?', in G. Esping-Andersen (ed) *Welfare states in transition: national adaptations in global economies*, London: Sage, pp 256–67.

Fraser, N. (2000) 'After the family wage: a postindustrial thought experiment', in B. Hobson (ed) *Gender and citizenship in transition*, New York, NY: Routledge, pp 1–32.

Fujiwara, R. (2006) *Families' lives with children with severe disabilities: caring mother and gender*, Tokyo: Akashishoten (in Japanese).

Goodman, R. and Peng, I. (1996) 'The East Asian welfare states: peripatetic learning, adaptive change, and nation-building', in G. Esping-Andersen (ed) *Welfare states in transition: national adaptations in global economies*, London: Sage, pp 192–224.

Group YOU (2010) *Research on work–life balance of carers of children with disabilities*, Sendai City, Miyagi: Group YOU (in Japanese).

JILPT (Japan Institute of Labour Policy and Training) (2011) *Data book of international labour statistics*, Tokyo: JILPT (in Japanese).

Knijn, T. and Komter, A. (2004) 'Introduction', in T. Knijn and A. Komter (eds) *Solidarity between the sexes and the generations: transformations in Europe*, Northampton: Edward Elgar, pp xii–xxii.

Knijn, T. and Kremer, M. (1997) 'Gender and the caring dimension of welfare states: toward inclusive citizenship', *Social Politics*, vol 4, no 3, pp 328–61.

Maeda, D. (2004) 'Societal filial piety has made traditional individual filial piety much less important in contemporary Japan', *Geriatrics and Gerontology International*, vol 4, pp S74–6.

MHLW (Ministry of Health, Labour and Welfare) (2005) *Survey on children/persons with intellectual disabilities*, Tokyo: MHLW (in Japanese).

MHLW (2006) *Survey on the actual status of children/persons with physical disabilities*, Tokyo: MHLW (in Japanese).

MHLW (2009) 'White Papers & reports: annual health, labour and welfare report'. Available at: http://www.mhlw.go.jp/english/wp/wp-hw3/

Nakano, T., Tazawa, A., Kaneko, T., Nakaune, T., Iwasaki, M., Takizawa, K., Dobashi, T. and Narita, S. (1995) *Family support based on user-orientation: children with disabilities and their family lives*, Chiba: Taiyousha (in Japanese).

Nakano, T., Matsumura, M., Iwasaki, T., Kato, K., Tashiro, N., Fuku, C., Takizawa, K., Narita, S., Ibaraki, N. and Urano, K. (1999) *A research of family supports for children with disabilities in the community: report of disability studies (1996–1997)*, Tokyo: Nakano Office, Meijigakuin University (in Japanese).

Park, M. and Chesla, C. (2007) 'Revisiting Confucianism as a conceptual framework for Asian family study', *Journal of Family Nursing*, vol 13, no 3, pp 293–311.

Preston, P.W. (2001) 'Elite political-cultural projects, economic growth and the achievement of social welfare in East Asia', in C.J. Finer (ed) *Comparing the social policy experience of Britain and Taiwan*, Aldershot: Ashgate, pp 307–32.

Sung, K.-T. (2001) 'Elder respect: exploration of ideals and forms in East Asia', *Journal of Aging Studies*, vol 15, no 1, pp 13–26.

WHO (World Health Organization) (2002) 'International Classification of Functioning, Disability and Health (ICF)'. Available at: www.who.int/classifications/icf/en/

Yokohama City (2007) *Research of actual status of children with disabilities and families' lives*, Yokohama: Child and Youth Department of Yokohama City and Yokohama Allied Conference for Supporting and Advocating Children with Disabilities (in Japanese).

PART THREE

Working partner-carers

NINE

Reconciling partner-care and paid work in Finland and Sweden: challenges and coping strategies

Anu Leinonen and Ann-Britt Sand

Introduction

In Finland, among caregiving paid workers aged 44 to 63, 3% of women and 4% of men reported having care responsibility for their partner in 2009 (Kauppinen and Jolanki, 2012). In Sweden, no exact figures on the numbers of working partner-carers are collected. Numbers of carers and informal helpers are largest among middle-aged women and adult daughters in both countries (see *Chapter One*), although among retired couples, both women and men often care for their partners (Szcbehely, 2005a, 2005b; Voutilainen et al, 2007; Kattainen et al, 2008).

In research and policy debate in Finland and Sweden, the circumstances of working partner-carers have received little attention: instead, care between partners has been studied almost exclusively among older retired people (Mossberg Sand, 2000; Mikkola, 2009). Finland's (1929) and Sweden's (1987) Marriage Acts impose no statutory obligation to provide personal care for one's spouse, although spouses are expected to help and support each other financially. However, the disability of one partner raises particular issues in how work and care play out in the family lives of middle-aged, usually co-resident, couples and this chapter explores these issues in the Nordic context. What type of problems and challenges do Finnish and Swedish working partner-carers have in their everyday lives? What are the means – the practical arrangements and policy support – by which they manage these challenges? How well are they supported by recent welfare state developments? And do those who need workplace flexibility to manage work and care receive any assistance from their employers? The chapter addresses these questions by exploring case material from two recent empirical studies.

The chapter is organised in three main parts. First, it provides a short overview of the services and support available to working partner-carers in the two countries. Second, it draws on two new qualitative studies of working carers in Finland and Sweden[1] – alongside other existing research on work–care reconciliation – to highlight some of the challenges partner-carers face in relation to work, care and their personal lives. Two case studies – one from each country – are presented to illustrate the different coping strategies partner-carers adopt to help them better manage the situations in which they find themselves. Third, the chapter considers the policy implications of this research.

Support and services available to partner-carers

Chapter Two has already noted some developments relating to partner-care among working-age people in Finland and Sweden, where regular help for sick, frail or disabled adults has long been central to the relationship between the individual and society. In both countries, family members' contributions have been made voluntarily and disabled people's right to receive formal help is well established in law and policy (more securely than that of frail older people). In recent years, however, cuts and reorganisations in public health and social care provision have transferred some care responsibilities to family members, and service users have increasingly been treated as consumers who can privately purchase tax-funded (eg by using service vouchers[2]) or tax-deductible care from the market (Kröger and Leinonen, 2012; Szebehely and Trydegård, 2012).

In general, home-based care for sick partners and their families in Finland and Sweden – including home help and home nursing, day care services, and services such as safety alarms and meals on wheels – is rather similar to help available there for older people and their families (see *Chapters Two* and *Three*). Severely disabled people in Finland have the right to personal assistance, which can mean services provided either by a personal assistant they employ or by publicly funded home care workers. In Sweden, too, people with extensive care needs have the right to personal assistance,[3] and in both countries, family members may be employed as personal assistants.

The support provided by municipalities for carers in general – including allowances, respite care and counselling – is also relevant to working partner-carers. In Finland, every second 'supported carer' (the term used for carers receiving Carer's Allowance) cares for a partner. Carer's Allowance recipients are split roughly equally between those who are retired and aged 65 or over and those of working age (Voutilainen et al, 2007), so while many supported partner-carers are above working age, many are not. In Sweden in the 1990s, about a quarter of family carers employed by municipalities cared for a partner (Mossberg Sand, 2000), and in the Swedish system, carers employed by municipalities can, and sometimes do, also hold another paid job.

As discussed in *Chapter Two*, concrete measures to help citizens respond to the challenges of reconciling work and care are in their early stages in both countries. Like other working carers in Finland, working partner-carers are eligible, in agreement with their employer, for (unpaid) temporary 'absence for an unforeseen family situation' or 'absence for care for a family member or other close person'. In Sweden, workers whose partner is terminally ill may claim End of Life Care Allowance, an income-related payment available to relatives, irrespective of the actual provision of care (see *Chapter Two*).

Other schemes – semi-retirement, part-time work, career breaks, work-sharing and job alternation schemes – can all also be used to make partner-care more manageable. Partner-carers often make informal workplace arrangements, based on more general options for arranging working time to fit with private life. These arrangements include: working from home; adjusted or flexible work schedules; short leaves (as distinct from annual holidays or unpaid breaks); flexitime; substitution of holiday bonuses for free days; and negotiation with colleagues about working hours (Kauppinen, 2010; Sand, 2010).

In both countries, disabled people are eligible for financial benefits, transportation and interpretation services, aids, home repairs, and rehabilitation services (Försäkringskassan, 2011; Socialstyrelsen, 2011; KELA, 2012; Sosiaaliportti, 2012). These measures are designed to improve and maintain the well-being of disabled people but are also relevant for their partners and have implications for the well-being of the whole family.

The next part of this chapter highlights the experiences of interviewees who were caring for their partners in Finland and Sweden. It illustrates the challenges they faced in relation to work, to the care they provided and in other aspects of their lives. Interviewees, who lived in different parts of Finland and Sweden, were interviewed separately Each had a partner who needed daily help or care because of a serious illness or physical and/or mobility disabilities. Each respondent's personal circumstances are detailed in Table 9.1.

Table 9.1: Finnish and Swedish partner-carer interviewees

Interviewee	Partner	Employment	Living	Current formal help and support	Informal practical help in care tasks
Finnish					
Seija-Reetta (female), 60	Husband, 59 (physical disability, neurological disease), disabled for two years.	Office work. Full-time (works partly from home because of care).	Co-resident.	No home care services; Carer's Allowance (financial, lowest level); publicly financed physiotherapy, occupational therapy, rehabilitation periods; transportation services (municipal disability services); aids in bathroom and sauna.	Practically nothing; son visits his family monthly; a female friend of the family sometimes keeps her husband company (and stays with him when Seija-Reetta is away).
Harri (male), 59	Wife, 59 (mental problems, memory disease), ill for decades, need for help has increased recently.	Office work. Full-time. Flexibility in daily working hours.	Co-resident.	Municipal home care several times a day; Carer's Allowance (financial, lowest level); municipal day care services and respite care during Harri's work travels; safety wristband.	Practically nothing; son visits with his girlfriend at times.
Irja (female), 65	Husband, 79 (memory disease, neurological disease), ill for 1.5 years (disability retirement for decades).	Office work. Full-time. Flexibility in daily working hours.	Co-resident.	Home care worker delivers medicines weekly (purchased by service voucher provided by the municipality); no Carer's Allowance (financial); publicly financed aids, eg safety wristband.	Co-resident son helps daily; daughter visits with her husband regularly.

Interviewee	Partner	Employment	Living	Current formal help and support	Informal practical help in care tasks
Marketta (female), 60	Male partner, 78 (neurological disease, other health problems), ill for five years, help needed earlier too.	Education. Part-time (based on wish to have more personal free time). Plans part-time retirement to get more time for herself and partner. Flexibility in daily working hours.	Separate apartments (150km apart).	Municipal home care visits once/ twice per week; support and activities organised by third-sector organisations; transportation services (municipal disability services); no Carer's Allowance (financial); publicly financed physiotherapy; publicly financed aids, e. safety wristband.	Practically nothing; companion services from a volunteer organisation; partner's son visits with his wife regularly, daughters live far away and visit at times.
Seela (female), 58	Husband, 62 (physical disability), disabled for 15 years.	Factory work. Part-time retired (based on disability). Shift-working, but only day shifts.	Co-resident.	Publicly financed physiotherapy; publicly financed aids in bathroom; Carer's Allowance (financial, lowest level).	Practically nothing; relatives and colleagues help occasionally.
Elli (female), 65	Husband, 77 (pulmonary disease), ill for decades.	Social and health care. Part-time retired (based on age; care was one reason to apply). Flexibility in daily working hours.	Co-resident.	Medical care in hospital, publicly financed respirator; no Carer's Allowance (financial).	Daughter helps regularly, son visits and supports emotionally, grandchildren visit regularly, meetings of a patient organisation.

Interviewee	Partner	Employment	Living	Current formal help and support	Informal practical help in care tasks
Swedish					
Anna-Lena (female), 68	Husband, 69 (early dementia), ill for 10 years.	Office work. Self-employed (retired but works part-time from home).	Separate (husband living in a nursing home for the past two years).	When husband lived at home: day care, home-help services, respite care when asked for.	Practically nothing; only mental support from the family.
Berit (female), 56	Husband, 60 (early dementia), ill for 10 years.	Office work. Full-time. When partner was living at home, she worked 50%.	Separate (husband living in a group home for the past four months).	When husband lived at home: day care, home-help services, respite care when asked for.	Practically nothing; daughter gives emotional help and support.
Eva (female), 57	Husband, 63 (blindness), ill for 30 years but condition has worsened lately.	IT consultant. Full-time.	Co-resident.	No formal help. Husband goes regularly to eye consultant at hospital.	Practically nothing; daughter (from earlier relationship) gives emotional support. His daughter (from earlier relationship) visits her father.
Bengt (male), 54	Wife, 52 (physical disability), ill for 15 years.	Craftsman. Self-employed (works part-time + employed as a family caregiver).	Co-resident.	Transportation services, walking assistance once per week; for past two years, employed as family caregiver (SKR9,800) (approximately €1,070/month).	Their two children give some help, parents and other relatives give some support.

Managing the tension

Challenges and coping strategies

Our analysis is based on the principles of qualitative content analysis (eg Marvasti, 2003). All 10 interview transcripts were examined to identify differences and similarities in how respondents talked about managing work and care. Much of the existing research literature discusses the tensions people feel in trying to manage these situations. Instances where respondents talked about such pressures were noted so that shared (or disparate) experiences could be recorded. Similar issues were identified in both the Finnish and Swedish interviews, although there were also some differences of emphasis in each country. Many interviewees said that as their partner's condition deteriorated, it had become impossible to leave them alone at home for long periods or that if they did so, this caused them great anxiety. At this point, they had needed to consider how to adjust their working hours and/or place of work and/or to apply for (municipal or private) assistance. Those who had considered changing their hours or place of work had negotiated this with their employers and co-workers, succeeding in varying ways. Some reported difficulties in accessing or obtaining social care services and benefits, and others talked about financial problems. Many spoke of inadequate time for rest, their own interests or other intimate relationships, while some mentioned that their partner's personalities and attitudes or the attitudes and expectations of other relatives and acquaintances sometimes caused them concern or additional stress.

The interviewees had responded to these problems and challenges in various ways. For some, coping strategies were rather structural in nature, and included accessing work time flexibility, social care services and financial benefits or allowances. Others gained support through informal help from other people. Some responses were more individual and familial; they were affected by (marital) commitments between partners, the meanings attached to work and personal resources. Individual strategies were often combinations of these different responses, chosen because of personal values.

When interviewees talked about the challenges they faced and the coping strategies they adopted to better reconcile work and care, four themes emerged: (1) work-related issues, such as arrangements at work; (2) care-related issues, such as the accessibility and quality of available services; (3) issues related to personal time, that is, time for rest, friends, hobbies and interests; and (4) issues related to interpersonal matters, such as relationships at work and between those close to the interviewees.

Work-related issues

For Nordic women and men, participating in paid work appears to be very significant. While the right of both partners to work was not questioned, the disability of one partner caused the non-disabled partner to re-evaluate her/his attachment to work. Some Finnish interviewees found that *postponing* their (part-time) retirement plans was a way of preventing their care responsibilities from becoming overwhelming, although when interviewed, some had already started to prepare for (part-time) retirement (Leinonen, 2011a). One interviewee explained: "I would feel like a prisoner. Now, when I leave to go to work, I feel

I get a break from it all. I get to visit another world." Another Finnish interviewee, by contrast, was already semi-retired – having reached normal retirement age – but said her husband's serious illness had been a significant factor in the timing of her retirement. The Swedish interviewees also felt that employment and being able to continue working were important for their own well-being. While their multiple duties were a potential source of stress, work also provided self-esteem and a counterbalance to caring, as British (Phillips et al, 2002; Arksey and Glendinning, 2008) and Nordic (Autio and Reivilä, 2005; Sand, 2010) studies have also found. A demanding partner-care role may make work even more significant, as partners usually live together and the workplace can offer a 'refuge' from round-the-clock caring responsibilities and the demands of the care relationship.

A second aspect, found throughout the data, related to the need to reduce working hours and the options available to do this. The partner's illness had often forced the interviewees (whether employed or self-employed) to reduce their working hours, especially in Sweden. This was not usually the preferred solution, however, and many partner-carers increased their working hours again as soon as they could. Finnish partner-carers seemed to manage the situation by making changes in *where* they worked or in their daily hours of work. Options for reorganising daily hours of work were important for carers, but depended on the nature of the work and the intensity of their caring responsibilities. Finnish interviewees in office jobs or education, for example, were able to start work later in the morning and to attend health and other appointments with their partners during the day. Working shifts or flexitime also gave some the opportunity to run care-related errands during the day. Two Swedish interviewees were self-employed. While, in theory, this gave them much flexibility in combining work and care, in practice, the intensive support their partners needed made working complicated. One said that she had "tried to keep the business going in the evenings and at night when he was asleep", but in the end had been forced to decline orders from her customers.

The interviewees did not report substantial difficulties in negotiating working time adjustments with their employers. This may be because the arrangements they used were based on general options that, depending on the type of work, allow workers to arrange their working hours to suit personal circumstances. Specific care leave in Finland and Sweden is a new and (in Sweden) little discussed topic, however, and those interviewed had few concrete expectations of how carers should be treated at work. In general, the Finnish interviewees welcomed the new care leave arrangements (see *Chapter Two*), although as most did not wish to take on care responsibility 24 hours a day, they did not necessarily feel that they were relevant to their own situation.

The data also revealed the spatial dimension of work and care. Two interviewees worked partly from home. While this could offer a good solution for partner-carers concerned about their husband's or wife's condition during the day, it was available only to those whose work could be taken home. As well as 'remote working', the spatial aspect also included issues of residential proximity and separation. In the future, caring from a distance (Neal et al, 2008) may become more common as partners may live considerable distances apart due to work or other family commitments (such as children from previous relationships). This has two implications, as the case of one Finnish female interviewee showed: living and working in a different environment provided valued room for one's "own thoughts", but arranging support for a partner far away involved extra concern and expense.

Finally, interviewees drew attention to the family economy and the management of housing costs. When the other partner was out of the labour market because of illness or disability, work was a significant source of income, as some Swedish interviewees pointed out. When partners live together, sharing the expenses of daily life, one partner's illness or disability may involve extra costs, which put pressure on the household budget. If the lost salary of one partner is accompanied by reduced working hours for the other, serious financial problems can arise. Although, in principle, Carer's Allowance (in Finland) and Employment as a Family Carer (in Sweden) are available to offset this reduced income, in practice, all three officially recognised Finnish partner-carers interviewed felt that the allowance was low, and that its significance was mainly symbolic, as other Finnish carers have also reported (Autio and Reivilä, 2005). In the Swedish data, one interviewee employed as a family carer also felt that the carer's salary was low and merely a symbolic gesture (see also Sand, 2007). Moving a partner into a nursing home or into assisted living can raise further financial difficulties. Where this happened, some Swedish interviewees found that it became too expensive to remain in the home they had previously shared with their partner.

Care-related issues

In both countries, interviewees whose partners received disability services – transport services, medical consultations and rehabilitation for disabled people – generally felt that these were important for the disabled person's well-being and functional capacity. These carers felt that the services affected the mood of the whole family, but it was home-based care services, day care and respite care that were especially significant in relation to the tension between work and care.

For interviewees in both countries, sharing the care tasks with home care workers was important. Often, it was a precondition for participating in work. Today, publicly funded home care services are targeted towards people with the highest needs (Kröger and Leinonen, 2012; Szebehely and Trydegård, 2012) and the problems in quality and accessibility of home care, and a failure to tailor services to individual needs, could mean extra stress. In addition, some interviewees saw the help they gave to their partner as just a normal part of their relationship and did not want to use home care services. As also found in studies of older people's attitudes to service use (Mossberg Sand, 2000; Mikkola, 2009; Leinonen, 2011b), some partners who were ill or disabled did not want to accept unfamiliar home care workers or other external help.

While some interviewees were happy with the quality of home care services, others said that turnover among home care workers and their varied levels of knowledge and skill caused additional problems (Sand, 2010; Leinonen, 2011b). Interviewees in both countries lived in different municipalities, where practices and resources differed, perhaps explaining their varied experiences. Non-Nordic studies of care services (see, eg, Mahmood and Martin-Matthews, 2008) have found that municipal home care does not always fit well with the routines, habits and wishes of partners. The interviewees saw their home as a place they left each day to go to work and to which they returned when work was over. Once free from work routines, they wanted to retain the flexibility of private life rather than follow the schedules of home care workers.

Many interviewees mentioned the lack of suitable respite care for people of working age, although one male interviewee in Finland stressed that working carers could be better off than other carers: "What I do want to say is that the city tries to arrange respite care for working caregivers, primarily." In his case, periods of respite care had been related to work trips, although he was planning to ask about respite care at other times, unrelated to his work, to get more time for rest and undisturbed sleep. Currently, Finnish municipalities can contract with a 'deputising' carer who works in the home during the statutory free days of the supported primary carer, an arrangement that may help some working carers and their partners.

(Inter)Personal issues

As found in other countries (Mooney et al, 2002; Gautun and Hagen, 2010), the Swedish and Finnish interviewees indicated that demanding care responsibilities reduce the opportunities working carers have to devote time to others close to them or to their own activities and interests, and prevent them from using their annual leave for rest. Constraints on personal time are also reported by working carers studied in other research in Finland and Sweden (Autio and Reivilä, 2005; Sand, 2010; Leinonen, 2011b). Some said that they missed activities they had previously shared with their partner and that it took a long time to adapt to changes in the relationship. In making these adjustments, carers regretted their own loss of free time, which was now taken up with care tasks; as one Swedish interviewee explained, carers are often "too tired to have fun". Other interviewees stressed that they tried to make time for exercise, hobbies and personal interests by setting aside 'unimportant' issues, like make-up or keeping the house tidy. Nordic women and men seemed keen to keep 'personal time' and time for their own activities and friends, and to maintain each partner's independence. Nevertheless, their caring commitments often displaced leisure activities, and long trips abroad became "only dreams". The attitudes of their partner's relatives sometimes put extra pressures on a wife or husband who would have liked to retain a life outside the partnership, which had now become a care relationship. The relatives of a husband with a serious illness did not always understand the distress of living, as one Swedish interviewee put it, as "a widow with a living husband". This involved juggling the feelings of commitment to the partner and the need for individuality and time for personal interests.

In both countries, relationships at work were important for many carers. Work provided social contacts and a chance to talk about care with people in similar family situations. Not all interviewees wanted to discuss their family life with colleagues, however, and some preferred to keep a boundary between private life and work (Clark, 2000). This may be especially true when care is given to a partner, where changes in sexuality sometimes affect intimate relations (Mossberg Sand, 2000; Hayes et al, 2009). Some interviewees also reported that work was a place where they could discuss issues other than the demands of care and that they valued this support.

In Nordic countries, many carers expect to share ongoing daily care tasks with formal care workers rather than with other family members (Mossberg Sand, 2000; Vilkko et al, 2010; Leinonen, 2011c). Nevertheless, most interviewees studied received (or had received) some sort of support from their adult children, other relatives or acquaintances. This was often occasional help rather than regular emotional or practical support. They did not normally expect (or receive) long-term help from their children, and this usually occurred in cases where the services provided by home care workers were unsatisfactory. Nevertheless, adult children in some family situations have more time available for care than their working parent, sometimes due to unemployment (Henz, 2010). While retired Finnish and Swedish partners usually see themselves as the primary and obvious source of help for a partner needing care (Jansson et al, 2001; Mikkola, 2009), when the partner is employed, this raises additional issues. In one Finnish case, the son's unemployment enabled his mother to remain in full-time work despite her husband's care needs. She was satisfied with her son's help, but nevertheless wanted him to have his own home and career.

Our interviewees' accounts of real-life situations showed considerable variation and each had many different elements. In what follows, a single case from each country is described to illustrate this diversity and complexity. Although these examples draw on individual narratives, they also hint at values shared by all interviewees: the importance of workplace flexibility; the significance of accessible and high-quality services; and the importance of rest and self-care.

Case examples

Seija-Reetta from Finland: working from home as a solution

For Seija-Reetta,[4] managing the family situation depended on the options available to her to manage her place of work, support from her employer and her attachment to work. She nevertheless reported several problems: unsupportive attitudes among her co-workers; a lack of time for her own personal interests; and unsuitable respite care. She saw her relationship ("partners naturally help one another") and her own ability to prioritise things as key to how she managed everyday life.

When Seija-Reetta was at work, she was concerned about the welfare of her partner, who was partly paralysed. She had been 'forced' to rethink what to do after he experienced a serious epileptic fit. Her solution was to apply to work from home for part of her working day. Before the epileptic fit, her husband had managed alone and she had come home in her lunch hour, but afterwards, what had been a short distance between her home and workplace seemed much further. She obtained permission to work from home, and stressed that negotiating this had been surprisingly easy; indeed, her employer had granted her wish immediately. This 'remote working' released her from continuous anxiety and enabled her to attend doctors' appointments with her partner during working hours and make the time up by working in the evenings. However, other problems arose: co-workers started to assume that she was only working in the mornings and made rude remarks.

When interviewed, Seija-Reetta said that she was not ready to take part-time retirement, as she enjoyed her work and the social contacts work brings. She and her husband had not considered formal home help, as they felt that helping each other was the natural thing for partners to do. Prioritising things, for example, compromising on the tidiness of the house, released time to relax. However, she stressed that their very limited informal care resources – one son lived far away and friends had disappeared once her husband became ill – meant that when she was travelling, her husband needed a place in respite care, although the lack of suitable places for people of working age was a problem. Consequently, Seija-Reetta found that caring was a tie. Travelling during annual holidays or trips associated with her personal interests always involved additional arrangements and she had given up participating in work-related evening training courses.

Berit from Sweden: relief through formal help and services

Berit's husband had moved to a group home at the time of interview. Her caring continued, but was now different. For Berit, publicly funded home care and the chance of a place in an assisted living facility were a way of coping with her circumstances. Her problems were linked to the family's financial difficulties arising from her husband's inability to continue working in his business, the need to reduce her own working hours and her husband's group home costs. She also found that other people's expectations caused additional stress.

Berit had worked in the same company for 25 years and when caring for her partner intensively, had reduced her working hours by half. This arrangement was made possible by a supportive employer, although she found it irritating that her boss defined her caregiving as a 'personal choice'. Before her husband became ill, Berit had also worked part-time in his business, but his illness had reduced the family income and they had been forced, in the end, to sell the firm. Nowadays, Berit said, most of her husband's pension went on his group home expenses, and their joint income was only half what it had been in the past. She could afford to continue living in her house following her husband's move only because she was able to increase her working hours.

When Berit first had formal home help she found it hard to have other people in her private home. She felt that she had to plan everything for the care workers, and keep her house tidy, as the workers were there only to take care of her husband. Despite this, she felt that she could not have handled the situation without their help and had not wanted to leave her partner alone for too many hours. Although her husband had been eligible for respite care, Berit felt that he was too young, compared to others using this facility, and had hated leaving him there. When his condition worsened, Berit had tried to find a group home more suitable to his age. She was very satisfied with the quality of the care he was receiving in the new living arrangement. However, she was not used to living alone. She visited her husband as often as possible and spent time with her daughter and her husband's daughter's family, but found her life rather empty. During this period, her work gave her both pleasure and feelings of continuity. However, other sources of resentment remained. Her partner's parents had been displeased when Berit arranged the long-term care facility for him and, she said, thought that she wanted to get rid of him, although what she really wanted was to maintain her husband's and her own well-being.

Conclusions

The starting point for the research reported here was the almost complete lack of previous research or policy debate on working partner-carers in Nordic countries. The care given by this group of carers was a 'blind spot' in how work and care are related. In Finland and Sweden, the carers interviewed faced quite similar challenges and had quite similar ways of managing these. Respondents stressed different aspects of the interface between work and care, however. The Finnish interviewees said little about financial problems, which were among the greatest challenges for the Swedish partner-carers. For both Finnish and Swedish interviewees, their lack of time for their own personal interests and for others close to them was a substantial problem. The accessibility and quality of publicly funded assistance was an important issue for carers in both countries. The Swedish interviewees had reduced their working hours, while the Finnish ones had rearranged their daily working hours and place of work.

Due to the different practices and resources of Finnish and Swedish municipalities, access to services varied (Larsson and Szebehely, 2006; Kröger, 2011). Opportunities for flexibility at work also varied, by type of work, employers' attitudes and local workplace cultures. In Sweden, municipalities are not legally obliged to pay carers – via Attendance

Allowance or Employment as a Family Carer – and in Finland, municipalities allocate Carer's Allowance and respite care only when budgets allow. Although a growing body of research is uncovering the unequal situation of carers (Saraceno, 2010; Häikiö and Anttonen, 2011; Leinonen, 2011b), it is clear that more work is needed to explore partner-care among Nordic women and men.

Working carers' life situations are all in some way unique and characterised by considerable diversity, yet their need for support and recognition is universal. All working carers deserve respect, an opportunity to organise suitable working hours, compensation for reduced working hours and high-quality services. Working partner-carers are no different from others in this sense and should have the chance to live their lives without their caregiving being stigmatised. However, some particular issues need to be taken into account when support and services are planned for them. First, home care needs to be sensitive to the family practices and routines of working-age people. Second, tailored respite care services for middle-aged and younger adults are needed. Third, good services and supportive work–life practices are necessary to ensure that carers can access some personal free time of their own. Paid work is highly valued in Nordic and European countries (Lewis, 2007), but although policies may support carers' participation in the labour market, their right to have time free from both paid and unpaid work is rarely acknowledged.

The analysis of the challenges and coping strategies of partner-carers hints at themes that are strong in the Nordic countries and that, historically, have differentiated Finland and Sweden from other welfare regimes: (1) participation in paid work is prioritised over full-time care by both sexes; (2) where the partner-carer is the primary carer, she/he expects to have assistance with personal care and long-term help from formal care providers rather than from children or other unpaid helpers (although children are expected to visit and to help occasionally or in a crisis); and (3) time for oneself and for personal interests is valued as an individual right, that is, it is considered important that the boundary between time devoted to care and time devoted to one's own interests should be protected.

Notes

[1] The Finnish interviews (n = 6) were conducted as part of the 'Working Carers and Caring Workers' (WoCaWo) research project in 2008/09 by Anu Leinonen. Anu Leinonen's contribution to this chapter was supported by a postdoctoral research grant from the Academy of Finland (grant number 131870). The Swedish interviews (n = 4) were conducted by Ann-Britt Sand

as part of the research project 'The Cost of Care: Caring Responsibilities and Gainful Employment in Middle Age'. This project is funded by the Swedish Research Council.

[2] A service voucher is a tax-free fixed sum that LAs can – if they so wish – grant to users and carers who are eligible for municipal services. In Finland, service vouchers are an alternative to municipal provision of services and are meant for purchasing services from for-profit providers (Mikkola, 2004).

[3] While a person over 65 may not become a user of personal assistance, he/ she retains this right if personal assistance was awarded at a younger age.

[4] All names have been changed.

References

Arksey, H. and Glendinning, C. (2008) 'Combining work and care: carers' decision-making in the context of competing policy pressures', *Social Policy and Administration*, vol 42, no 1, pp 1–18.

Autio, T. and Reivilä, S. (2005) *Tietoa työssäkäynnin ja omaishoidon yhteensovittamisesta* [*Information on reconciliation of work and care*], Helsinki: The Association of Care Giving Relatives and Friends.

Clark, S.C. (2000) 'Work/family border theory: a new theory of work/ family balance', *Human Relations*, vol 53, no 6, pp 740–70.

Försäkringskassan (2011) *Social insurance in figures 2011*, Stockholm: Swedish Social Insurance Agency.

Gautun, H. and Hagen, K. (2010) 'How do middle-aged employees combine work with caring for elderly parents?', *Community, Work and Family*, vol 13, no 4, pp 393–409.

Häikiö, L. and Anttonen, A. (2011) 'Local welfare governance structuring informal carers' dual position', *International Journal of Sociology and Social Policy*, vol 31, nos 3/4, pp 185–96.

Hayes, J., Boylstein, C. and Zimmerman, M.K. (2009) 'Living and loving with dementia: negotiating spousal and caregiver identity through narrative', *Journal of Aging Studies*, vol 23, no 1, pp 48–59.

Henz, U. (2010) 'Parent care as unpaid family labor: how do partners share?', *Journal of Marriage and Family*, vol 72, no 1, pp 148–64.

Jansson, W., Nordberg, G. and Grafström, M. (2001) 'Patterns of elderly partner caregiving in dementia care: an observational study', *Journal of Advanced Nursing*, vol 34, no 6, pp 804–12.

Kattainen, E., Muuri, A., Luoma, M.-L. and Voutilainen, P. (2008) 'Läheisapu ja sen merkitys kansalaisille' ['Informal help and its significance for citizens'], in P. Moisio, S. Karvonen, J. Simpura and M. Heikkilä (eds) *Suomalaisten hyvinvointi 2008*, Helsinki: National Research and Development Centre for Welfare and Health, pp 218–31.

Kauppinen, K. (2010) 'Who cares when grandmother gets sick? Ageing, employment and intergenerational family support in contemporary Europe', in T. Addabbo, M.-P. Arrizabalaga, C. Borderías and A. Owens (eds) *Households and well-being in modern Europe: gender, inequalities, work and consumption*, Farnham: Ashgate, pp 163–75.

Kauppinen, K. and Jolanki, O. (2012) 'Työn sekä omais- ja läheishoivan yhdistäminen – työssäjatkamisajatukset' ['Reconciling work and caregiving: to continue working or retire?'], in M. Perkiö-Mäkelä and T. Kauppinen (eds) *Työ, terveys ja työssäjatkamisajatukset*, Helsinki: Finnish Institute of Occupational Health, pp 133–56.

KELA (Kansaneläkelaitos, The Social Insurance Institution of Finland) (2012) *Guide for benefits*, Helsinki: KELA.

Kröger, T. (2011) 'Re-tuning the Nordic welfare municipality: central regulation of social care under change in Finland', *International Journal of Sociology and Social Policy*, vol 31, nos 3/4, pp 148–59.

Kröger, T. and Leinonen, A. (2012) 'Transformation by stealth: the retargeting of home care services in Finland', *Health and Social Care in the Community*, vol 20, no 3, pp 319–27.

Larsson, K. and Szebehely, M. (2006) 'Äldreomsorgens förändringar under de senaste decennnierna' ['Changes in elderly care in recent decades'], in J. Vogel (ed) *Äldres levnadsförhållanden*, Stockholm: SCB, pp 411–20.

Leinonen, A. (2011a) 'Masters of their own time? Working carers' visions of retirement', *European Journal of Ageing*, vol 8, no 4, pp 243–53.

Leinonen, A. (2011b) 'Informal family carers and lack of personal time: descriptions of being outside the sphere of formal help', *Nordic Social Work Research*, vol 1, no 2, pp 91–108.

Leinonen, A. (2011c) 'Adult children and parental caregiving: making sense of participation patterns among siblings', *Ageing and Society*, vol 30, no 2, pp 308–27.

Lewis, J. (2007) 'Gender, ageing and the "new social settlement": the importance of developing a holistic approach to care policies', *Current Sociology*, vol 55, no 2, pp 271–86.

Mahmood, A. and Martin-Matthews, A. (2008) 'Dynamics of carework: boundary management and relationship issues for home support workers and elderly clients', in A. Martin-Matthews and J.E. Phillips (eds) *Aging and caring at the intersection of work and home life: blurring the boundaries*, New York, NY, and London: LEA, pp 21–42.

Marvasti, A.B. (2003) *Qualitative research in sociology*, Thousand Oaks, CA: Sage.

Mikkola, H. (2004) 'Vouchers in social and health care', *Health Policy Monitor*, Issue 03. Available at: www.hpm.org/en/Surveys/THL_-_Finland/03/Vouchers_in_social_and_health_care.html

Mikkola, T. (2009) *Sinusta kiinni: Tutkimus puolisohoivan arjen toimijuuksista* [*Depending on you: a study of partner care, everyday life and agency*], Helsinki: Diak.

Mooney, A., Statham, J. and Simon, A. (2002) *The pivot generation: informal care and work after fifty*, Bristol: The Policy Press.

Mossberg Sand, A.-B. (2000) *Ansvar, kärlek och försörjning: Om anställda anhörigvårdare i Sverige* [*Responsibility, love and maintenance: on family carers employed as caregivers*], Göteborg: University of Göteborg.

Neal, M.B., Wagner, D.L., Bonn, K.J.B. and Niles-Yokum, K. (2008) 'Caring from a distance: contemporary care issues', in A. Martin-Matthews and J.E. Phillips (eds) *Aging and caring at the intersection of work and home life: blurring the boundaries*, New York, NY, and London: LEA, pp 107–28.

Phillips, J., Bernard, M. and Chittenden, M. (2002) *Juggling work and care: the experiences of working carers of older adults*, Bristol: The Policy Press.

Sand, A.-B. (2007) 'The value of the work: on payment for informal care', in I. Paoletti (ed) *Family caregiving to older disabled people: relational and institutional issues*, New York, NY: Nova Science Publisher, pp 295–317.

Sand, A.-B. (2010) *Anhöriga som kombinerar förvärvsarbete och anhörigomsorg: Kunskapsöversikt* [*Relatives combining paid work and family care: a literature overview*], Stockholm: National Family Competence Centre.

Saraceno, C. (2010) 'Social inequalities in facing old-age dependency: a bi-generational perspective', *Journal of European Social Policy*, vol 20, no 1, pp 32–44.

Socialstyrelsen (2011) *Swedish disability policy*, Stockholm: The National Board of Health and Welfare.

Sosiaaliportti (2012) 'Vammaispalvelun käsikirja' ['e-Handbook of disability services']. Available at: http://www.sosiaaliportti.fi/fi-FI/vammaispalvelujen-kasikirja

Szebehely, M. (2005a) 'Care as employment and welfare provision: child care and elder care in Sweden at the dawn of the 21st century', in H.M. Dahl and T. Rask Eriksen (eds) *Dilemmas of care in the Nordic welfare state*, Aldershot: Ashgate, pp 80–7.

Szebehely, M. (2005b) 'Anhörigas betalda och obetalda äldreomsorgsinsatser' ['Unpaid and paid old-age care'], in *Forskarrapporter till Jämställdhetspolitiska utredningen*, Stockholm: Fritzes, pp 133–203.

Szebehely, M. and Trydegård, G.-B. (2012) 'Home care for older people in Sweden: a universal model in transition', *Health and Social Care in the Community*, vol 20, no 3, pp 300–9.

Vilkko, A., Muuri, A. and Finne-Soveri, H. (2010) 'Läheisapu iäkkään ihmisen arjessa' ['Informal help in the everyday life of older persons'], in M. Vaarama, P. Moisio and S. Karvonen (eds) *Suomalaisten hyvinvointi 2010*, Helsinki: National Institute for Health and Welfare, pp 104–33.

Voutilainen, P., Kattainen, E. and Heinola, R. (2007) *Omaishoidon tuki sosiaalipalveluna: Selvitys omaishoidon tuesta ja sen vaihteluista 1994–2006* [*Support for informal care as a social service: a study of support for informal care and variations in it in 1994–2006*], Helsinki: The Ministry of Social Affairs and Health.

TEN

'In sickness and in health' and beyond: reconciling work and care for a partner in Australia and England

Gary Fry, Cathy Thomson and Trish Hill

Introduction

This chapter examines the issue of combining paid work with the care of a disabled or seriously ill partner in England and Australia. It begins by outlining the prevalence and characteristics of partner-carers of working age in each country, using survey data on their demographic characteristics, participation in paid employment, the services and welfare benefits they access, their reasons for leaving paid work, and their future employment plans. Case studies are then used to illustrate the challenges faced by partner-carers in trying to reconcile their caring and employment roles in the English and Australian contexts, and recent policy developments in each country and their implications for this group of carers are discussed. The chapter concludes by considering the effectiveness of the support available to partner-carers and the implications of the evidence available for future policy development.

Partner-carers: prevalence and characteristics

England

In 2001, the Census of Population showed that England and Wales had 5.2 million carers (ONS, 2003: 8). Survey data suggest that around one fifth to one quarter of all carers care for a partner, figures ranging from 18% (Maher and Green, 2002) to 26% (NHSIC, 2010). A survey of working-age carers in Great Britain in 2007 found that half of those caring for a partner were men, a much higher percentage than for carers of other people (Yeandle et al, 2007a).

Partner-carers emerge consistently as one of the three largest groups of carers, along with carers of a sick or disabled child and carers of a parent, and tend to be older than other carers. Ross et al (2008) found that 39% of carers over the age of 52 were caring for a partner, their average age being 68 (men) and 67 (women), while Yeandle et al's (2007a) study of carers of working age found that among 504 partner-carers, 60% were aged 50 to 64.

Partner-carers have especially heavy care responsibilities. In the latter study, 86% cared for an average of 20 hours per week (compared with 79% of other carers) and 63% for 50 or more hours per week (compared with 57%). That study also found that two thirds of partner-carers had been caring for at least five years. Official surveys in both 2000 and 2009/10 also showed that partner-carers had high weekly hours of care (Maher and Green, 2002; NHSIC, 2010).

These demanding roles are almost certainly linked to co-residence, as most partner-carers live with the person they care for. The 2001 Census showed that 48% of carers lived in the same household as someone with a long-term limiting illness (Buckner and Yeandle, 2008) and subsequent national surveys have shown that just over half of co-resident carers are caring for their partner (Maher and Green, 2002; NHSIC, 2010).

Yeandle et al (2007a) found that two thirds of working-age partner-carers supported someone with a physical disability (66%) and just over half (54%) cared for someone with a long-term or terminal illness, figures that were far higher than for other carers. Their study also found that 44% of partner-carers cared for someone who was frail or had limited mobility, 27% for someone with a mental health problem, 19% for someone with a sensory impairment, and 9% for a partner with dementia.

Despite providing high levels of care, 58% of working-age partner-carers in Yeandle et al's (2007a) study had paid jobs and they were more likely than other carers in the study to work full-time (34%, compared with 25%). Over half of working partner-carers said that their employer was carer-friendly (58%) and two thirds felt that they had the support of family and friends (67%). However, only a minority (23%) said that their caring did not affect their work and just 28% felt that they had adequate services to support them in combining work and care. The financial circumstances of partner-carers in the study were similar to those of other carers: 30% were 'struggling' financially; 30% were 'managing to get by'; and 35% described themselves as financially 'reasonably comfortable'.

The employment status of these carers compared with that of people caring for 50 or more hours per week as recorded in the 2001 Census of Population is shown in Table 10.1.

Table 10.1: Employment status of carers of working age in Great Britain, partner-carers and all carers by gender (%)

Data described[a]	Working full-time	Working part-time	Self-employed	Seeking work	Looking after home or family	Other
Women						
Partner-carers (CES, 2007; n = 307)	32	22	3	1	24	18
All other carers (CES, 2007; n = 990)	23	26	4	3	30	14
All caring 50+ hrs/week (2001 Census for England and Wales; n = 408,330)	13	18	4	2	45	18
Men						
Partner-carers (CES, 2007; n = 162)	38	17	4	1	24	16
All other carers (CES, 2007; n = 143)	35	12	3	7	25	18
All caring 50+ hrs/week (2001 Census for England and Wales; n = 262,276)	33	3	9	5	20	30

Notes: [a] Most carers in the CES data set provided 50+ weekly hours of care (Yeandle et al, 2007b: 7, Figure 2.3). Data from the 2001 Census for England and Wales for people 'caring 50+ hours per week' are presented for comparative purposes. It is not possible to distinguish partner-carers from other carers in Census data as relevant questions were not asked. As shown, CES data *over-represents* female carers employed full-time and male carers employed part-time and *under-represents* self-employed male carers and female carers looking after home and family.

Sources: 2001 Census data, Buckner and Yeandle (2006: 8, Table 4), derived from Census Commissioned Tables, Crown Copyright (2004), and special analysis of CES data for this chapter (for a description of the CES data, collected from carers in England, Scotland and Wales, see Yeandle and Buckner [2007: 49–55]).

The needs of working-age partner-carers in England have not otherwise been extensively studied. Most published research on this group – in England and elsewhere – focuses on the needs of older people caring for a partner with a particular condition (typically, dementia/Alzheimer's disease; stroke; Parkinson's disease; multiple sclerosis; or spinal/muscular disorders). Studies of these carers show them to have: lower socio-economic status than other carers (Llacer et al, 2002); heavier carer duties, giving rise to strain (Blake et al, 2003); and restricted recreational/social lives (O'Reilly et al, 1996; Wright et al, 1999). They also experience emotional difficulties linked to the care they give (Dickson et al, 2010) and strain on the couple relationship (Shim et al, 2011). Ross et al (2008) found that compared with non-carers, partner-carers aged 50 or older with demanding caring roles – including those who were employees – had lower incomes and less family wealth, took fewer holidays, and were less likely to belong to clubs or other recreational groups.

These data suggest that partner-carers experience negative impacts affecting their financial, social and physical welfare. This almost certainly arises from their typically long-term, demanding caring roles, the difficulties they have in reconciling work and care, and their limited opportunities for recreation, breaks and holidays.

Australia

Australia's 2009 Survey of Disability, Ageing and Carers (SDAC) identified 529,000 working-age partner-carers – 27% of all carers of working age – comprising an almost equal number of men and women (ABS, 2011). It also identified 188,000 'primary' partner-carers, who constituted the largest group of working-age primary carers (34%). Just over half (55%) of this group were women. As in England, partner-carers in Australia tend to be older: 70% of working-age partner-carers were over 45, and over 40% were aged 55–64, although there were few gender differences in their age profiles (ABS, 2011).

The evident late onset of caring roles for partner-carers may increase their vulnerability as older workers in the labour market, and time spent caring will affect labour force participation. Among working-age primary carers, nearly half the partner-carers spent less than 20 hours per week providing care, but around 20% cared for 20–40 hours per week and a third intensively (40+ hours per week). Across all age groups, women were more likely than men to provide intensive levels of care (ABS, 2011). Since other research has shown that many carers do not recognise the support they give to a partner as 'care', these figures may be underestimates (Bittman and Thomson, 2000).

The duration of the caring role has implications for career progression and financial security (Thomson et al, 2008). In general, female partner-carers had provided care over a longer period of time than males: among primary partner-carers, 58% of men and 63% of women had been caring for five years or more (ABS, 2011).

Partner-carers in Australia, as in England, tend to provide high levels of support because they are likely to live with the person for whom they care. The SDAC data show that nearly half of all carers, and over 90% of primary carers, assisted a spouse with a profound or severe limitation. Most primary partner-carers (73%) supported a person with a head injury, stroke or other brain damage and 15% cared for a person with mental illness (ABS, 2011).

Among those of working age, partner-carers were less likely to be employed full-time, or employed at all, than both other carers and non-carers (see Table 10.2), and those aged 55–64 were less likely to be employed than their younger counterparts (ABS, 2011). Underscoring the intensity of caring roles for primary carers, a lower proportion of primary carers were employed compared to other partner-carers.

Table 10.2: Employment status of carers in Australia by gender and carer type, 2009 (%)

	Employed full-time	Employed part-time	Total employed	Non-employed
Men				
Primary partner-carers	42	16	57	43
Other primary carers	43	13	56	44
All partner-carers	58	12	71	29
All other carers	62	12	74	26
Non-carers	68	14	82	18
Women				
Primary partner-carers	11	25	35	65
Other primary carers	23	31	54	46
All partner-carers	20	28	48	52
All other carers	31	35	66	34
Non-carers	37	33	71	30

Source: ABS (2011), authors' calculations.

In view of partner-carers' lower rates of participation in employment, it is not surprising that they were twice as likely overall to live in financially disadvantaged households (compared with both other carers and with non-carers). Two fifths of male partner-carers and nearly half of female partner-carers lived in households with income in the bottom two quintiles of the household income distribution (ABS, 2011). Caring had negatively affected the finances of many primary carers: one third said that their income had decreased because of caring; one in five had additional expenses; and almost half (43%) reported difficulty meeting everyday living costs. The main unmet need – identified by 14% of employed and non-employed working-age primary partner-carers – was for more financial assistance (ABS, 2011).

There is solid Australian evidence that caring can adversely affect employment due to the difficulties of reconciling work and care (Edwards et al, 2008; Thomson et al, 2008). Among employed primary partner-carers, 28% needed time off at least once a week to care for their partner and 30% had changed their working hours since commencing caring. Around one quarter of primary partner-carers were not employed when surveyed but had worked prior to taking on their caring role (ABS, 2011). Carers who had left their jobs said that their main reasons for dropping out of paid work were a preference for caring full-time and a need to fulfil emotional obligations. Other factors included workplace arrangements, financial considerations and a lack of alternative care arrangements.

Among primary partner-carers, about 30% had not been in paid work prior to becoming a carer or were permanently unable to work. Over a quarter of non-employed primary partner-carers said that they would like to work, however (ABS, 2011). Perceived barriers to re-entering the workforce while caring included: a lack of alternative care arrangements; disruption to the care recipient; difficulty in arranging working hours; loss of skills due to being out of the workforce; and age.

Limited research is available in Australia specifically focusing on partner-carers and how they reconcile work and care. Consistent with findings in English and international studies (O'Reilly et al, 1996; Cannuscio et al, 2004; Pinquart and Sörensen, 2011), qualitative research in Australia has indicated that partner-carers' caring role may impact on their health (Cahill and Shapiro, 1998), their participation in employment (Cahill and Shapiro, 1998) and the timing of their retirement (Watson, 2003).

The profile of Australian partner-carers in many ways mirrors that seen in England. Generally, these carers provide intensive levels of care over prolonged periods. This adversely affects their economic, employment and social participation and has far-reaching implications for their financial security, health and well-being. The support and services available to partner-carers are the focus of the next section of the chapter.

Services and support for carers of a disabled or seriously ill partner

There are currently no policies or services in England specifically designed to meet the particular needs of partner-carers. Nevertheless, this group of carers has the same access to policies and initiatives as is available to carers in general (described in *Chapter Two*). These include: Carer's Allowance (CA), which can be combined with part-time work; the right to request flexible working, subject to employer agreement; and direct payments, which small numbers of carers have used to help them manage work and care. Services that their partner may need, subject to a minimum level of assessed need, can be accessed through their local authority (LA). Much of this support is means-tested, however, so service users may have to pay, or co-pay, for it, and those with assets above a certain level may not be eligible for publicly funded support.

Yeandle et al's (2007a) survey showed that about 40% of the partner-carers studied spent their own private resources on the services their partner required, while 37% said that services were received for which there was no charge; about 12% had a partner with a direct payment in place (figures that varied only slightly from those for all carers). A quarter of partner-carers (26%) said that there was home care support in place in their caring situation and 20% said that their partner attended a day centre, but few (10%) had access to carers' breaks or 'respite' services.

A study of CA claimants in 2010 (Fry et al, 2011) found that some partner-carers preferred not to use formal care services, either because they felt that they did 'a better job' than home care workers or because their partner did not wish anyone else to provide care (a finding also reported in Nordic countries, see *Chapter Nine*). Others had been unable to access support through their LA as, in most localities, services were available only to those with needs assessed as 'substantial' or 'critical'.[1]

Recognition of the needs of carers in Australia, in legislation and through Carers' Action Plans, Carers' Charters and the National Carers' Strategy (see *Chapter Two*), is more recent than in England. At the national level, no legally enforceable responsibilities or obligations currently exist, although the National Employment Standards (NES), as set out in the Fair Work Act 2009, aim to assist employees to better manage work and care. The NES established a minimum entitlement for several categories of paid and unpaid leave, including carers' leave

(FWO, 2009). As in England, there is no legislation specifically designed to support partner-carers. In 2012, the Australian government was reviewing the Fair Work Act 2009, amid calls to expand the right to request flexibility to include other carers, such as partner-carers.

According to the 2009 SDAC, employed partner-carers use a variety of workplace arrangements to reconcile their work and care responsibilities (ABS, 2011). In the previous six months, one fifth had accessed paid leave, such as recreational leave or personal leave, 16% had used flexible working hours, 10% had used unpaid leave, and 8% had had an informal arrangement with their employer (carers may have used more than one of these arrangements). Other workplace arrangements used included rostered days off, working from home and part-time hours. Of employed partner-carers, 10% indicated that they would like to use more workplace arrangements to assist them in their caring role, but 57% had not accessed any workplace arrangement to assist them to provide support at home.

A similar picture emerges with respect to income support and services for partner-carers. Carer Payment (CP) and CA are the main sources of income support for Australian carers but do not target partners, and CP is available only to those in paid employment for 25 hours per week or less (see *Chapter Two*). Among primary carers, 27% of those supporting a partner received CP, compared with 20% of other primary carers (ABS, 2011). No services are specifically designed to meet the needs of partner-carers, but their households can access a range of support services through the Home and Community Care (HACC) programme (DoHA, 2011a).

Research shows that carers' use of services in Australia is low (Edwards et al, 2008) due to costs, inflexibility and lack of access (Thomson et al, 2008) and that most working-age primary partner-carers had never used respite care (96%, compared with 85% for other primary carers) (ABS, 2011).

Reconciliation of paid work and family life for partner-carers

Seeking or sustaining paid work is clearly challenging for partner-carers in both countries, and employment opportunities have been shown to be reduced for adults providing care to someone living in their own home (Arber and Ginn, 1995). Partner-carers are more likely than other carers to be co-resident, to provide many weekly hours of care over long periods and to access only limited support services.

Yeandle et al's study of carers in Great Britain, including England, included a number of qualitative interviews with carers, including 44 people who were caring for a seriously ill or disabled partner (Yeandle and Buckner, 2007). Three cases from that research are summarised here to highlight some of the issues encountered by partner-carers who wished to combine paid work and care.[2]

Case examples from Britain

John

John, in his 40s, had been caring for his wife, who had been diagnosed with multiple sclerosis, for five years. He had agreed flexible working arrangements with his employer, but relied on his mother-in-law to help care for his wife and enable him to continue in work. John needed to remain employed because his wife (who had not been in paid work before her illness) was not eligible for contributory sickness benefits. As his mother-in-law grew older, John became uncertain about how long she could continue providing this support. He wanted to work until retirement age but feared that he would need to leave his job to care for his wife, a situation that he felt would 'reduce him to poverty'.

Combining full-time work with caring for his wife was only possible for John with the additional help of a relative. Without this, he said that he would need to give up his job and try to arrange a formal support package for his wife. Although his employer had agreed a flexible working arrangement, her care needs were too complex and demanding for him to manage without additional support. This problem may be widespread, as several studies report that limited access to services is more important in causing carers to leave work than difficulty in accessing flexible working arrangements (Yeandle and Buckner, 2007; Fry et al, 2011).

John also found his role difficult because he sometimes felt uncomfortable providing the personal care his wife needed. Other studies have shown that men may find it especially difficult to offer personal care (such as bathing and dressing) as it can conflict with traditional masculine behaviour (Graham, 1983). While Ungerson (1987) claimed that the taboo against 'cross-sex caring' in Western cultures does not commonly apply to married couples, Parker (1993) argued that this type of care may nonetheless cause tensions between husbands and wives.

Arnold

Arnold, in his 50s, cared for his wife who experienced mental illness. He had left his well-paid, full-time job to care for her. To bring in income, he found local work as an 'odd job' man and claimed CA, but felt frustrated that his earnings had to be kept low to avoid losing this allowance. Arnold spoke of feeling exhausted and incompetent as a carer and guilty about being unable to provide financial support for his teenage sons at university. Despite having his own needs reviewed (through a LA carer's assessment), he did not consider the support offered suitable and felt that mental health conditions were poorly understood within the health and social care system.

Arnold's care affected more than his relationship with his wife: being unable to provide for his sons at university meant that he also felt bad about himself as a father. Being restricted to working locally (in case of a caring emergency), he felt that he had little choice but to claim welfare benefits, even though the combination of these and his reduced earnings was insufficient to cover his mortgage payments and bills.

Because the earnings threshold for CA claimants effectively limits them to part-time work, many carers receiving CA feel that they are restricted to low-paid, low-skilled jobs. In Fry et al's (2011) study, a quarter of CA claimants were partner-carers. They included both men (44%) and women (56%), and 90% were people of working age. With demanding caring roles, many of these carers had given up well-paid jobs and accepted lower-level positions despite their experience and qualifications, as Arnold had done.

Jennifer

Some partner-carers manage to remain in paid employment with the support of a direct payment to the person they care for (Yeandle and Stiell, 2007).[3] This option, still used in only a minority of cases, provides cash in place of services, and greater flexibility. Jennifer's knowledge of this, as well as her capacity to operate the scheme, enabled her to retain her job.

In her 40s, Jennifer cared for her husband, who required constant attendance following a stroke. Her job as a part-time schoolteacher was important to her and she did not want to give it up. Following a needs assessment, Jennifer's husband was allocated a direct payment by the LA, enabling the couple to directly employ home care workers of their choice. Despite early difficulties with administering the direct payment and the technical aspects of employing staff, Jennifer was able to retain her job, although she experienced using direct payments as quite challenging, mentioning that anyone lacking her skills would find this very difficult.

Case examples from Australia

The Australian case examples presented here are drawn from focus groups undertaken for the *Negotiating caring and employment* project in 2005 (Thomson et al, 2008; see also *Chapter One*). They highlight the diverse circumstances of partner-carers and their varied attempts to reconcile work and care, and show that the complex nature of a couple's relationship – even before care needs arise – can accentuate the difficulties encountered. The couples described had to acknowledge changes in their relationship, increased dependency and the need for formal services. Denial of need and a lack of formal and informal support can prevent carers from balancing the competing demands of family, care and job, and can lead to reduced working hours or leaving employment. Australian data suggest a significant group of primary partner-carers (43%) did not have a fallback carer to assist them in their role (ABS, 2011).

For many partner-carers, trying to combine often-conflicting caring and employment roles can lead to high levels of carer strain, increased stress and poor health. Maya, described in the following, had found the competing demands of care and employment over a prolonged period too burdensome and eventually left paid work.

Maya

Maya, in her early 60s, cared for her husband, who had a long-term mental illness, cardiac disease and diabetes. Maya had combined caring and employment for over 10 years but left paid work due to exhaustion and the difficulties of balancing multiple responsibilities, particularly as her husband's level of need increased. She stated:

> "You're both the housekeeper, the gardener. You're everything, plus you hold down a full-time job.... I used to get up about 5.30 to 6 o'clock ... prepare breakfast or sort out clothes or whatever ... and then you come home in the evening and you're either washing, cleaning, cooking and doing those sorts of things. So, one of the things for me was that it was like doing two full-time jobs all the time."

Although her workplace was fairly sympathetic towards her care responsibilities, Maya felt obliged not to take too much time off. She did not access carer's leave but instead used her own annual leave entitlement, as she did not want to be perceived as taking advantage of her situation. She did not seek help from formal services until she reached a crisis and had to leave work. After this, Maya felt isolated and missed the intellectual stimulation, social interaction and income work had given her. When interviewed, she was in contact with counselling services. She felt that if she had accessed support earlier, she might have remained in employment.

Maya's situation shows that without adequate support from accessible and appropriate support services, working carers can find it difficult to sustain employment, even when they value their work. Despite working in an environment sympathetic to her care situation and being able to access carer's leave, Maya was reluctant to take time off. If work–family balance was promoted for all employees, carers like her might more readily use the flexible options available.

Brad

The difficulties faced by partner-carers with multiple care responsibilities are evident in Brad's case. Brad, in his 40s, had left work to care for his wife, who had a mental illness and was not coping with caring for their 10-year-old autistic child. He hoped to return to work in the coming year if his wife's health improved. While employed, he had found juggling work and care responsibilities increasingly difficult. The unpredictable nature of his wife's illness meant that he could not plan when he needed to take time off. His working conditions were not flexible. He had found it hard to ring in and explain his situation to his employer and ask for time off. Leaving work resulted in financial hardship for the family, despite receiving CP. He had delayed applying for income support until they "didn't have any money for the week" due to the onerous bureaucratic processes involved.

Brad's care situation highlights the problems faced by an employed partner-carer with unpredictable care needs and an unsympathetic and inflexible workplace. Access to flexible working arrangements and a sense of job security have been shown to be important in supporting carers to stay in employment (Hill et al, 2008). Brad's circumstances also starkly illustrate the financial consequences of leaving employment and having to rely on income support. The financial difficulties associated with care are also evident in Jane's situation.

Jane

Jane cared for her husband, who had a degenerative neurological disease. The couple lived in a small regional town where Jane, in her 50s, was self-employed and worked from home. Her working hours were flexible but she had reduced them to accommodate her increasing care responsibilities. The family was financially secure and she received CA. They had extended their house and built a disabled access bedroom and bathroom to meet her husband's needs. They incurred substantial costs associated with travelling to the city for medical appointments and treatment. Jane was aware of available support services in the region but had not accessed them, mostly due to her husband's desire to remain as independent as possible, even though he depended on her for almost all his care needs. She worried about the future, often staying up late or waking early in the morning unable to sleep. Her situation was, she said, "on my mind 24/7".

Recent policy developments affecting partner-carers

As explained in *Chapter Two*, some additional carers' services were developed in England in the 2000s following national commitments made in successive National Carers' Strategies (in 1999, 2008 and 2010). These provided some additional resources for local services, including some England-wide developments, such as a training programme (Caring with Confidence) and 'demonstrator sites', where partnerships between health, social care and voluntary agencies offered carers health and well-being support. When these time-limited programmes were evaluated (Yeandle and Wigfield, 2011, 2012), they showed that nearly half the carers who accessed them were partner-carers. Both programmes helped some carers pursue employment opportunities. Other developments during the 2000s included 'Carers Direct', a national helpline offering carers telephone and web-based support and advice. For carers seeking paid work, help to access local employment support schemes was also made available in some, but far from all, localities. This offered training and guidance on applying for jobs, in some cases, with financial support to purchase replacement care while carers attended job interviews or vocational training (Fry et al, 2009). Some LAs install 'telecare' packages, including emergency alarms and household sensors, in the homes of sick or disabled people, and these have been shown to help some carers retain or seek paid work by providing reassurance, 'peace of mind' and a safer home environment (Jarrold and Yeandle, 2009).

Successive governments have pursued a policy goal of 'personalising' care and support in England (DH, 2010). This approach claims to offer service users and carers choice, control and dignity and seeks to help sick and disabled people remain at home with appropriate support for as long as possible. English LAs now offer 'cash-for-care' options in the form of 'personal' or 'individual' budgets and 'direct payments', which are expected to play a greater role in the future, both for service users and their carers. While these initiatives still reach only a small minority of carers, by facilitating care delivered in the home, supporting carers to have 'a life of their own' and developing carers' confidence in seeking leisure, educational or employment opportunities, they could in future have a positive impact on partner-carers.

A recent policy initiative relevant to partner-carers in Australia is Consumer Directed Care (CDC). This includes Consumer Directed Respite Care (CDRC), which aims to give carers more control over the design and delivery of respite services. The programme targets carers of frail older people and older people who are carers, however, and is not specifically designed to support partner-carers of working age. While its implications for partner-carers are yet to be investigated, it also has the potential to give them greater control over the types of services accessed (DoHA, 2011b).

The funding and policy development for the HACC programme in Australia is also changing. The Commonwealth (national) government became responsible for the policy and funding of HACC aged care services for people aged 65+ (50+ for Indigenous Australians) from mid-2011 and for the administration of this programme from 2012. Australia's state and territory governments are responsible for basic community care services for people aged under 65 (under 50 for Indigenous Australians) (DoHA, 2011a). It is too early to speculate on how this will affect partner-carers, as they do not fit precisely into either age category and it is possible that their needs may yet again be overlooked. Similarly, the impact of the proposed National Disability Insurance Scheme on partner-carers (see *Chapter Two*) cannot be predicted. A scheme of this type may provide care recipients with significant new support, however, and has possible implications for supporting partner-carers to remain in or re-enter employment.

Discussion

Partner-carers in England and Australia display a number of similarities with respect to their age and gender profiles. In both countries, partner-carers constitute the largest group of working-age carers, yet there are few policies that aim to address their specific needs. This oversight is particularly salient given that in both countries, workforce activation policies identify mature-age workers as a key group whose employment retention or re-entry needs to be encouraged.

Many partner-carers provide intensive levels of care over protracted periods and the negative impact of partner-caring on employment participation is highlighted by their relatively low employment rates. Loss of jobs, reduced income and increased stress impact on couples at a time when the illness or disability of one partner is creating fundamental changes in the nature of their relationship and future aspirations for retirement. In both countries, there is relatively little research or policy discourse around the care, employment careers, financial security and well-being trajectories of partner-carers.

Partner-carers in both countries employ a range of strategies to reconcile caring and employment roles. Some reduce hours to part-time employment, adopt flexible working practices, take paid or unpaid leave, or negotiate informal arrangements with employers, although little is known about the support available to them in their workplaces.

In both countries, partner-carers make modest use of services available to all carers as they attempt to reconcile work and care, although income support payments for carers place restrictions on permitted earnings or hours of employment. The implementation of new 'personalisation' and 'self-directed support' initiatives may create opportunities to address the needs of this large and particularly strained group of carers, many of whom wish to access or remain in employment, although neither country has policies specifically targeting partner-carers as yet. The success of such initiatives thus depends on the extent to which the needs of this overlooked group can be articulated and recognised within the spheres of policy and public discourse.

Notes
[1] The Department of Health (DH) issues guidance to English LAs on 'Fair Access to Care Services' (FACS), which defines four levels of care need; 'low', 'moderate', 'substantial' and 'critical'. LAs may decide the level of need they will meet using public funds, but must apply locally agreed criteria to all local residents equally (DH, 2003).

[2] All names are pseudonyms.

[3] LAs may also make direct payments to carers in their own right, although this happens less often (Clements, 2005: 37–8).

References

ABS (Australian Bureau of Statistics) (2011) *Disability, ageing and carers Australia: basic Confidentialised Unit Record File* (CURF, Release 3 CD-ROM), Canberra: ABS.

Arber, S. and Ginn, J. (1995) 'Gender differences in the relationship between paid employment and informal care', *Work, Employment and Society*, vol 9, no 3, pp 445–71.

Bittman, M. and Thomson, C. (2000) 'Invisible support: the determinants of time spent in informal care', in J. Warburton and M. Oppenheimer (eds) *Volunteers and volunteering*, Sydney: Federation Press, pp 98–112.

Blake, H., Lincoln, N.B. and Clarke, D.D. (2003) 'Caregiver strain in spouses of stroke patients', *Clinical Rehabilitation*, vol 17, no 3, pp 312–17.

Buckner, L. and Yeandle, S. (2006) *Who cares wins: the social and business benefits of supporting working carers: statistical analysis – working carers, evidence from the 2001 Census*, London: Carers UK.

Buckner, L. and Yeandle, S. (2008) 'Analysis of 2001 Census of Population for the Department of Health's pre-publication impact assessment of the National Carers' Strategy 2008', unpublished report, University of Leeds, Leeds.

Cahill, S. and Shapiro, M. (1998) '"The only one you neglect is yourself": health outcomes for carers of spouses or parents with dementia, do wives and daughter carers differ?', *Journal of Family Studies*, vol 4, no 1, pp 87–101.

Cannuscio, C., Colditz G., Rimm, E., Berkman, L., Jones, C. and Kawachi, I (2004) 'Employment status, social ties, and caregivers' mental health', *Social Science and Medicine*, vol 58, no 7, pp 1247–56.

Clements, L. (2005) *Carers and their rights: the law relating to carers*, London: Carers UK.

DH (Department of Health) (2003) *Fair Access to Care Services: guidance on eligibility criteria for adult social care*, London: DH.

DH (2010) *A vision for adult social care: capable communities and active citizens*, London: DH.

Dickson, A., O'Brien, G., Ward, R., Allan, D. and O'Carroll, R. (2010) 'The impact of assuming the primary caregiver role following traumatic spinal cord injury: an interpretative phenomenological analysis of the spouse's experience', *Psychology and Health*, vol 25, no 9, pp 1101–20.

DoHA (Department of Health and Ageing) (2011a) *General information on Home and Community Care (HACC) transition frequently asked questions (FAQs)*, Canberra: DoHA.

DoHA (2011b) *Consumer directed care*, Canberra: DoHA.

Edwards, B., Higgins, D., Gray, M., Zmijewski, N.A. and Kingston, M. (2008) *The nature and impact of caring for family members with a disability in Australia*, Melbourne: Australian Institute of Family Studies.

Fry, G., Price, C. and Yeandle, S. (2009) *Local authorities' use of Carers' Grant*, London: DH.

Fry, G., Singleton, B., Yeandle, S. and Buckner, L. (2011) *Developing a clearer understanding of the Carer's Allowance claimant group*, London: DWP.

FWO (Fair Work Ombudsman) (2009) *Factsheet: personal/carer's leave and compassionate leave and the National Employment Standards*, Canberra: Commonwealth of Australia.

Graham, H. (1983) 'Caring: a labour of love', in J. Finch and D. Groves (eds) *A labour of love: women, work and caring*, London: Routledge and Kegan Paul, pp 13–31.

Hill, T., Thomson, C., Bittman, M. and Griffiths, M. (2008) 'What kinds of jobs help carers combine care and employment?', *Family Matters*, no 80, pp 27–32.

Jarrold, K. and Yeandle, S. (2009) *'A weight off my mind': exploring the impact and potential benefits of telecare for unpaid carers in Scotland*, Glasgow: Carers Scotland.

Llacer, A., Zunzunegui, M.V., Gutierrez-Cuadra, P., Beland, F. and Zarit, S.H. (2002) 'Correlates of well-being of spousal and children carers of disabled people over 65 in Spain', *European Journal of Public Health*, vol 12, no 1, pp 3–9.

Maher, J. and Green, H. (2002) *Carers 2000*, London: The Stationery Office.

NHSIC (NHS Information Centre) (2010) *Survey of carers in households 2009/10*, London: The NHS Information Centre for health and social care. Available at: http://www.ic.nhs.uk/pubs/carersurvey0910

ONS (Office for National Statistics) (2003) *Census 2001: commentaries by theme and region*, London: ONS.

O'Reilly, F., Finnan, F., Allwright, S., Smith, G.D. and Ben-Shlomo, Y. (1996) 'The effects of caring for a spouse with Parkinson's disease on social, psychological and physical well-being', *British Journal of General Practice*, vol 46, no 410, pp 507–12.

Parker, G. (1993) *With this body: caring and disability in marriage*, Buckingham: Open University Press.

Pinquart, M. and Sörensen, S. (2011) 'Spouses, adult children, and children-in-law as caregivers of older adults: a meta-analytic comparison', *Psychology and Aging*, vol 26, no 1, pp 1–14.

Ross, A., Lloyd, J., Weinhardt, M. and Cheshire, H. (2008) *Living and caring? An investigation of the experiences of older carers*, London: National Centre for Social Research on behalf of ICL-UK.

Shim, B., Landerman, L.R. and Davis, L.L. (2011) 'Correlates of care relationship mutuality among carers of people with Alzheimer's and Parkinson's disease', *Journal of Advanced Nursing*, vol 67, no 8, pp 1729–38.

Thomson, C., Hill, T., Griffiths, M. and Bittman, M. (2008) *Negotiating caring and employment*, Sydney: Social Policy Research Centre, University of New South Wales.

Ungerson, C. (1987) *Policy is personal: sex, gender, and informal care*, London: Tavistock.

Watson, E.A. (2003) 'I'm just doing it: a study of men caring for partners with MS', PhD thesis, University of New South Wales, Sydney.

Wright, L.K., Hickey, J.V., Buckwalter, K.C., Hendrix, S.A. and Kelechi, T. (1999) 'Emotional and physical health of spouse caregivers of persons with Alzheimer's disease and stroke', *Journal of Advanced Nursing*, vol 30, no 3, pp 552–63.

Yeandle, S. and Buckner, L. (2007) *Carers, employment and services: time for a new social contract?*, CES Report Series No 6, London: Carers UK.

Yeandle, S. and Stiell, B. (2007) 'Issues in the development of the Direct Payment Scheme for older people in England', in C. Ungerson and S. Yeandle (eds) *Cash for care in developed welfare states*, Basingstoke: Palgrave Macmillan, pp 104–36.

Yeandle, S. and Wigfield, A. (eds) (2011) *New approaches to supporting carers' health and well-being: evidence from the National Carers' Strategy Demonstrator Sites programme*, Leeds: CIRCLE, University of Leeds.

Yeandle, S. and Wigfield, A. (eds) (2012) *Training and supporting carers: the national evaluation of the Caring with Confidence programme*, Leeds: CIRCLE, University of Leeds.

Yeandle, S., Bennett, C., Buckner, L., Fry, G. and Price, C. (2007a) *Diversity in caring: towards equality for carers*, London: Carers UK.

Yeandle, S., Bennett, C., Buckner, L., Fry, G. and Price, C. (2007b) *Managing caring and employment*, London: Carers UK.

ELEVEN

Partner-care in the East Asian system: combining paid work and caring in Japan and Taiwan

Mei-Chun Liu and Machiko Osawa

Introduction

Although partner-care is one of the main types of caring in Japan and Taiwan, it has received less research attention than other forms of caring. In both countries, a rapidly ageing population and a sharply decreasing birth rate pose challenges for care systems that have long been and remain primarily family-based. Working-age partners with dual work and caring roles often encounter real hardship. This chapter examines their current situation and the challenges they face, using case examples from qualitative research from both countries to exemplify inadequacies in the present system and the urgency of overhauling current arrangements.

Working and caring for a partner

Partner-carers in Japan

In Japan, caring is a topic receiving increasing attention, as already noted in this book. The number of people needing care has increased from 2.5 million in 2000 to 4.8 million in 2009 (MHLW, 2009) and almost half of all carers (44%) while caring for family members are also working (MIAC, 2006). Some 144,000 people left their jobs to provide care for a family member in 2006, an increase of 160% from 2002 (JIWE, 2011). Most were people in their 50s and 60s – and many were women – but an increasing number of men are leaving their jobs to care for family members too (Tsutome and Saito, 2007).

In Table 11.1, data on the relationship between the primary carer and the person receiving care are shown at three points in time: 1968, 1993 and 2007 (Kasuga, 2010). Direct comparison is not possible, as the data are from separate surveys, but some shifts in patterns of primary care by family members in Japan can be identified. In 1968, the oldest son's wife was the main carer, and 60% of older women needing care relied on their daughter-in-law. However, at the later dates, this proportion was much smaller – 37% in 1993 and 34% in 2007 – suggesting that a major change occurred in the 1970s and 1980s.

Table 11.1: Primary carers in Japan by relationship to care recipient and gender of care recipient, 1968–2007 (%)

Relationship to care recipient	1968		1993		2007	
	Men	Women	Men	Women	Men	Women
Spouse (partner)	50	8	70	14	44	39
Son and daughter-in-law	36	64	15	43	2	34
Daughter and son-in-law	9	19	10	30	51	24
Grandchild	1	4	–	–	–	–
Paid care attendant	–	–	1	3	–	–
Other	4	6	4	11	3	4

Source: Kasuga (2010).

An interesting change in recent years of particular relevance to this chapter has been husbands' increasing role as carers. In 1968, only 8% of older women needing care were cared for mainly by their husbands. In 1993, this figure was 14%, and by 2007, nearly 39%. The difference between the figures for 1993 and 2007 is exceptionally large. The 2007 data showed that husbands had become the primary carers of older women, displacing care by their children, the usual arrangement in the past. The survey also asked respondents who they thought would be their main carer in the future when they needed care: most expected to rely upon their spouse, 80% of respondents in 'couple–only' households and 66% in extended households (Kasuga, 2010).

As well as changing family structure, urbanisation in Japan has also played a role in shaping these changing arrangements. In the late 1950s and 1960s, many Japanese migrated from rural to urban areas to work and establish new lives. As Kasuga (2010) points out, people in the generation born before the Second World War, who established new households during the era of rapid economic growth in the 1950s and 1960s, tend to regard their spouse as a partner: they shared hardships and raised their children together. In this sense, they have been liberated from the traditional family or '*ie*' system.[1] Husbands in this generation consequently feel both a strong attachment to their wives and that they have a duty to care for them when needed. Wives by contrast have long been accustomed to taking care of their husbands. Meanwhile, traditional marriage matchmaking has given way to marriage based on love, and this blossoming of romantic love after the Second World War has also contributed to the rising trend of partner-care in Japan.

Although partner-care is increasing among couples and a growing number of husbands take care of their wives, some problems have emerged as these changes have occurred. Men were not used to household work or to communicating regularly with neighbours, creating a tendency for them to become isolated when a partner requires constant care at home. Their lack of local support causes them stress as it often means that they receive no assistance from neighbours or friends (Tsutome and Saito, 2007).

Partner-carers in Taiwan

As noted throughout this volume, care issues have become a significant policy concern in most industrialised countries, and Taiwan is no exception here, especially given its rapidly ageing population and rising female labour force participation rate (see *Chapter One*). As in Japan, studies of care and caring have been conducted in Taiwan, but most have been focused on childcare, eldercare and care of people with disabilities.

Partner-care has received less attention in research and policymaking. Among the few studies of partner-carers that exist, most have focused on older couples over working age. A few studies of 'foreign brides' – typically women of working age – have concentrated on the care they give to their sick or disabled husbands, but these have not explored the competing demands of care and work, and the Taiwanese literature has thus so far offered no clear understanding of this dynamic.

Partner-care is intrinsically different from other kinds of care relationships. In Taiwan, the moral and legal bond between the carer and the care recipient is defined by social, legal and cultural norms (see *Chapter Two*). Obligations of conjugal loyalty, the legal responsibility to care for a disabled partner and the fear of social ostracism that partners can face in the outside world thus shape the partner-care relationship. This is quite different from a parent–child relationship, such as a son or daughter caring for a parent, where the bonds are established mainly through blood ties. As the examples presented later in this chapter suggest, partner-care involves rather intricate emotional processes and may involve conflict or other struggles. Yet, if a partner becomes disabled, marital intimacy can also strengthen, reinforcing the voluntary aspects of caring. Indeed, as Allen et al (1999) suggest (based on US data), intimacy enhances the likelihood that a person will care for his or her disabled partner, especially in situations of temporary disability. Yet, in the moral and legal context in Taiwan, even if there is discord in the marital relationship, partners are obliged to take on a caring role. In such cases, partner-care is involuntary and can involve grievances, even anger.

Although it has become one of the main types of care given, there is almost no research on people of working age who give care to their partner, and the subject needs, but currently lacks, serious policy attention in Taiwan. Nevertheless, a few official statistics demonstrate the importance of partner-care. A serious shortage of hospital nurses means that bedside care in Taiwan is predominantly handled by family members and in 2009, 45% of hospitalised people aged 55–64 were cared for by their partners (MOI, 2009). In cases of temporary disability among people aged under 65, a substantial minority (15%) were cared for by their partner, the next most important category of carer after parents (52%) (MOI, 2009).

Gender asymmetry in caring has been observed in many parts of the world, with women predominating as primary caregivers. Earlier studies in other parts of the world showed that it was mainly women who gave care to a partner (Stone et al, 1987; Rose-Rego et al, 1998), although, as seen here in relation to Japan (and also in *Chapters Nine* and *Ten*), this may be changing in some places. The situation in Taiwan is no different: in 2009, an official survey found that 63% of those caring for a disabled partner aged under 65 were female (MOI, 2009).

Services and support for sick and disabled adults and their partner-carers

Services available in Japan

For Japan's seven million disabled people, the most important legislation is the Basic Law for Persons with Disabilities 1993, revised in 2004. In 2002, the Japanese cabinet implemented an action plan to further the goals of this legislation relating to 'rehabilitation and normalisation'. The law aims to create an inclusive social environment in which disabled people enjoy the same rights and opportunities as non-disabled people, including medical care, pensions, welfare, employment, education, transportation, housing and accessible buildings. A special department within the cabinet is charged with promoting the welfare of people with disabilities and with coordinating and improving services.

In the past, disabled people in Japan received services from a service provider selected by their local authority (LA), but since 2003, they have been able to choose their own care provider. The new legislation also ensures that within each LA, all types of disability are handled by a single department. Partner-carers of disabled adults can get publicly funded assistance with household tasks such as cooking, bathing and washing. In such cases, the disabled person pays 10% of the cost of the services they receive and the LA covers the remaining 90%.

To encourage self-reliance among disabled people, the government also provides physical training, and job training for those who wish to work. To access this service, they must be medically examined to establish their level of impairment or disability and assessed for their eligibility for services such as physiotherapy, more extensive medical attention and skills training. In addition to services provided by LAs, there are also independent living centres for disabled people. These were established in 1991 to improve the living conditions of disabled people. Run by disabled people themselves, they disseminate information about available services, help disabled people access services and advocate for policy reform.

Although the government promotes 'full participation and equality', disabled people in Japan face a reality different from these laudable goals and experience considerable isolation and segregation. Special education facilities and the curriculum offered are good, but also foster segregation between disabled and non-disabled people. Disabled graduates face bleak career prospects and many disabled people end up working in rehabilitation centres, where the pay and benefits are too low to enable them to live independently. The partners of disabled people often bear a considerable economic responsibility, only partially offset by the meagre welfare benefits available, making their participation in paid work especially important.

Services available in Taiwan

Taiwan's care system has been modified in recent decades to cope with the rising need for care (see *Chapter Two*). Nevertheless, family members still provide most support. Over 93% of people with disabilities live at home, receiving scant assistance from either the government or the community and, in general, there is a distinct lack of resources families can draw upon to meet the care needs of their members, whether as carers or care recipients.

Policy on long-term care, long anticipated as a major development in Taiwan's care system, has been highly contested for more than a decade. When the Long Term Care (LTC) Bill currently under consideration will become law remains an open question, as in its present form, it leaves enormous controversies unresolved, including who is to be insured by the planned LTC insurance system, the level at which premiums for this should be set and how extensive insurance coverage should be.

The Disability Act 1980, amended most recently in 2007, is the major legislative instrument through which care services in Taiwan have been provided over the past two decades. However, as it involves a means test based on family income and a medical assessment set at a very high threshold, only the neediest are covered. Consequently, most families in need of support are denied services and benefits. The problem lies not only with the financial threshold and the disadvantages that follow from this, but also with the population targeted. People experiencing temporary disability arising from acute illness, disease or accident are not covered by the Act. Although they need as much, or more, care when they are hospitalised or recuperating at home than those with a permanent disability, they are not entitled to respite care or related social support, and rely heavily on their partners and other carers.

The pressures of this situation have led many families to look to the government for alternative solutions. There has been mounting pressure on Taiwan's migrant worker policy, with calls for relaxation of the number who may be admitted. As a result, the number of migrant care workers increased between 1996 and 2011 from 30,255 to almost 200,000. While this heavy reliance on migrant care workers relieves the immediate pressure on the government to establish an effective care system, paradoxically, it is slow progress in developing the care system that gives legitimacy to hiring them. Thus, migrant care has become a way of compensating for the care deficits that stem from the government's passivity in responding to the public outcry that has demanded support for care. Even so, eligibility criteria for hiring a migrant care worker are too strict to include most families, who are left alone without even this alternative form of care.

Migrant care workers are not always welcome as substitutes for the care a partner would otherwise give. Before turning to the support of a migrant care worker, two types of negotiation and decision need to be taken into consideration. First, caring often involves intimate interactions and close bodily contact. Most migrant care workers are women and unless they have no other alternative, many Taiwanese wives are reluctant to turn to these potential substitutes to care for their disabled husbands (Lan, 2006). Second, women's identity is socially constructed and reaffirmed through roles socially imposed upon them.

In Taiwan, being a good wife is very important for many women's self-esteem and for their own sense of identity. Caring is an integral part of enacting the duties of a 'good wife' in Taiwanese society, and women often fear that by delegating their caring roles to a female 'outsider', they risk losing their identities as a mother, wife or daughter-in-law (Lan, 2006).

Experiences of combining work and partner-care

So far, this chapter has considered the wider context in which partner-care takes place in Japan and Taiwan. In this section, two case studies from both countries are given to show how partner-care is managed and some of the tensions involved. These cases, based on personal interviews, form the focus of the discussion of how personal circumstances and societal arrangements play out for partner-carers in the two countries.

Case examples from Japan

Mr Okada

Mr Okada holds a managerial post in one of the largest public relations (PR) companies in Japan. He is now 55 years old. Five years ago, soon after her 50th birthday, his wife collapsed at home following a subarachnoid haemorrhage. She required two operations that left her with minor brain damage, although she can still manage many aspects of her everyday life with very little assistance.

Mr Okada usually leaves home at about 8am to go to work, and at 9am, his wife is picked up and taken to the nearby eldercare centre. This is a facility where older people can be taken during the day and brought back to their homes in the evening. Users can also stay overnight if this is requested. As it takes Mr Okada only about 15 minutes to travel from his office to the eldercare centre, he can, if necessary, remain at work until about 8.30pm and still manage to pick his wife up before 9pm

Although she is only 55, his wife goes to the eldercare centre each weekday, except on Wednesday afternoons, when her friend picks her up from the centre and takes her to a Braille writers' meeting. She also participates in activities organised on Mondays by her friend, as a volunteer. When the activity is over, her friend brings her home and they cook together.

Mr Okada is able to combine work and care relatively easily. He feels that this is because of the nature of his work and the understanding attitude of his work colleagues. He has been with the same company since he graduated from university and had worked for over 20 years in the same section. A year before his wife's collapse, however, he was transferred to a different division of the organisation. At the time, he felt ambivalent about this, as his new job was mainly a clerical role and he missed the excitement and busy schedule he previously had. Now, he feels that he is lucky to have this position, as it gives him the time he needs to care for his wife. Occasionally, he needs to leave the office at about 4pm to take her to the clinic to treat her depression, which she began to experience after leaving hospital.

Mr Okada does not cook, but his wife can. Since she has short-term memory lapses, for safety purposes, she cooks only while he (or someone else) is there. Her elder sister recently retired. She and her niece visit often and help take care of his wife.

Mr Tanaka

Mr Tanaka has lived in a suburb of a major Japanese city with his wife and mother-in-law for almost 15 years. Because the town they live in is a new development, they cannot rely on community ties and traditional forms of mutual assistance. Mr Tanaka works at a funeral parlour and his job is to prepare bodies for the coffin-viewing ceremony.

The couple were already living with his wife's mother when, in February 2002, Mr Tanaka's wife, then only 52 years old, was diagnosed with Alzheimer's disease. In 2004, her mother gave up her job to take care of her daughter, but she is becoming old and finds it very difficult to look after her daughter by herself and Mr Tanaka has now become heavily involved in his wife's care.

In 2005, the back pain Mr Tanaka suffers from worsened. He felt that it was becoming impossible to manage both his work in the funeral parlour and his wife's care. He considered quitting his job and talked this over with his supervisor. The supervisor advised him that if he left his job, he would face serious financial problems as he was still paying off a mortgage on his home. His boss instead arranged a transfer to the clerical section of the funeral parlour. Mr Tanaka's schedule in this role allows him to combine work with the care of his wife, although his income in the new position is 40% lower than his previous earnings.

In 2005, Mr Tanaka came across an association for families caring for dementia patients, which helps families to find out what services are available to them. When he applied for the municipal home-nursing care service in 2006, the care manager assessed his wife's care needs at the highest level (level 5). This means that he can use the day service operated by the care insurance system, which picks up and drops off patients and looks after them during the day: this enables him to continue to go to work. Although Mr Tanaka faces many difficulties in his everyday life, he says that he loves his wife more than ever. He feels that he now has a new purpose in life, to see his wife's smile and make his loved one's life better.

With the introduction of Japan's Long-Term Care Insurance (LTCI) system in 2000 (see *Chapter Two*), support for older people has improved. However, the system is not designed to provide care for people under the official retirement age of 65, even though, in Japan, there were 37,000 dementia patients under this age in 2012. Fortunately for him, the public officials dealing with Mr Tanaka's situation were understanding and helpful. Japan's LTCI system is also designed to provide supplementary assistance to a primary carer. There is an implicit assumption that this person will be the wife or daughter-in-law or a husband already retired from work, but Mr Tanaka's case is not so unusual, as one in three carers are men (Tsutome and Saito, 2007). To enable main household earners to combine work with the care of a partner, it is important to introduce flexible working schedules in Japanese workplaces, and this is beginning to happen (see *Chapter Two*).

Case examples from Taiwan

Mrs Tang

Mrs Tang is 50 years old and is a full-time assembly line worker in a medium-sized factory. Her husband is a 56-year-old taxi driver and they have two daughters aged 16 and 12. The family lives with the husband's mother, now in her late 80s. Recently, Mrs Tang's husband fell seriously ill and when she was interviewed, her husband had been hospitalised for two months. In her employment, Mrs Tang has strict and inflexible working hours: she will be penalised if she breaks these rules. To keep her job – now even more important to the family as her husband is unable to work – Mrs Tang can, in general, only provide care for her husband at night, when she is off work. Twice, when he needed a high level of care immediately after being released from the intensive care unit at the hospital, she took time off during the day to care for him. In doing this, she used up all her statutory leave, which means that she has no leave left this year to make a trip back to visit her parents in China.

Mrs Tang generally helps her husband with bathing and dressing, leaving other kinds of assistance to be provided mainly by her brother-in-law, who is also a taxi driver and has more time flexibility, enabling him to help in the daytime. Her mother-in-law has helped take care of the granddaughters. Although Mrs Tang is lucky enough to have relatives to help and has not needed to give up her job or become impossibly overstretched between hospital and home, she finds managing both work and care difficult. She seldom comes home for a break as she needs to care for her husband in the hospital at night, and has slept at her husband's bedside continuously for two months. During this time, she has lost a lot of weight and is greatly affected by the stress and fatigue involved in the effort to combine work and care. As she explained:

> "Sleeping at my husband's bedside in the hospital is not easy. You simply cannot sleep all night through without being disturbed. Yet, regardless of the sleep quality of the previous night, I have to go to work anyway. There are times when I can hardly focus on my job and lose concentration, especially after a poor night's sleep the night before."

As Mrs Tang's husband suffers from an acute illness, he is not entitled to any official care support and she has to mobilise informal care resources on her own. Luckily, she can turn to other family members for help.

Mr Deng

Mr Deng is a mid-level public official in a tax office. He was in his early 40s when his wife, a junior high schoolteacher and director in her late 30s, was diagnosed with cancer. At this time, their daughter was aged 11 and their son aged seven. During the medical treatment period, Mr Deng took over the domestic chores previously handled by his wife, including buying meals, picking up the children from school, taking them to their out-of-school activities and managing household chores. Sometimes, he accompanies his wife to hospital appointments. He also searches for medical information and professional expertise to help his wife make decisions about the various treatment choices offered by her doctors.

When asked whether he encounters insurmountable hardships in combining work and care, he answers:

> "I did not feel under particular strain during the time my wife was sick. During the first two months when undergoing cancer treatments, she was in a really bad situation. I am so grateful to my mother, who moved in to live with us

and helped by cooking special meals to help my wife gain strength and who took care of our two children. As for the household chores, they are relatively easy to handle. I can fetch dinner easily around the street corner, as there are lots of different kinds of food shops available locally."

Mr Deng says that the situation has not created too much difficulty for him because his job is flexible enough to accommodate the needs of his wife and children. His work usually involves going to different locations to check on employers for possible tax evasion. This means that he is usually out of the supervisor's eye and can benefit from the flexibility available in his job to adapt to the new situation his wife's illness has created.

Mr Deng did not stop working or make job changes to adapt to these new circumstances. He is able to combine work and care without much difficulty for two main reasons: first, the considerable work flexibility he enjoys, which means he can adjust his hours to the children's school times and is able to get to inexpensive fast-food shops, where meals are ready and packed up to go, as is typical for city life in Taiwan; and, second, the help from his mother. She moved in to take care of her daughter-in-law while she was undergoing her chemotherapy treatment. His family and job flexibility have helped the couple cope during this tough time. This case also shows the importance of informal care support, given the insufficiency of formal services. Over 60% of older people in Taiwan say that they prefer living with their adult children. Elderly parents moving to live with married adult children in Chinese culture was long thought of as the way things ought to be, and the arrangement continues to create many opportunities for healthy older women to take on caring roles.

Policy debates and developments affecting partner-care

Developments in Japan

Japan's LTCI system provides nursing support for primary carers, based on an official assessment of need, which is periodically adjusted to accommodate changes in the patient's condition. Although this is of great benefit to families coping with challenging caring situations, often referred to in the media as 'nursing hell', changing norms, employment patterns and gender roles are undermining this family-based model of care. In the future, it is unlikely that younger women will take on these tasks to the same degree that their mothers and grandmothers have done. For them, at some point, assisted living and other institutional arrangements are likely to be necessary.

The LTCI system provides assistance for any family member who needs care for more than two weeks. Many workers can take up to 93 days' unpaid care leave (see *Chapter Two*), but this arrangement excludes about 35% of the workforce (some 10 million people) who are 'non-regular' workers (about half of them people in 'working poor' households who often cannot afford to take unpaid care leave even if eligible). A further difficulty is that the maximum care leave period is too short for many partner-carers.

Although 60% of companies have a written paid leave policy, in practice, very few workers actually use it. This is both because of a deeply ingrained work culture that prioritises job over family, and because workers know that if they take care leave, their colleagues' workload will increase, as many companies do not hire replacements for those taking a leave of absence.

Japan faces an acute shortage of nurses and care workers, but has not enacted policies that would address this problem effectively. In addition, as families become less able or inclined to care for older people at home, the current family-based model will come under pressure, stoking demand for professional care services. In this situation, it makes sense to consider drawing upon foreign labour. The government has negotiated agreements with Indonesia, the Philippines and Vietnam to recruit more care workers, although the terms of these agreements (also discussed in *Chapter Five*) are inadequate and deeply flawed.

Combining work and care is an increasingly pressing problem in Japan. The current LTCI system relies on spouses to act as primary carers, but since both spouses work in 55% of married-couple households, it is very difficult for spouses to perform this function when a partner becomes ill or disabled. Full-time workers usually have rigid work schedules and long hours, and are thus unable to combine work and care. The lack of flexible work options and the rarity of telecommuting suggest that reforms in employment practices might help some households better manage caring tasks. There is also an acute shortage of assisted living facilities, a half-way option between home-based care and long-term hospitalisation. The acute ageing crisis in Japan is creating a sense of urgency about the need for reform. It is being used as a rationale for increasing taxes to support services targeting older people, and for rationing such services. There are expectations that the minimum age for LTCI premium contributions will be lowered from the current age of 40 and the government wants incrementally to double the existing 5% consumption tax applied to goods and services, partly to fund social services. While partner-carers face the same problems other family members face in providing care for people needing support, the major difference is that there is little public discourse about their specific problems and, hence, little movement towards policies tailored to their needs. The government's dire financial circumstances – a public debt to Gross Domestic Product (GDP) ratio exceeding 200%, by far the highest in the Organisation for Economic Co-operation and Development (OECD) – mean that policymakers are more focused on trimming existing programmes than on promoting reforms that would genuinely help partner-carers.

Developments in Taiwan

Given Taiwan's very narrow formal care services and the fact that the services available are not specifically addressed to partner-carers, many partner-carers of working age endure extreme hardship as part of their dual burden of managing to provide care while remaining at work, which is often essential to compensate for the lost family income associated with their partner's illness or disability. As exemplified in this chapter, both work flexibility and a kin network can alleviate partner-carers' situation. But not all partner-carers have such resources.

Some aspects of the socio-economic context in Taiwan may help working-age carers cope with caring roles. The lower labour force participation rates of middle-aged and older women – 46%, 24% and 4%, respectively, for women aged 45–54, 55–64 and 65+ (see *Chapter One*) – suggest that many are potential partner-carers should the need arise. Quite a high proportion of Taiwanese workers (18% in 2010) are self-employed or unpaid family workers, and may have more work flexibility than other employees, which would help them cope if they need to care. Early retirement may also ease conflicts between the demands of work and care. For the past decade, the average retirement age has been around 56 years: in 2005, only 33% of workers retired at age 60 or older, compared with 72% in 1991. Retirement statistics show that in 2009, 33% of people retired at age 45–55, over half when aged 55–64 and just 8% at 65+, and that some early retirements were made in response to family care needs.

Workplaces are not care-friendly in Taiwan. Long working hours and limited leave provisions mean that workers have few ways of reconciling work and care. In addition, the shortage of assisted living facilities, the inadequacies of home-care services and the absence of financial support for care seriously jeopardise working-age partner-carers' capacity to balance their dual roles.

Discussion

Both Japan and Taiwan are predominantly family-based care regimes in which care is delivered at home, primarily by relatives, with limited public support. Both countries are latecomers in building a care system able to cope with the increasing care needs of their people. The two countries nevertheless have different socio-economic contexts and population profiles, leading to differences in the development of their care systems. Japan entered the so-called 'aged society' much earlier than the rest of the world and experienced a sharply declining birth rate in the late 20th century, creating a care crisis to which it responded by introducing its LTC Insurance Act 2000, the first Asian country to recognise carers' needs in this way. Its response to the crisis, and progress over the last two decades, left Taiwan far behind.

In contrast, the development of Taiwan's social services has been very slow. Only in 2007, with its substantial revision of the Disability Act 1980, did carers' needs receive official recognition. They have finally been put on the public agenda, but their needs remain unmet: paid care leave is available only for childcare and is denied to carers of older people and other disabled adults. In Taiwan, in marked contrast to Japan, where carers can have up to 93 days of care leave per year, carers are entitled to a total of only seven days' unpaid care leave per year. The late start and consequent inadequacies of Taiwan's public care provision and care leave policies make it very difficult for working people to cope with care needs in the family. Workers in the informal sector may have more flexible schedules to cope with their caring roles, but such jobs are poorly paid and lack security.

Although Japan has introduced paid care leave for up to 93 days and part-time employment with flexible work schedules is quite widespread, Japanese workers still face difficulties in balancing work and care. This arises from low take-up of care leave – caused by the low compensation rate of 40% – and a relatively high labour force participation rate.

Labour market characteristics have a significant impact on workers who need to care for disabled family members. The much lower labour force participation rate in Taiwan – especially among the 45–64 age group – suggests that a large latent pool of potential partner-carers exists, should care needs arise. Self-employed and unpaid family workers are another group of potential carers. By contrast, high labour force participation rates among middle-aged and older workers in Japan and a low rate of self-employed and unpaid family workers limit the pool of potential carers there.

To help working-age partner-carers balance work and care, reforming the care system should command top policy priority in both countries. Governments, non-governmental organisations and employers all have important roles to play in enabling working-age carers to cope effectively with their dual roles.

Note

[1] '*Ie*' is a Japanese term for household and refers to the traditional patriarchal family structure. It also serves as the basis for the official family registration system (known as '*koseki*') which is maintained in government offices and includes basic information such as births, marriages and deaths of family members.

References

Allen, S.M., Goldscheider, F. and Ciambrone, D.A. (1999) 'Gender roles, marital intimacy, and nomination of spouse as primary caregiver', *The Gerontologist*, vol 39, no 2, pp 150–8.

JIWE (Japan Institute of Workers' Evolution) (2011) *Kaigo wo okonau roudousha no ryouritsu shiensaku ni kakawaru kenkyu hokokusho* [*Report on studies of those who combine paid work and caring*], Tokyo: JIWE.

Kasuga, K. (2010) *Kawaru kaigo to kazoku* [*Changing caregiving and family*], Tokyo: Kodansha.

Lan, P.C. (2006) *Global Cinderella: migrant domestic and newly rich employers in Taiwan*, Durham, NC: Duke University Press.

MHLW (Ministry of Health, Labour and Welfare) (2009) *Kaigohoken Jigyo joukyo Houkoku* [*Annual report on nursing care insurance: business report*], Tokyo: MHLW.

MIAC (Ministry of Internal Affairs and Communication) (2006) *Shakai Seikatsu Kihon chosa* [*Basic survey on social life*], Tokyo: MIAC.

MOI (Ministry of Interior) (2009) *Report of the Senior Citizen Condition Survey*, Taipei: MOI.

Rose-Rego, S.K., Strauss, M.E. and Smyth, K.A. (1998) 'Differences in the perceived well-being of wives and husbands caring for persons with Alzheimer's disease', *The Gerontologist*, vol 38, no 2, pp 224–30.

Stone, R., Cafferata, G.L. and Sangl, J. (1987) 'Caregivers of the frail elderly: a national profile', *The Gerontologist*, vol 27, no 5, pp 616–26.

Tsutome, M. and Saito, M. (2007) *Dansei Kaigosya Hakusho* [*White Paper for male caregivers*], Kyoto: Kamogawa Shuppan.

CONCLUSIONS

Reconciling work and care for older parents, disabled children and partners: convergent or separate paths in three welfare systems?

Sue Yeandle and Teppo Kröger

Introduction

This book, while not the first to address the reconciliation of paid work and the care of older, sick or disabled people in an international context, offers an updated and extended perspective on an issue whose importance is increasingly recognised around the world. The book is characterised by three features: (1) the distinction it makes between caring in three different relational contexts; (2) its focus on the influence of carers' organisations as well as of demography and labour force participation; and (3) its coverage of Nordic, liberal-democratic and East Asian societies. It aims to offer readers insights into the personal worlds of working carers in varied cultural and social contexts, to present available statistical evidence about the scope and nature of the care they give, and to review trends and developments in relevant policy fields in six countries.

As mentioned in *Chapter One*, two earlier books first analysed issues affecting working carers using an international comparative perspective almost 20 years ago. Judith Phillips' (1995) edited collection *Working carers: international perspectives on working and caring for older people* broke new ground in the mid-1990s, bringing the relationship between caring and employment into international focus for the first time. Her collection centred on research findings from Britain and North America and also presented early analysis of the circumstances of working carers in Ireland and Germany. It emphasised that since in every country, women were increasingly needed in the labour market but also remained the main carers of older people, caring should be understood as a workplace issue. The book developed a discussion that had begun in Britain and presented examples of workplace initiatives and empirical findings from different countries.

Work and caring for the elderly: international perspectives, edited by the American researchers Viola M. Lechner and Margaret B. Neal (1999), both broadened earlier US studies on working carers and offered an extensive international comparison. Aiming to heighten awareness of the options available to address the 'work–eldercare dilemma', their book presented a range of approaches used in supporting people to combine work and care in 11 countries. Its objectives – similar in some ways to those of the present volume – were to explore support for older people and their employed carers in different national contexts, including three of the countries covered here. That collection concluded that while combining work and care had become quite widespread in the countries studied, awareness of (and support for) employed caregivers remained recent and limited; indeed, in many countries, it barely existed.

No book offering comparable international analysis of combining family care of older, sick and disabled people with paid employment was published in the 2000s, although a volume edited by Anne Martin-Matthews and Judith Phillips (2008) gave further attention to working carers, and in Europe, the topic received increasing attention in journal articles. These drew variously on the Survey of Health, Ageing and Retirement (see: www.share-project.org), the EUROFAMCARE project (Lamura et al, 2008) and other studies (Kröger and Sipilä, 2005; Addabbo et al, 2010; Saraceno, 2010; Suanet et al, 2012).

The significance of supporting employees to combine the care of sick, frail or disabled family members with their professional lives has certainly not diminished since the 1990s, however. Trends in population ageing and in female labour market activity have accelerated in the last 20 years (see *Chapter One*). Past confidence in the availability of unpaid and unsupported family care has been eroded, not only in Europe and North America, but also around the world. As a result, there is growing awareness that both women and men need help to lead a satisfying family life while also, within the increasingly prevalent 'adult worker model' (Lewis, 2001), making a full contribution to working life.

The present volume analyses the experiences and circumstances of three separate groups of working carers: (1) those supporting older parents; (2) those helping their sons or daughters who are disabled or seriously ill; and (3) those caring for their disabled, sick or dying partners. It has explored how these carers are supported in six countries, looking in each case at the state's role (legislation, welfare services and financial support) and at the contribution of employers (mainly through modified working arrangements). Compared with the earlier collections mentioned, this book aims to provide an updated, extended and more specified analysis. Updating previous work by highlighting the many developments affecting working carers that have taken place since the late 1990s, it extends the focus of work–care reconciliation by bringing three countries (Australia, Finland and Taiwan) not previously examined in comparative perspective into the frame. By focusing on experiences (carers' lived realities) and policies (the frameworks and guidelines that shape the social, legal and economic context for family care) in different relational contexts, it also offers a more specific analysis. In *Chapters Three* to *Eleven*, the book contrasts developments in two countries, each with broadly similar welfare arrangements and traditions. This final chapter draws the main findings of the book's previous chapters together. It discusses the comparative lessons learned, considers future challenges in work–care reconciliation and highlights some new and still unanswered questions that the editors hope future researchers will continue to address.

Work–care reconciliation in different caring situations

Care of older parents

Of the three types of caring circumstances considered in this book, the care of older people has received most policy attention. Policymakers in the countries studied are increasingly alert to low fertility and rising longevity in their populations, and keen to develop systems capable of supporting much larger numbers of very aged people. Many now believe that, in the future, the care family members give to their older relatives will be increasingly important in underpinning aged care arrangements. The old are the largest group using health services and requiring care, and younger citizens, most of whom aspire one day to reach old age themselves, also have an interest in creating sustainable systems capable of meeting older people's needs.

In the six countries studied here, most aged people already live alone or in aged-couple households, or are increasingly likely to do so. In late old age, many have conditions that affect their activities of everyday living and need regular help; some require constant care and attention (see *Chapter One*). Most nevertheless spend the majority of their aged years outside hospitals or residential/nursing homes, unless or until their care needs become very intensive.

Even today, strong traditions and values normalise middle-aged sons' and daughters' concern for their parents' well-being, and family members play a role in supporting their older relatives in all six countries. The support they give takes different forms, variously including helping an aged parent with practical tasks, arranging care services for them, accompanying them to medical appointments, providing emotional or financial support, and providing personal care. In Finland, Sweden, England and Australia, far fewer older people reside with their sons or daughters than in previous generations: with pensions and more varied housing options, many choose to retain their independence, and some families are geographically dispersed. Even in East Asia, the number of older people living with younger relatives fell in the 2000s, to under half in Japan and barely two thirds in Taiwan. Unpaid carers, mostly daughters or daughters-in-law, sometimes sons, nevertheless continue to be the primary resource on which these more independent and solitary older people rely in all six countries if care needs arise.

In some nations, helping people of working age to sustain employment alongside eldercare activities is now an explicit policy objective, although in others, it remains an unrecognised issue or is overshadowed by other official responses to the growing need for aged care (see *Chapters Three, Four* and *Five*). Key issues occupying decision-makers have included: cost containment; ageing in place; service rationing; care outside hospital; personalisation/self-directed support; and the regulation of paid caring labour (Ungerson and Yeandle, 2007). In recent decades, this has brought growing acknowledgement of the need for new approaches and considerable changes in public policy. Although the detail of these policy developments lay beyond the remit of this book, all have implications for family members involved, willingly or otherwise, in supporting their older relatives and suggest a larger role for them in the future.

Australia and England are liberal democracies whose welfare states still offer, in the 2010s, little more than a 'safety net' for older people needing social care (see *Chapter Four*). Even in Finland and Sweden, Nordic states offering some of the world's longest-established universal provision for older people, support systems have come under financial pressure in recent decades and more is now expected of family carers (see *Chapter Three*). On the other hand, Japan and Taiwan, East Asian countries that previously lacked welfare systems and relied almost exclusively on co-resident family care until recently, have found that new policies are needed to keep pace with population ageing and other social changes (see *Chapter Five*).

In all six countries, many working-age people, especially women, provide care that complements, or substitutes, support to older people provided or funded by the state. Although much eldercare is provided by the old themselves, caregiving to older family members is nevertheless relatively common among the working-age population, especially those in their mid-40s and older. In the countries studied, demographic changes also mean that these workers tend to have fewer siblings to share in the care of their frail older parents. Family care and support takes different forms in the six states and is framed by different policy and cultural arrangements in each. When eldercare is needed, however, in each country, family care is a more usual care arrangement than the use of either home care (whether public, private or grey market) or residential eldercare services.

The state's legal responsibility for older people's well-being and services is well established in the two Nordic countries (see *Chapter Three*). Service provision and entitlements are nevertheless locally variable and the financial sustainability of these systems is increasingly questioned. Swedes are committed to their universal welfare state and favour public care provision. Surveys show that they are even less likely than Finns to feel that family members 'should' care for their older relatives. Yet, in both these countries, many older employees, especially women, provide care, help or support to an older relative alongside their job, and some find this challenging or stressful. In Australia and England, caring for an older relative is also common among mature working-age people (see *Chapter Four*). If needs arise, carers in these countries sometimes give up work or reduce their working hours, although most find some way of combining work and care. In the East Asian states, most workers who give up paid work to care for older relatives are women, although surveys show that some men are doing this too. Here again, combining work with the care of an older relative is an increasingly prevalent arrangement, although in East Asia, it is still often provided on a co-resident basis, reflecting the strength of the traditional familial model, which has only very recently begun to change (see *Chapter Five*).

The way each state supports those who combine paid work with the care of older relatives is summarised in Table 12.1. Limited paid leave options, in rather tightly specified circumstances, have recently been introduced in Australia, Finland, Sweden and Japan. Valued though these may be, they are not yet how most carers of older people manage work and care, however. Under the paid care leave arrangements described, workers nearly always lose at least some income, even where (as in the Nordic countries, Australia and Japan) the state contributes to their cost. Short periods of unpaid carer's leave are available for emergencies (in England and Taiwan) or for longer periods (in Australia, Finland and Japan), but, in truth, such leave is only accessible to the better-off or those with other forms of financial support. The law in England, Finland and Japan now requires employers to respond to requests for flexible working arrangements made by their employees who are carers, subject to managerial discretion. In the liberal democracies, quite high numbers of part-time jobs – 25% of all jobs in both Australia and England – offer a further way of combining work and care, although most part-time positions are low-paid (see *Chapter One*). Such work is harder to find in the Nordic states (less than 15% of jobs) and East Asia (Japan, 20% of jobs). In all six countries, some, mostly larger, employers offer those with care responsibilities leave or flexibility that goes beyond their statutory obligations, although organisations seem to provide this more often for working parents than for working carers (Colombo et al, 2011: 123; see also *Chapter Two*). Some employees find their colleagues and managers supportive when they need to care for older family members, but, as earlier chapters reported, others say that they dare not mention their eldercare responsibilities, fearing negative impacts on their reputation at work or their promotion chances.

At home and in local communities, some workers who care for elderly parents receive support in combining work and care through local carers' services. These somewhat variable services rarely reach more than a small minority of carers, even in the Nordic states and the liberal democracies, where there are networks of not-for-profit carers' centres (see Table 12.2). Other differences between the three welfare systems, notably the services and support available to older people themselves, are rather more visible. Sweden, and to a lesser degree Finland, ensures that older people who require support in daily living need not rely on relatives for personal care or daily support, making carers' input (unless individuals choose otherwise) complementary to what the state provides (see *Chapter Three*). In Australia and England, services for older people usually involve means-testing, are much less widely available than in the Nordic states and are often restricted to those with significant care needs. Consequently, many carers of older people in these countries consider the care they give essential to their parent's well-being (see *Chapter Four*). In the East Asian states, charging policy (in Taiwan), taboos arising from Confucian beliefs, values based on filial piety and (in Japan) shame and social pressure ('*sekentei*') still limit many families' willingness to access services (Asai and Kameoka,

Table 12.1: Support available to carers through statutory employment rights and working time/place flexibility

Country	Carers of seriously ill or disabled children	Carers of frail, sick or disabled older people	Carers of sick or disabled partners
Australia	**Paid** personal/carer's leave for 10 days per year, paid at employee's normal hourly rate. Emergency short-term **unpaid** carer's leave for two days per occasion.		
	Legal right to request **flexible working** for parents of children under school age or children with disability under 18 years old, employees with 12 months' service only.		
England	No paid leave rights for carers. Emergency short-term **unpaid leave** can be taken to care for a family member. Legal right to request **flexible working**, employees with six months' service, caring for spouse/partner, relative or co-resident person; can be refused only for clear business reasons, no time limit.		
	Right to **unpaid parental leave** (disabled child <18 years old). Like all mothers, up to 52 weeks' part-paid maternity leave (can part-share with father); all fathers, two weeks' paid paternity leave.		
Finland	**Paid** job alternation leave for 90–359 days; must take as minimum 90 successive days, employees with 12 months' service and 10 years' experience only, 70% of unemployment benefit rate; costs covered by state. **Unpaid care leave**, maximum six months per request, available at employer's discretion.		
	Like all parents, childcare **leave** until the child is three years old, **paid** flat-rate allowance, with means-tested and possible municipal supplements.		
Sweden	**Paid leave** for terminal care for 100 days, paid at 80% of wage, requires doctor's certificate, workers up to age 67. No unpaid leave rights.		
	Like all parents, **paid parental leave** for 480 days (60 days each parent, rest distributed as parents wish), can be taken at any time until the child is eight years old.		
Japan	**Paid** family care leave, maximum 93 days for each family member (self-employed not eligible). **Paid or unpaid** nursing leave for five days per year (10 days per year if more than one dependant). Legal right to request **flexible working**: employers must offer carers: 1) shortened working hours; 2) flexible working time; or 3) limitation of extra working hours, up to one year per application.		
Taiwan	**Unpaid** parental leave for two years (until child's third birthday), parents without labour insurance. **Paid** parental leave (60% of salary), parents (one at a time) with children aged six months–three years, parents with labour insurance. **Paid** care leave, five days per year, children < 12 years old, civil servants only. **Flexible working** or unpaid one-hour early leave, employees with children <3 years old, companies with 30+ employees only.	**Unpaid** leave to care for relatives.	

2005; see also *Chapter Five*). Services for older people are not available for all, in any case, and in these East Asian states, very few carers' services have been developed.

Table 12.2: Publicly funded support available to carers through national social and health care systems

Country	Carers of seriously ill or disabled children	Carers of frail, sick or disabled older people	Carers of sick or disabled partners
Australia	Publicly funded (Commonwealth, state and territory level) **carers' services**; carer support groups, respite services, counselling and so on. Mainly state-funded **health care** system, most general practitioners do not charge a co-payment (80% nationally); if additional co-payment charged, this is not privately insurable.		
	Early intervention support service.		
England	Right to an independent LA **carer's assessment.** **Free universal** state-funded **health care.** **Social care services**; subject to means and needs tests administered by LAs; support may involve user co-payments or charges.		
	LA **carer's services.** **'Short breaks' services** (legal duty on LAs to provide). **'Early support'** LA/NHS **programme.**	Small minority get discretionary **carer's services** (respite, training, health checks, direct payments, etc).	
Finland	**Public universal health care** (with moderate user fees). **Home care and residential social care services** (with moderate user fees). Variable, discretionary **carer's services**, such as short-term respite care (with moderate user fees).		
Sweden	**Carer's assessment.** **Public universal health care.**		
	Home-based and residential social care services (in principle, free of charge). Variable, discretionary **carer's services**, such as short-term respite care (in principle, free of charge).	**Home-based and residential social care services** (with moderate user fees). Variable, discretionary **carer's services**, such as short-term respite care (often free of charge).	
Japan	**Health care** system (with 30% user fees).		
	Early intervention support services. **Nursing care** at home. **Short-term hospitalisation.** **Day service** for disabled children. **Specialist medical care.**	Community **carer support programme** within LTCI (training, carer exchange, support schemes).	
Taiwan	Variable, discretionary LA-funded **carer services** (respite, training, support groups, counselling, information). **Universal** insurance-funded **health care** (NHI) system.		

Care of disabled children

In all the countries studied, the large majority of children with disabilities or serious illness live with, and are mainly cared for by, their parents (see *Chapter One*). Many continue to receive parental care throughout their adult lives. In East Asia, it is still usual for adults with disabilities to reside in their parents' home, receiving most of their care from their mothers and supported financially, even in adulthood, by their families (see *Chapter Eight*). By contrast, for some decades, policy in the Nordic countries – especially in Sweden, where significant public resources have been committed to supporting the independence of disabled people – has been to encourage disabled children to live independently as they reach adulthood. This usually means moving to supported housing with suitable disability services in place, often with assistance to participate in paid employment (see *Chapter Six*). The two liberal democracies sit between these extremes in policy terms: Australia and England both have arrangements in place to help disabled adults live independently without needing to rely on their parents, but compared with Sweden, offer less comprehensive services to support this goal. As in East Asia, parents in England and Australia, especially mothers, thus often have lifelong caring roles. In both these liberal democracies, disabled adults (if unable to work or needing help with the costs of disability) receive financial support from the state, but the benefits they are offered are less generous than in the Nordic systems, causing many to need their parents' ongoing financial (and other) support (see *Chapter Seven*).

Caring for a sick or disabled child has acquired greater visibility in public policy in all six countries in recent decades. This arises from altered public attitudes to disability and, thanks to continuing health care improvements, larger numbers of seriously disabled and very sick children surviving into adulthood and to older ages (see *Chapter One*). While parent-carers receive some extra support (compared with other parents) in all six countries (Table 12.3), their children's improved life chances have not been accompanied by commensurate improvements in the help parent-carers get to reconcile work and care. The additional supervision, medical appointments, special transport arrangements and other support their children need, often into adulthood, cause many parents difficulties at work (see *Chapters Six* to *Eight*). Many nevertheless wish to retain a 'worker' identity and need to generate income for their household's financial well-being.

Table 12.3: Financial support available to carers through state welfare benefits and social security arrangements

Country	Carers of seriously ill or disabled children	Carers of frail, sick or disabled older people	Carers of sick or disabled partners
Australia	**Carer's Allowance** (supplementary payment, not means-tested).		
	Carer Payment/child (income support payment, income/assets tested).	**Carer Payment/adult** (income support payment, income/assets tested).	
England	**Carer's Allowance** (not means-tested, carers caring 35+ hours per week and earning under £100/€125 per week from paid work only). **Carer Premium** (additional payment that carers who are claimants of certain other allowances may claim).		
	Disability Living Allowance (paid to/in respect of the person cared for, including disabled children, determines carer's eligibility for CA).		
Finland	**Carer's Allowance.** **Job Alternation Leave Benefit.**		
	Special Care Allowance (during treatment of a child). **Disability Allowance** (to parents of under 16-year-old disabled children to support care at home).		
Sweden	**Personal Assistance** (if user eligible before age 65).		
	Care Allowance (extra state financial support payable to parents of a disabled child, in line with the child's needs).	**Paid kin caregiver.** **End of Life Care Allowance.**	
Japan	**Family Care Leave Supplement** (through unemployment insurance, for carers with prior employment record only).		
	Special Child Rearing Allowance. **Welfare Allowance for Children with Severe Disabilities.** **Income tax allowance.**	**Family Caregiver Benefit** (some municipalities only).	**Income tax allowance.**
Taiwan	**Income tax allowance.**		
		Special Care Allowance for low-income citizens (family carers aged 16–64 and without a full-time job only).	

Note: This is a policy field where changes happen regularly. This table describes the situation in October 2012.

This type of caring affects women more than men. In the Nordic countries and liberal democracies, mothers of a sick or disabled son or daughter are considerably more likely than other mothers to live with their child but to do so without the support of a partner. In all six countries, such mothers are particularly likely to face lifelong challenges in combining work and care and many experience significant and ongoing financial pressure. Those with sole caring responsibility find it especially difficult to work and many report that their caring role limits the hours they can work and the type of work they can undertake (see *Chapter Seven*). Since parental responsibility for a disabled child usually begins in a mother's late 20s or 30s, these pressures may affect them – and those fathers who, less commonly, provide this type of care – throughout their working lives. Statistically, mothers of disabled children are more likely than other mothers to have low incomes, to be outside or on the margins of the labour market, and to face difficult challenges in combining work and care (see *Chapters Six* to *Eight*). Although many receive some support from other relatives, single parent-carers can face acute difficulties and experience isolation and difficult time pressures in all six countries.

In the Nordic countries and in England, cash-for-care systems of various kinds enable some disabled people to employ personal assistants (PAs), sometimes with transformative impacts on their lives. Uniquely in the countries studied, Sweden permits the employment of parent-carers as their child's PA, creating a form of kin-caregiver employment (see *Chapter Six*). This arrangement is not found elsewhere. While it may suit some families, it seems not to offer a model suitable for widespread use. Many parent-carers value the opportunity paid work gives for experiences outside the family setting, and working as one's child's PA can limit younger disabled people's ability to achieve autonomy and independence.

Everywhere, even in the Nordic countries, where a good range of disability services is available, caring for a disabled child can mean that parents have to give up or reduce their paid work in order to meet their child's needs or give their child the quality of life they think appropriate. Many face stark choices: their ability to combine work and care depends on the nature of their child's disability, the quality and flexibility of their personal networks, their access to suitable services, and the attitude and adaptability of their employer. Only when an appropriate configuration of support is in place is combining work and care possible for parent-carers. In the six countries included in this book, such configurations are rare in Taiwan, not common in Finland, Japan, England and Australia, and more usual, although by no means universal, in Sweden.

Care of sick, disabled or dying partners

The unpaid care given to a non-elderly, usually co-resident, partner who is sick or disabled has received least attention in the wider policy debates about care, although, in several respects, such care is distinctive.

First, much more often than happens in the care of elderly parents or disabled children, partner-care frequently involves care by men as well as by women. Second, the care needed, which must often be managed alongside full-time employment, commonly arises unexpectedly. Third, it is frequently intensive (as in the care of a partner who is dying), can be unpredictable or progressively demanding (as in the care of a partner with a fluctuating mental health problem or long-term condition), and may need to be carried out alongside the care of the couple's children or elderly parents (Yeandle et al, 2007; see also *Chapter Ten*). Finally, because the partner needing care may have lost earnings through inability to continue at work, many couples in these circumstances face very challenging financial pressures, making retaining their job or occupational status especially important for many partner-carers.

In England and Australia, where researchers have now studied family caring over many decades, it is clear that wider shifts in gender relations and more companionate marital relationships lie behind men's greater tendency to provide partner-care themselves when the need arises. Today, if their partner has care needs, men quite often provide this support themselves, rather than turn – as their fathers might have done – to female family members for help (see *Chapter Ten*). There are hints of similar changes in male behaviour in contemporary East Asia too (see *Chapter Eleven*). In the Nordic states, individualism and egalitarian values are central to social arrangements and underpin these countries' universal care systems: here, mutual support within a relationship is a normative expectation, although couples have no legal obligation to provide each other's personal care. Nordic couples do not wish to turn to their children for regular assistance and expect to receive formal support (see *Chapter Nine*).

These observations help us understand why many people who seek to combine significant amounts of care with a *full-time* job are partner-carers. These carers are often men and women who are well established in their jobs or careers and whose livelihoods and future economic well-being depend upon their ability to continue working. Especially when caring needs arise unexpectedly, for example, when a partner has a major accident, acute health crisis (like a stroke or heart attack) or serious medical diagnosis (such as cancer or neurological disease), large changes in home life may be needed and some partner-carers need leave from or greater flexibility at work. Examples of such circumstances were seen in all the countries studied, and supportive employers, effective services and good personal networks seem to be critical to the successful combination of work and care in all types of welfare system (see *Chapters Nine*, *Ten* and *Eleven*).

Only a small minority of partner-carers have access to carers' services, such as respite, counselling and advice, which could be helpful in supporting them to reconcile work and care. Support of this kind is most developed in those states (England and Sweden) where carers have the right to have their own needs as a carer assessed. In the Nordic states and the liberal democracies, the importance of flexible respite, mentoring and alternative care services is recognised, with state funding available to enhance and develop services, most of which originated as voluntary or charitable provision (see *Chapters Nine* and *Ten*). There is evidence that similar services are beginning to develop in the East Asian states too, mainly in response to the awareness-raising activities of voluntary organisations (see *Chapter Eleven*). In all the countries studied here, however, partner-carers with access to supportive carers' services or leave from their jobs are the exception. When care needs arise within the couple, sustaining work and care is a challenging and often stressful experience in which the carer's health and financial well-being come under pressure, with social and familial networks often unable or inadequate to provide the support the couple needs. Partner-carers called upon to provide care intensively or over long periods are at risk of falling out of work in all six countries. In England and Australia, where carer benefits are available only to those with low earnings or short working hours, social security policy discourages partner-carers from staying in employment (see *Chapter Ten*). In all six societies, the needs of partner-carers are often poorly understood by their employers and managers (although some report positive experiences), and are rarely discussed or considered by researchers and policymakers. Many partner-carers require more flexible and accessible systems of support than are currently available.

Convergence and differentiation

Societal arrangements for the delivery of care to sick, frail or disabled parents, children or partners are changing in all the countries studied. The research reported in this book shows that in the early 21st century, both family members and the state play a role in each of these types of care. Each country offers some support services, either to those requiring care, to their family carers or to both. Such services are usually provided either by local authorities (LAs) or independent organisations, sometimes operating as charities or not-for-profit organisations, sometimes as private companies or as individuals offering commercial services. In all six countries, the state considers it its business to regulate and shape some aspects of these, notably, where migrant workers and commercially provided home care agencies or residential homes are concerned. In the East Asian states, care services are relatively new, but rapidly developing: they have been established for much longer in the liberal democracies and the Nordic countries, although in the latter, in the four countries considered in this book, the state has increasingly withdrawn from directly providing care, turning variously to stricter targeting, outsourcing of services and privatisation.

The changes under way are shaped by both common and distinctive factors. Values and cultural differences are undoubtedly important influences. Individual responsibility and independence in adulthood plus a shared commitment to meeting dependency needs through universal welfare arrangements distinguish the Nordic states from the other countries considered here. The continuing influence of Confucian and familial values is undeniable in the East Asian states. The liberal democracies still mainly organise their systems on the basis that families should rely on what the state provides only *in extremis*, or in special circumstances. 'Pure' models shaped by these values are under pressure in all three types of welfare system, however. Demographic change, urbanisation and geographical and social mobility have greatly changed attitudes towards disability and the longer, home-based lives of people with serious illness, as well as towards the responsibility of the state.

Some differences between the Nordic, liberal-democratic and East Asian models are apparent, but how far is each of the three types of welfare system studied coherent? In the two Nordic countries, our examples mostly display similarity, both in policies and in the experiences of carers. Finland and Sweden have tended to ignore the needs of working carers of older parents, who remain largely invisible and lack specific support (see *Chapter Three*). Where parent-carers are concerned, however, Finland offers considerably less flexible and individualised support than Sweden, leading to longer spells of caring responsibility and delayed independence for young disabled adults (see *Chapter Six*). Partner-carers, again, face broadly similar conditions in both countries: lack of attention, limited personal time and large variations in the flexibility available in the workplace or in local services (see *Chapter Nine*). The Nordic welfare model thus seems to be rather coherent, despite some variations in the Finnish and Swedish cases.

The two liberal democracies, England and Australia, have adopted very similar policies and approaches. Both have taken steps to support working carers of older people by promoting flexible working and modest unpaid emergency or care leave. Each has developed programmes to enhance carers' health and well-being (see *Chapter Four*). Both have gradually given attention to parent-carers, promoting (at least in their policy statements) their participation in paid work. Nevertheless, these countries' complex benefit systems and limited service provision make the implementation of such policy aims difficult (see *Chapter Seven*). In the case of partner-carers, England and Australia also display broadly comparable tendencies: few, if any, specific measures address the needs of this group, but carers in both countries use the strategies of part-time work, flexible working, taking emergency leave and breaks, and negotiating informal workplace arrangements (see *Chapter Ten*).

The two East Asian states have responded very differently to working carers. In the past two decades, Japan has developed policies providing long-term care, care leaves and workplace support for carers. Comparable policy steps are under discussion in Taiwan but are not yet enacted, let alone implemented, leaving its carers far behind those in Japan. The situation is different for carers of older parents (Japan offering them some new 'quasi-rights', while Taiwanese families increasingly turn to migrant care workers), for parent-carers of disabled children (Japan making flexible working and carer leave available; Taiwanese parents still relying on their informal networks) and for partner-carers (for whom, work–care reconciliation is most difficult in Taiwan, resulting in low labour force participation rates among middle-aged and older workers) (see *Chapters Five*, *Eight* and *Eleven*).

As they respond to population ageing and increased longevity, all six countries now nevertheless expect disability, illness and extreme old age to be ever-present features of their societies and are beginning to reshape their social arrangements and systems to cope with this. Policymakers recognise that dementia and mobility problems as well as other impairing conditions will be increasingly common, placing greater demands on health and social care systems. All societies expect to provide more health care at home, not least to keep medical costs manageable, although what this will mean for families and carers is less widely discussed.

Sick and disabled people themselves expect more, and respond less passively to their circumstances than in previous generations. Disabled people have successfully asserted their right to autonomy and social participation, which is now internationally recognised, if still unevenly and inadequately implemented (WHO, 2011). At the end of life, individuals more often expect some choice in how and where they die, and greater policy attention is being given to how those who wish to die at home rather than in institutional or medical settings can be enabled to do so. Family carers, as this book has shown, now more often claim the right to better support and services: their advocates have been robust in demanding recognition of their role and the right to care without becoming socially excluded. Both carers' and disability movements now operate worldwide and, albeit at a different scale and pace in the six countries studied here, exercise significant influence in each.

Population ageing changes the balance between older and younger people, bringing new labour force participation imperatives. Reinforced by altered gender relations – spearheaded in the Nordic states, but now evident worldwide, including in the feminist movements of Taiwan and Japan – all six states today recognise the importance of enabling women as well as men to participate in paid work. Across the life course, most families in all six countries now depend for household financial well-being on at least some form of joint breadwinning.

These multiple trends and pressures are contributing to some convergence in the way the societies studied here approach work–care reconciliation. As shown in Tables 12.1–12.3, all six states now offer at least some support for carers: over recent decades, this has been extended and its tendency over time is to increase in range and form. Despite this, most family carers, in each of the countries studied, still provide care largely unsupported and bear most of the pressure of work–care reconciliation at the individual level. Nevertheless, all six countries now provide carers with some, rather minimal, employment rights and flexibility, give some carers modest financial support or compensation, and offer some types of services and respite to carers. Since none of these arrangements existed 50 years ago anywhere in the world, this is a remarkable policy change, even though the impact for carers themselves has been rather weak to date.

Future challenges and developments

It is clear that there are additional challenges ahead. While not a specific focus of this book, although touched on in some chapters here, one issue of growing importance is the increasing tendency for people of working age to be juggling, simultaneously, not only paid work and the care of older, sick or disabled family members, but also the care, support and financing of children, teenagers and young adults. These triple pressures, which involve financial, advisory, caring and emotional support to both older and younger generations (sometimes called 'sandwich' caring), serve only to underscore the importance of the policies and services debated here (Künemund, 2006).

Policy ideas sometimes 'travel' in the area of employment and social policy. This does not mean that systems can be translated, wholesale, from one country to another, but the exchange of ideas, through international networks of carers' organisations, the Organisation for Economic Co-operation and Development (OECD), European Union (EU) and academic channels, has self-evidently enabled some policies to transfer from one state to another (Glendinning et al, 2009; Colombo et al, 2011). It is perhaps especially to be expected that carers' right to flexible working arrangements may extend quite rapidly to additional countries, as this appears to have quite low costs for employers or the state and is being spread voluntarily by some multinational corporations (Cullen and Gareis, 2010).

The six states examined in this book are already considering a number of difficult questions and grappling, at policy level, with how to answer them. Should the state's role be to provide, enable or regulate care? Is care best conceptualised as a commodity that can be purchased by care consumers or as a publicly provided support service for individuals and families with care needs? What are the most cost-effective ways of sustaining carers' contributions? Will investment in carer training and in respite and relief arrangements make their care more sustainable in the longer term, and will it encourage future generations to be willing to care? In organisations and workplaces, what will change managerial perceptions towards combining work and care, and how can taking carers' leave or accessing workplace flexibility become normal responses, which do not prejudice a worker's reputation or career development? Perhaps most fundamental of all, could jobs be designed differently so that they fit better with longer working lives, normalise episodes of caring responsibility and maintain carers' incomes when caring occurs?

In recent decades, governments in all the countries studied here have been pressed by national – and, in some cases, also local – carers' organisations and advocacy groups to respond to the difficulties faced by those caring for their elderly parents or their sick or disabled children and partners. While policy debate has centred on population ageing and the need for both women and men in future generations to work longer and to contribute to their parents' care, all three types of care covered in this book now command a degree of policymaker attention.

Australia and England have outlined strategic carers' policy aims at the national level, making long-term commitments to supporting carers. In England, this includes an explicit focus on those combining work and care. The law in these liberal democracies now also gives carers limited access and nascent rights to information, assessment, services, workplace flexibility and care leave. These rather modest gains appear reasonably secure and campaigners aim to build upon them. In England, workplace flexibility for workers with care responsibilities seems sustainable and is supported by some influential employers (DH,

2010). Both countries provide well-established financial allowances for carers unable to work through care, or those receiving low pay due to reduced working hours because of care. However, the growing numbers of carers receiving these, and the disincentives to work that some claim they involve, may put these arrangements under pressure in the future (Colombo et al, 2011; Fry et al, 2011).

Policymakers in Sweden and Finland, by contrast, have been less explicit in promoting national policies to support carers, although, arguably, almost as much carer support provision exists there as in the liberal democracies. This may be, in part, because a significant role for carers is more controversial in these states, where welfare services should, in theory, meet all citizens' needs without obliging them to depend upon family support. Carers in both these states nevertheless have access to some forms of care leave and can try to negotiate remuneration for caregiving (under a contractual arrangement with their LA). In Sweden, this involves comparatively generous payments, although the arrangement's use has declined, perhaps because although it turns care into a formal 'job', it still separates the carer from mainstream working life. On the other hand, the personal assistance that disabled children and adults can access in Sweden (also gradually emerging in Finland) offers a new way of employing family carers using public resources. Sweden and Finland spend proportionately more on disability and care services than the other countries studied in this book, producing better-quality services for adult and non-adult disabled people as well as for older people (see *Chapter One*). This situation is clearly beneficial for family members who contribute to their care. However, even though Swedish parents of disabled children have a formal right to work part-time, if they wish, until their child reaches adulthood, fewer Nordic carers use part-time work as a way of reconciling work and care compared with those in the liberal democracies.

Carer support is much less developed in Japan and Taiwan, although some local support programmes exist, linked in Japan to the LTCI system and offered in Taiwan, at their discretion, by a few LAs. Income support for carers in the East Asian states is very limited and available only to those in lower-income households. By contrast, paid care leave from work is more generous in Japan than in Finland and still does not exist as a workers' right in England. In Taiwan, following the path of Japan, support initially developed to help workers with childcare responsibilities (which carers of disabled children can access like other parents) may, in time, become available to carers of adults. This is certainly an aspiration of the carers' movement there. Theoretically, therefore, there is a basis in both East Asian states upon which more systematic support could be built in the future.

Conclusion

Our investigation of carer support and carers' circumstances in the six countries studied in this book suggests that as the 21st century progresses, policymakers will be forced to address the need for better work–care reconciliation in every nation. This will happen irrespective of the type of welfare regime or of differences in family culture and values, because population ageing and rising female labour force participation – the two megatrends identified in *Chapter One* – continue to push care up the policy agenda worldwide. Effective policy in this field requires imagination and vigour, but can make a difference to the quality of life of carers, and of those they care for and about. Since few people will avoid caring or being cared for in their longer 21st-century lives, at stake here is the quality of life of all.

Reviewing the evidence presented in this book, we conclude that varied and adaptable configurations of support will be needed in every society. Creative policy options and much more flexible and responsive services are required. Each caring situation is, and always will be, different. This is why the rhetoric of 'personalised' or 'consumer-directed' support is so attractive to policymakers and families alike (Yeandle et al, 2012). Yet, as we have seen, without coherent policy arrangements, clarity about entitlements and effective information about the support options available, carers' lives too easily become difficult, stressful and unhealthy, compromising the sustainability of the support they give.

Our comparative international analysis has shown the value of responsive services and of even quite modest legislative entitlements. This suggests that clear and fair national policies, local services tailored to community and family needs, and employers capable of finding flexible responses to working carers that do not compromise organisational objectives can make a difference to carers' well-being. This book has also highlighted the importance of taking carers' views and experiences into account. The role and influence of carers' organisations is evident in many of the policy changes observed, not just in Australia and England, where their influence and impact is undeniable (Cook, 2007; Carers Australia, 2010), but also in the East Asian countries and Nordic states. The pressure carers' organisations have been able to exert, especially when working together with groups supporting the interests of older people, disabled people and women, has also had an identifiable impact on policies and services.

Uniform policy prescriptions cannot be the way forward in countries with very different policy traditions, cultural expectations and systems of values and belief. It is nevertheless evident that work–care reconciliation will be more easily facilitated if countries learn from each other about how employment rights, leaves from work, systems of financial compensation and local support arrangements can benefit carers and the people they care for, in all their diversity. Such arrangements, well configured, can enable carers to remain active citizens, effective workers and supportive family members – parents, partners, daughters and sons – without bringing these different but equally valued roles into damaging or stressful conflict with each other or with the needs of their frail, ill or disabled family members.

References

Addabbo, T., Arrizabalaga, M.-P., Borderias, C. and Owens, A. (eds) (2010) *Households and well-being in modern Europe: gender, inequalities, work and consumption*, Farnham: Ashgate.

Asai, M.O. and Kameoka, V.A. (2005) 'The influence of *Sekentei* on family caregiving and underutilization of social services among Japanese caregivers', *Social Work*, vol 50, no 2, pp 111–18.

Carers Australia (2010) *Annual report 2008–9*, Deakin: Carers Australia. Available at: http://www.carersaustralia.com.au/publications

Colombo, F., Llena-Nozal, A., Mercier, J. and Tjadens, F. (2011) *Help wanted? Providing and paying for long-term care*, Paris: OECD Publishing.

Cook, T. (2007) *The history of the carers' movement*, London: Carers UK.

Cullen, K. and Gareis, K., with Peters, P., Byrne, P., Mueller, S., Dolphin, C., Delaney, S. and Lilischkis, S. (2010) *Company initiatives for workers with care responsibilities for disabled children or adults*, Dublin: Eurofound.

DH (Department of Health) (2010) *Recognised, valued and supported: next steps for the Carers' Strategy*, London: DH.

Fry, G., Singleton, B., Yeandle, S. and Buckner, L. (2011) *Developing a clearer understanding of the Carers' Allowance claimant group*, London: Department for Work and Pensions.

Glendinning, C., Tjadens, F., Arksey, H., Morée, M., Moran, N. and Nies, H. (2009) *Care provision within families and its socio-economic impact on care providers*, York: University of York, Social Policy Research Unit.

Kröger, T. and Sipilä, J. (eds) (2005) *Overstretched: European families up against the demands of work and care*, Oxford: Blackwell.

Künemund, H. (2006) 'Changing welfare states and the "sandwich generation": increasing burden for the next generation?', *International Journal of Ageing and Later Life*, vol 1, no 2, pp 11–30.

Lamura, G., Döhner, H. and Kofahl, C. (on behalf of the EUROFAMCARE Consortium) (2008) *Services for supporting family carers of older people in Europe: characteristics, coverage and usage: a six-country comparative study*, Hamburg: Lit Verlag.

Lechner, V.M. and Neal, M.B. (eds) (1999) *Work and caring for the elderly: international perspectives*, Ann Arbor, MI: Brunner/Mazel.

Lewis, J. (2001) 'The decline of the male breadwinner model: implications for work and care', *Social Politics*, vol 8, no 2, pp 152–69.

Martin-Matthews, A. and Phillips, J. (eds) (2008) *Aging and caring at the intersection of work and home life: blurring the boundaries*, New York, NY: Lawrence Erlbaum Associates/Psychology Press.

Phillips, J. (ed) (1995) *Working carers: international perspectives on working and caring for older people*, Aldershot: Avebury.

Saraceno, C. (2010) 'Social inequalities in facing old-age dependency: a bi-generational perspective', *Journal of European Social Policy*, vol 20, no 1, pp 1–13.

Suanet, B., Broese van Groenou, M. and van Tilburg, T. (2012) 'Informal and formal home-care use among older adults in Europe: can cross-national differences be explained by societal context and composition?', *Ageing and Society*, vol 32, no 3, pp 491–515.

Ungerson, C. and Yeandle, S. (eds) (2007) *Cash for care in developed welfare states*, Basingstoke: Palgrave Macmillan.

WHO (World Health Organization) (2011) *World report on disability*, Geneva: World Health Organization.

Yeandle, S., Bennett, C., Buckner, L., Fry, G. and Price, C. (2007) *Stages and transitions in the experience of caring*, London: Carers UK.

Yeandle, S., Kröger, T. and Cass, B. (2012) 'Voice and choice for users and carers? Developments in patterns of care for older people in Australia, England and Finland', *Journal of European Social Policy*, vol 22, no 4, pp 432–45.

Index

Note: Page numbers in *italics* indicate tables.